33/81 40 Bt
3/81

WITHDRAWN

HISTORIC FORESTS OF ENGLAND

RALPH WHITLOCK

Historic Forests
OF ENGLAND

A. S. BARNES & COMPANY

SOUTH BRUNSWICK AND NEW YORK:

© 1979 Ralph Whitlock
Published in the U.S.A. by A. S. Barnes & Company, Inc.
Cranbury, New Jersey 08512
ISBN 0–498–02429–6
Library of Congress catalog card no. 79–1924
Printed and bound in England

Contents

THE PRIMEVAL FOREST	page 7
CELTS, ROMANS AND SAXONS	13
THE ROYAL CHASE	17
AFTER THE MIDDLE AGES	26
MEN OF THE FOREST	35
WILD LIFE IN THE FORESTS	55
THE NEW COMMERCIAL FORESTS	96
GAZETTEER: *the historic forests*	101
BIBLIOGRAPHY	171
INDEX	173

The Primeval Forest

In Britain the advance of first grassland and then trees in the wake of the receding glaciers of the last Ice Age began about 8200 B.C. The first colonists were doubtless dwarf willows, then birch, followed by pine. Hardwood trees, such as oak, elm, alder and ash, with hazel underwood, arrived before 5000 B.C. and were probably accompanied by crab apple, hawthorn, blackthorn, holly, rowan, wild cherry and several other familiar species. Towards the end of this *Boreal* period, as it is called, lime, beech, hornbeam, several of the poplars, whitebeam and wild service trees moved northwards into our islands (not then islands, for a land-bridge where the Straits of Dover now impose a sea barrier linked Britain with continental Europe).

The *Atlantic* period, to which the dates 5500 to 3000 B.C. have been assigned, is thought to have been relatively warm and wet. The pine forests retreated to the north, and the breaching of the land-bridge by the Straits of Dover ended the free spread of new species into Britain. From 3000 to 1 B.C. is designated the *Sub-Boreal* period, when the climate became drier and many of the peat bogs which had been formed during the preceding millennia dried out.

From the year A.D. 1 to about A.D. 1000 (the *Sub-Atlantic* period) the climate reverted to damp but mild weather, which favoured the growth of deciduous trees but also the formation of peat, so inhibiting the natural regeneration of pine. For when pine seeds fall upon peat beds instead of soil they do not germinate.

From about A.D. 1000 to the present date has been termed the *Recent* period. In spite of the stormy, cold interludes in the fourteenth and fifteenth centuries and again in the late seventeenth and eighteenth, there is held to be a general trend towards a drier and warmer climate. Intruding into this background the first men, our Mesolithic ancestors, appeared in Britain during the Atlantic period. They hunted, fished, trapped animals and searched for berries, nuts and roots, but as far as we know had no domestic animals. As they were also few in number their impact on their environment must have been negligible. Any fires they may have started to flush game would have no greater consequence than the occasional forest fires ignited by friction or lightning. Interference with the forest on any scale began with the arrival of Neolithic men around 3000 B.C. and has continued ever since. Thus 3000 B.C. is a suitable starting point for a survey of our forests. At that date, allowing a century or so either way, they were virtually intact—the original, primeval forests of Britain. From that date their decline begins.

The old saying that in Saxon times a squirrel could travel from the Severn to the Wash without once setting foot on ground is well known and undoubtedly correct. Britain was essentially a forest country. By the Saxon era, however, encroachment on the woodland had already advanced during the Roman centuries, and receded, so that much of the forest was secondary growth. At our starting point in about 3000 B.C. it is generally agreed that over much of the Highlands of Scotland pine and birch forest predominated. In lowland Scotland, most of northern England as far south as the Wash and most of Wales the most abundant species were oak and hazel. Over the rest of England the forest was of mixed deciduous species, among which it has recently been suggested lime was preponderant. In Cornwall and south-west Wales, as well as in most of Ireland, elm evidently tended to replace oak, though hazel was plentiful.

The information on which these generalisations are based comes mainly from the study of pollen deposits. Pollen grains remain intact for thousands of years, especially in layers of mud, silt and peat, and the species of plant from which they came can be identified in some, though not all, instances. The broad outline of dominant species does not imply that few others were present. Ash, for instance, was well established throughout most of England; there were oaks in the western Highlands of Scotland, and pines in East Anglia. The dry soils of much of southern and central England are not conducive to the preservation of pollen, so information about forest composition there is sketchy. We wonder what the chalk and limestone uplands were like. For centuries down to the last few decades they were open grassland and it is tempting to assume they must always have been so. The soil would seem to be too thin for tree growth. Yet since, in 1953 and 1954, myxomatosis almost wiped out the rabbit population, the vegetation of areas of old downland untouched by cultivation has progressively changed. First, coarse grasses have smothered the milkwort, thyme, bird's-foot trefoil and other lowly herbs. Then bushes have thrust their way up through grasses, and now trees are beginning to push above the tops of the bushes. The process is particularly noticeable in such military areas as Salisbury Plain, where no sheep or cattle graze to control the herbage. It is quite obvious, too, that some trees will flourish on thin soils. The chalk hills are often crowned by towering clumps of beeches, the roots of which probe into the chalk. Hawthorn, wild service tree, yew, birch, oak, lime and elm are other species which can live on thin, alkaline soils, though admittedly the oaks are often stunted.

Can we then visualise the whole country, including the chalk hills, buried in trees? Were Stonehenge and Avebury secret shrines in groves? Probably not. Even before Man appeared some control of tree and shrub growth must have been exercised by grazing animals. Deer and wild cattle (the great aurochs of northern Europe) probably retired to rest in the forest but emerged to graze on any existing open grassland, on which natural regeneration of trees would be effectively prevented by them. A study of human prehistory suggests that the early immigrants found the chalklands open.

On the other hand, the mixed but heavier soils of the Midlands were

undoubtedly thickly forested. At Rothamsted Experimental Husbandry Station in Hertfordshire in 1882 a half-acre plot in a wheat field called Broadbalk was fenced in and left to its own devices. At the end of four years competition by weeds had eliminated all but a few stunted wheat plants. Gradually the arable weeds were smothered by brambles and bushes, and these in their turn had to yield place to trees. Now the half-acre is a dense wood of trees 60 to 70 ft tall, the chief species of which are hawthorn, oak, ash and sycamore. In parts the tree-cover is so dense that only trailing ivy will grow beneath it; elsewhere there is a thick growth of bramble and dog's mercury. The natural vegetation of the heavy soil at Rothamsted, typical of the Midlands, is thus clearly demonstrated. Whether the forest everywhere was as dense as is suggested by Broadbalk is open to doubt. The abundance of hazel would seem to indicate that it was not. Hazel normally grows in open woodland under a thin canopy of taller trees. Later foresters arrived at a density of twelve per acre as ideal for oaks with a hazel undergrowth. We should perhaps therefore visualise much open forest with occasional glades but with some denser and more jungly areas, according to soil.

One of the first results of Man's impact on the forest when Neolithic immigrants began to practise agriculture around 3000 B.C. was a noticeable decline in the numbers of elms, or at least in the amount of elm-pollen deposited. The elms may still have been there, however, but pollarded and cut frequently so that they never produced flowers. The leafy branches of elm make useful cattle food when grazing is scarce, and elms tend to grow at the edge of woodlands rather than in the heart of dense forests. The process continued indefinitely for, as the human population and their skills increased, so more and more land was needed for growing crops and for grazing. The methods by which these early semi-nomadic agriculturists cleared patches of forest may well have been similar to those still employed by tribes at a comparable level of culture in Africa and South and Central America today. Commonly known as the 'slash-and-burn' technique, it consists of slashing down all the bushes and underwood, burning them and planting a crop amid the ashes. Seeds are placed individually, with the aid of a dibbing stick. One or two successive crops are grown, and the plot is then abandoned for a period of years (from seven to 15, according to local custom), the tribe moving on to other clearings in the forest. At the end of the cycle they return and repeat the process.

Once a series of clearings has been well established the periodical slashing and burning are relatively easy. The formation of new clearings, involving the destruction of large trees, is a more formidable task. It is accomplished by ringing, burning and long and patient sessions with axes. In this connection, although the contemporary tribesman uses an iron panga or machete, he used to employ the same techniques when only stone tools were available. People who have used stone tools claim that they are surprisingly effective. Almost certainly our Neolithic and Bronze Age ancestors tackled the forest by similar methods. One probable difference is that the British tribes possessed more grazing animals, the chief regions where slash-and-burn is practised in Africa being tsetse-fly areas. Cattle, sheep and pigs in sufficient numbers inhibit natural regeneration. On the other hand, many trees, notably elm, can renew themselves by suckers.

The plough was a late arrival on the prehistoric scene. The ploughs used to cultivate the small square 'Celtic' fields, which are a feature of chalk hillsides in southern England, were well-made, one-handled implements, usually drawn by a couple of oxen and designed only to scratch a groove in soft soil, not to turn a furrow. I have handled one of them and found that with practice I could achieve a very shallow furrow, but nothing like what could be done with a plough fitted with a mould-board. Such a plough, equipped with an iron tip or share, was introduced to Britain by invading Celtic peoples about 400 B.C. Among them were the Belgae and other tribes of southern Britain whose names are known from Roman records. We have arrived on the frontier of historic times.

A few clues exist as to the use of wood in the earlier ages. It is known, for instance, that the 'blue stones' of Stonehenge were brought from the Prescelly Mountains of Pembrokeshire. The most widely accepted theory about the route and methods employed is that the stones were mounted on rafts in Milford Haven, towed to the mouth of the Bristol Avon then upstream to the watershed with the river Wylye, then down the Wylye to its confluence with the Salisbury Avon, upstream to Amesbury and overland again for the last few miles. Apart from timbers for the boats, or rafts, huge ones would have been needed for rolling the stones down to the sea, over the watershed and finally to the selected site: the heaviest of the blue stones weighs four tons. The sarsen stones, which also had to be hauled for miles over the downs, weigh up to 45 tons each. The trees used to supply the timbers for this colossal task must have been massive and numerous. Again, the generally accepted explanation of how the stones were raised to an upright position and the great lintels (some of them weighing seven tons) placed on the tops is that log platforms were constructed alongside by stages to support them, while other huge timbers were employed as levers. The demand would have been for tree-trunks that were long and straight as well as of sufficient diameter. Dr Gerald Hawkins, in his book *Stonehenge Decoded*, estimates that the timber lattice or scaffolding required to put one lintel in position would have been 'about a mile of six-inch diameter logs cut into twenty-foot lengths, with notches similar to those in a log-cabin wall'.

Woodhenge, nearby, is a kind of timber replica of Stonehenge, in that it consisted of concentric rings of wooden posts which presumably supported some sort of roof. A rather similar timber construction existed on Sanctuary Hill, a mile or so from that other great stone circle at Avebury.

Beyond any doubt, the men who built Stonehenge and Avebury were skilled in the use of big timbers. Felling and shaping large trees would not have deterred them. Corroboratory evidence comes from the lake villages of the Somerset marshes, where timber and brushwood causeways were constructed to give access to the island settlements. Oak, ash, lime, alder, holly and hazel were the woods used. It has been pointed out that there are so many poles of uniform size that they could hardly have been

This giant beech in the New Forest was evidently subjected to coppicing when young

natural growths. They would seem to have been produced in coppices felled at regular intervals, perhaps of 20 or so years, a woodland management policy in widespread use within memory and still employed in places. It could, of course, have evolved naturally from slash-and-burn methods of cultivation. The earliest of the Somerset causeways dates from about 4000 B.C., which implies that in that corner of England Man was making his mark on the environment considerably earlier than our starting date of 3000 B.C.

Turning to specific trees, oak, elm, hazel, pine, alder and birch were widely distributed in Britain before the beginning of the Atlantic period (about 5500 B.C.). Ash, holly and lime seem to have become established during that period, and beech also found its way into southern England about the same time but did not extend its range far northwards. The beech is an enigmatic tree, for Julius Caesar reported that in 55 B.C. there were no beeches in Britain, and as recently as the seventeenth century the antiquary John Aubrey stated that the only beeches in his native Wiltshire were a hill-top clump in Groveley Wood. Both would seem to have been wrong, yet how could alert and interested observers miss such a conspicuous tree? Little information is so far available on the hornbeam, maple and several other species.

In attempting to visualise Britain when the forests were dominant, we should note that, besides the chalk and limestone downland concerning which some doubt exists, certain areas were never clad in trees. Sandy heaths were too dry and poor to support anything more than heather and gorse, which leads to the paradoxical conclusion that much of the New Forest, generally agreed to be one of the oldest surviving forests, was never woodland. The Fens of Cambridgeshire and the neighbouring counties were amphibious realms of mud, water and reeds and grew no trees, except on the islands. On the other hand, trees may have extended much farther up mountainsides than they do today.

Celts, Romans and Saxons

The heavy, iron-shared plough introduced by the Celts in the three or four centuries immediately preceding the Christian era did more than revolutionise farming by turning a furrow. It was powerful enough to cultivate heavy clay soils, thus enabling farmers to move down from the thin-soiled uplands to the more fertile lowlands. Already before the Roman invasion large areas of former forest land, especially in south-eastern Britain, had been claimed for the plough. Apart from political considerations, one motive behind the Roman annexation of Britain was a desire to get hold of the British wheat harvest, from which a sizeable surplus was already being exported. In the four centuries when Britain was a province of the Roman Empire immense areas of the south-eastern half of the island were under cultivation, and consequently many of the forests must have been virtually cleared. A district of south Wiltshire with which I am familiar will serve as an illustration of the pattern of the countryside during the Roman era.

On the thin chalk soil of the hill-tops the Celtic peasantry were cultivating their little holdings by the old traditional methods; the outlines of their small rectangular fields are still visible on hill-slopes. One of their villages which has been partially excavated shows the inhabitants to have been poor but independent people. Taxation would have been heavy and doubtless they had forced labour on the adjacent metalled highway and sundry other impositions to contend with, but otherwise they seem to have been left alone. They were not slaves.

Down in the broad and fertile valley, within sight of the poverty-stricken village, were at least three villas. Though termed 'Roman' they may as easily have been occupied by Romanised Celtic aristocracy as by gentlemen from the Mediterranean. One of them was exceptionally large. Professor J. A. Richmond, commenting in his book *Roman Britain* on a similar villa at Ditchley in Oxfordshire, suggests that, from the size of its granaries, it must have been the centre of an estate of some thousand acres. Three such villas, or country estates as they would be more properly termed, in the valley in question in south Wiltshire would have taken up most of the available acreage. Thus we have a picture of a thoroughly tamed countryside, laid out in cultivated fields—large ones in the valley, small ones on the hills. No doubt areas of woodland were left, much of it probably coppiced and well managed and only here and there, in waterlogged bottoms, remnants of the old primeval forest.

The frontier between the domesticated countryside and the more primitive landscape beyond was, roughly, the Fosse Way, slicing diagonally across England from Lincoln to the Devon coast near Axmouth. It is true that on the far side were islands of cultivation, as around Wroxeter, Ribchester and the East Riding of Yorkshire, but pastoral rather than arable farming was the rule, and vast areas of ancient forest and wasteland remained intact. On the near side even the Fens were reclaimed to some extent, to designs by skilful Roman engineers, the manual labour being provided by slaves and the hostages of war, notably the defeated Iceni. It has been demonstrated that once the main pattern of canals and fields was laid out the British peasantry was turned loose and allowed to farm it according to traditional methods, with the provision that at key points Roman tax-collectors waited to collect the lion's share of the produce.

Apart from the clearing of wooded land for agriculture, large inroads into the forest were made for industrial purposes. Trees were felled not only for timber but for fuel and for burning charcoal, then a commodity in great demand. Iron deposits were exploited in the Weald and the Forest of Dean, requiring much wood for smelting. Although in Roman times the Weald, one of the most difficult of woodlands to reclaim, was hardly encroached on by farmers, it housed numerous ironworks, mostly by the side of or within easy reach of roads linking London with south coast ports.

The last Roman legions are thought to have left Britain in A.D. 410, though some historians think that a military force returned for a short time in 418. Much of the economy had been wrecked by a co-ordinated raid by barbarians in 367, but the province continued to tick over without too much further disruption for a few more decades. Bishop Germanus, visiting southern Britain in 429, found flourishing cities, a reasonably prosperous countryside and most of the machinery of government still functioning. He encountered only one party of raiding Saxons, who were soundly defeated by a resolute band of British soldiers led by the militant bishop. Between then and the end of the century continually reinforced Anglo-Saxon irruptions played havoc with the Roman organisation in the south-eastern half of Britain. Settlements were established in Kent by the 450s and the Saxon tide had swept over half Britain by 500. Then it seems to have halted and indeed have been turned back for a time (the period of the semi-mythical Arthur). Very, very little is known about events for the next hundred years or so.

So, then, a gap of at least two centuries is interposed between the collapse of the Roman civilisation and the emergence of settled and modestly civilised Anglo-Saxon kingdoms. A period rather longer than from the French Revolution to the present day. Trees can grow to a great size in 200 years, but comparatively few of those in our existing forests are as old as that. The plot in Broadbalk Field, Rothamsted, we remember, has become covered with a dense wood, 60 or 70 ft high, in just short of 100 years. There was plenty of time for much of Britain to revert to its original forest state, and plenty of evidence that that is what happened. A contributory factor was that most of the villa estates were on the most fertile land which had been won from the forest. Abandoned and neglected, the sites followed the pattern of events on Broadbalk. The Anglo-Saxons had in most places to start again the process of reclamation from the beginning.

They started from a different angle. Roman-British civilisation moved downhill from the upland villages. Dorchester (Dorset) provides a typical example of the sequence of events. Here the Celtic population lived in a town of sorts protected by the mighty ramparts of Maiden Castle. Not long after it had been taken by assault by Vespasian's legions the survivors moved down and settled in the new town of Durnovaria which the Romans had laid out for them. The Anglo-Saxons, on the other hand, were boat people. They arrived in ships, rowed them up the rivers and settled within easy reach of a navigable waterway, which offered a line of retreat in case of necessity. Very few of their early settlements are not by rivers. Here they often constructed their first houses by up-ending their boats and building around them; here they found meadow-grazing for their cattle; here they later fabricated their water-mills. And from here they began their new assault on the forest.

Except in certain districts well populated in Roman times and taken over at an early date by the invaders, such as Kent, there is little continuity. Anglo-Saxon villages sprang up where no Roman habitations had been, and Roman sites remained for many more centuries buried in the deep forest. In general the Anglo-Saxons were a closely knit tribal community. Their leaders were 'first among equals'. Like the Celts, they possessed a heavy plough, capable of tackling stiff soils, but it was so cumbersome that it needed eight oxen to pull it. No one man was wealthy enough to own eight oxen, so ploughing and other major tasks were necessarily a communal effort. The usual arrangement was that in the nucleated villages which the early settlers favoured each free man had his hut and private plot around it, generally fenced in by stakes and hurdles. The reclaimed farmland around the settlement was divided into three main sections, one of which was, in any one year, devoted to wheat, another to barley, oats or rye, and the third left fallow, though at times during the summer grazed and cut for hay. Each of these large fields was further divided into strips of about an acre apiece. Every year a number of these strips were allocated to each household, according to its needs and status. In order that no man should have all the better land and another all the poorer, no two strips were, in the early allocations, contiguous to each other. And every year a new allocation was made. The strips tended to be long and narrow, simply because turning a heavy eight-oxen plough is such a difficult operation that the ploughman would go as far as possible. The ridge-and-furrow patterns still visible in many ancient fields, especially Midland pastures, were formed in this way. Each strip was theoretically 40 poles (a furlong or 'furrow-long') in length by four poles wide.

Beyond the open fields lay the waste. In fenland and marshy districts that could be swamps or meres; on the borders of the chalk hills it may have been grassy downland; but in most places it was forest. Here the households of the settlement had common rights. They could gather wood, collect nuts, dig turf, pick berries, hunt or trap wild animals and birds.

Here too they could turn their animals to graze and forage. At first the wild wood was apparently limitless. As the years passed and the population grew, the men would enlarge their cultivated fields and would push their foraging farther and farther into the waste. Eventually they would meet people from other villages probing into the forest from another direction. Then, peaceably or otherwise, it was necessary to delineate the boundary between the two villages. Now all of that part of the forest had been allocated. It belonged to somebody, or rather, to some community.

As the pressure on space increased many villages appointed a *woodward* to take charge of the woods. His duty was to organise the cutting of trees and underwood and to supervise grazing animals in the forest. In time the rights of each householder became exactly defined; one would be allowed to turn out 10 cows to graze, another only two; one could keep 12 geese on the common, another only six, and so on. Each householder maintained his rights jealously, and the woodward had to ensure that he did not exceed them. Among the perquisites of his office the woodward could claim all trees blown down by the wind. While that was the pattern of settled districts, there were still vast areas of Britain without human settlements. In spite of encroachments in easily settled districts, over probably the greater part of the country the forest was still supreme. Here the wild beasts and wild men (criminals and outlaws) lurked. Travel was dangerous but good hunting was to be had by men sufficiently exalted to be able to command a strong company of retainers. So, beyond the confines of the settlements the forest became the hunting-ground of Anglo-Saxon nobles and particularly of the king.

The Royal Chase

The moment has come for re-defining the word 'forest'. So far the assumption has been that it bears its modern connotation and is synonymous with woodland. For much of Britain in early times that was accurate enough; woodland was the natural cover of most of the country. Note has been taken, however, that there were exceptions, not only in special regions such as the Fens, but where the soil was too thin or poor to support trees, as on sandy heaths and steep mountainsides.

For hunting, Anglo-Saxon monarchs and nobility did not need woodland exclusively. Woodland harboured the game they sought, but open country had its own advantages. Any and all waste land could be and was included in a royal *chase*—which is a better word for it than *forest*, although the two words were frequently used indiscriminately. Confusion over this point has sometimes led historians to assume that certain areas, such as the New Forest, were entirely covered by trees, whereas the extensive heaths in its southern sector never were. Exmoor and Dartmoor too possessed more open moors than woodland.

Another point which may require clarification is the purpose and character of the hunts engaged in by early and medieval kings. Hunting, although exciting sport, served the more important function of providing meat for the royal table. Early and medieval royal courts moved around the kingdom not only to promote law and order but also because such large establishments quickly exhausted local food supplies. So the royal household became semi-nomadic, moving from royal manor to royal manor. Martinmas, 11 November, was the traditional date for the slaughter of all domestic livestock for which it would be impossible to find food during the winter. After much gargantuan feasting around that date, the populace tightened its belts, and thereafter salt meat was the order of the day for anyone lucky enough to eat meat at all. Under such circumstances fresh venison was always preferable to salt beef from a lean ox which had spent most of its life pulling a plough. Kings out hunting were therefore not only enjoying themselves, they were after a good dinner.

With that in mind, chasing a stag across the countryside was not the easiest method of killing one's quarry. Undoubtedly it was sometimes practised, but probably the more usual procedure was driving the deer towards concealed bowmen. These tactics were being used in the hunt which ended with the killing of William Rufus in the New Forest in the year 1100. They had the advantage that the line of beaters could allow hinds and fawns to dodge back into the forest and force only the stags to run the gauntlet in the killing zone. The importance attached to the edibility of the beasts of the chase is demonstrated by the fact that there were only four of them:

the red deer, the fallow deer, the roe deer and the wild boar. Foxes, badgers, otters, martens and wild cats were hunted for sport but were not considered as being in the same category as the other four and were not protected by the more stringent forest laws. In days when hawking was a popular sport, many more species of birds than today were regarded as worthy of attention; our ancestors evidently ate the flesh of, for instance, the heron and the coot, which we would regard as decidedly fishy. The most abundant quarry in some of the royal forests would seem to have been wildfowl, as in the Forest of North Petherton in Somerset.

The beasts of the forest require ample space, so there was good reason for monarchs and nobility to keep the forests or chases as extensive as possible. Encroachment was incessant. In times of national unrest or in the reign of a weak king it often assumed formidable proportions. There are many medieval instances of a stronger king demanding the restoration of land filched from the forest in the previous reign.

In the course of the centuries the term 'forest' became an administrative one. It referred to the area administered according to forest laws, as codified by several kings. Throughout most if not all of the Saxon era freemen had the right to kill any game on their own land but not to follow it into the king's forests. Until the reign of William I, freemen retained the right to take game other than the four beasts of the chase even in the forests. The forest laws had therefore not been unduly oppressive, and the savage code imposed by the first Norman king must to the English have seemed outrageous. Until about the end of the last century considerable weight was attached to the *Constitutiones de Foresta*, a collection of forest laws said to have been enacted at Winchester in the reign of King Canute, in A.D. 1016. The document is now considered to be, if not a complete forgery, at least a drastically edited version compiled by a Norman scribe, whose aim was to show to the indignant English that William's harsh code was no more than a revision of one that had been in existence for more than 50 years. The code comprises 34 paragraphs, some of which impose draconian penalties, though oddly some of the most severe are not for offences involving the game but for 'violence against the Chief Men [i.e. the King's deputies] of the forest'. It can be assumed that the laws of the alleged Canute's code were certainly honoured in the reigns of the early Norman kings.

The 'Chief Men of the Forest' in Norman times were the *Wardens*, also known as stewards, bailiffs or chief foresters. Apparently such officials also existed in Saxon times, too, for there are several instances of William the Conqueror reappointing Saxon noblemen who had held the posts in the previous reign. In later reigns and in some forests the office became hereditary. According to the laws incorrectly attributed to Canute, the Chief Man received annually from the King 'two horses, one saddle, one sword, five lances, one spear, one shield and two hundred shillings of silver'. Under the same code there were also *Middle Men* and *Tinemen*.

Less exalted than the Wardens but still of considerable importance were the *Verderers*. These were elected by the freeholders of the forest and so

Queen Elizabeth hawking. Herons appear to be the quarry

ostensibly represented their interests. In practice they were responsible to the Crown, and their most important duty seems to have been to ensure that the forest laws were kept. In some instances a Chief Verderer was appointed by the Crown. The number of verderers varied from two to six, according to the size and importance of the forest; four seems to have been the average. Verderers were naturally men of considerable substance, possessing extensive interests within the forest in question. They received no salary and usually no perquisites.

Foresters were in early times not simple woodmen but important forest officials. Each had authority over a walk, division, ward or bailiwick, in which his first duty was to protect the deer. That naturally included keeping an eye open for poachers, cutting twigs and evergreens for the deer to browse on in winter, and taking special care of the hinds during the *fence month*, a month around Midsummer Day, when the fawns were being dropped. The office of forester seems to have been one of considerable importance, sometimes held by minor local gentry, even women, who employed a deputy to do the actual work. It usually carried with it rights of pasture and pannage and certain other perquisites, such as the right to so many standing trees per year. Generally a forester was also entitled to take one or two deer during the year. In some forests the foresters were paid a wage or salary—on a daily basis in accordance with the principle that a forester must *always* be on duty. Twopence a day seems to have been a fairly standard rate throughout much of the Middle Ages.

In some of the larger forests a *Mounted Forester* was appointed. He exercised general supervision of the whole forest, making frequent patrols on horseback. From the fourteenth century onwards the Mounted Forester evolved in some instances into the *Chief Forester*, a local magnate appointed by the Crown. The office by then appears to have been one of some honour, considerable perquisites but few responsibilities. All that was expected of the Chief Officer in later times was that he should attend the king when hunting and supervise the arrangements for the hunt.

When about their business the working foresters were in early times entitled to bed and board in the houses of forest tenants, who were also required to provide food and lodging for the forester's horse and dog. As might be expected, these perquisites were not always willingly supplied and became in time a frequent source of friction. A Forest Charter of the year 1217 and subsequent enactments expressly prohibited foresters demanding such concessions, but the practice seems to have continued, and indeed in some instances a money payment was demanded in lieu of services in kind.

Another medieval forest official was the *Woodward*. His duties, somewhat different from those of the early Saxon woodward, lay chiefly in the extensive private properties which existed in many of the forests. Although privately owned, these lands were not exempt from the forest laws. The wellbeing of the king's deer was paramount, and the woodward's task was to ensure that it received due priority. No trees could be felled, buildings erected, land cleared or industries (such as charcoal-burning) set up without royal assent. The woodward was appointed to see that the regulations were observed. The owner of the private estate paid him but his responsibilities were to the Crown. *Rangers* performed similar duties in outlying or detached sectors of the forest; they are not mentioned in forest records until late in the fourteenth century.

A further set of forest officials were the *agisters*. Their duties consisted not so much of the allocation of pasturage rights in the forest—they were established by ancient custom and very familiar to everyone concerned—but the collection of payments due for those rights. They also had to ensure that no freeholder turned loose in the forest more animals than he was entitled to.

The existence of private property within the forest borders is noted above. In some instances this consisted of private estates in existence when the forest was created or enlarged; more often the estates were granted by the king, and often the recipient was an abbey or other ecclesiastical establishment. Although the owner had a title to the land the Crown retained the hunting-rights, and the forest laws still applied. In addition to hunting deer, the cutting of trees and the erection of high fences were expressly forbidden. There were, however, within some of the forests *Parks*, around which fences or walls, though not high ones, could be erected. Here too the Crown reserved the hunting-rights and forest law had to be observed. The parks called for the services of another set of forest officials, the *Parkers*, whose duties were much the same as those of woodwards and rangers.

Incidentally, although we have been regarding the two as synonymous, there was a legal and administrative distinction between a *forest* and a *chase*. A *forest* belonged to the king; a *chase* to a nobleman or some other subject. Hence the royal forest laws did not apply to a chase. In practice the distinction was usually lost, for many of the chases were granted to nobles and prelates by the king, who nevertheless retained jurisdiction and required the forest laws to be observed. There were also instances of the Crown acquiring chases from subjects, when the forest laws automatically became applicable. Outside the boundaries of the forest freeholders had the right to hunt wild animals on un-enclosed land. The activities of the Crown in claiming such land were so comprehensive that it is a matter for surprise that any un-enclosed and unclaimed land remained. Evidently it did, for further restrictions were devised for some of it.

In more recent times the term *Warren* has been given the more limited meaning of an enclosure for keeping rabbits (or, to use the medieval word, *conies*). In medieval England a warren was a legal term referring to land over which the king had granted rights to take certain game. The concessions usually applied to the lesser game such as hares, foxes, wildcats, badgers, rabbits and many birds, but not to deer or wild boars. They were made to local magnates, who were empowered to deal with poachers but only those trying to take the specified animals. On warren land a man might be arrested and have his dog impounded for hunting a hare but not a deer. A hare was a 'beast of the warren'; a deer was a 'beast of the forest'. A warren was generally a fairly extensive area, and it was not enclosed.

A *Purlieu* was a forest term which came into use in the later medieval period. It referred to land which had formerly been forest but was now outside the forest boundaries. The word may still be found in place-names in the New Forest and elsewhere. It is also more or less synonymous with the *Venville* parishes on the edge of Dartmoor, with the *Wynlands* of the Peak and with other similar local features. Generally, the forest laws still applied to purlieus, though with less severity than in the forest. For example, deer had to be protected but could be turned off if a farmer found them grazing on his crops, an action strictly forbidden in the forest. Some forest rights were retained by owners of purlieus, but usually not as extensive as those of forest freeholders.

Severe as the forest laws were, they offered some compensation to freeholders who lived in the forest. Many of these were, after all, men in direct employment of the Crown, engaged in the maintenance of the forest, and it must be recognised that, if they were to give adequate service, they needed to be reasonably contented and to have the chance of a fair standard of living. The rights of forest-dwellers were therefore as clearly defined as their duties. As at the present time in relation to forests and commons where rights are still exercised, the rights were normally attached to a property rather than an individual. Thus a forest holding would consist of a house, buildings, a few acres of enclosed land, the right to turn loose in the forest a specified number of livestock, and probably certain other rights mentioned below. *Pasturage* was the right to turn grazing animals loose in the forest and referred usually to cattle. Usually the cattle had to be branded, so that a forester or other official could recognise any that were there illicitly. *Pannage*, the right to turn pigs into the forest, was an important economic factor, for pigs can get much of their food by grubbing and rooting under trees. More particularly they can grow fat by feeding on acorns and beech-mast. In many forests pannage was confined to the 'mast' season, which was defined as from 14 September to 18 November. Before the start of the season each commoner had to notify how many pigs he intended to turn loose, the number being, of course, limited to the number for which pannage rights were attached to his holding. For each pig he had to pay a fee, which seems to have ranged generally from a halfpenny to fourpence (at a time when mature pigs were worth about 24 pence each).

Horses were less plentiful than cattle and pigs but were allowed to roam the forests on similar terms. As stallions were seldom cut and uncontrolled mating was therefore the rule, attempts were made by several monarchs, notably Henry VIII, to improve the size and quality of horse stock by stipulating that any stallions turned loose should be of a specified height. The ordinance was frequently disregarded.

Concerning sheep there was some conflict of opinion. It was held by some that, because sheep have similar grazing habits to deer, they compete with them and so should be excluded from forests. Those who held the opposite view could quote plenty of instances of deer and sheep grazing side by side. In the end arrangements were based on local custom. To some forests sheep were readily admitted; from others they were prohibited, transgressions being punished by swingeing fines. Goats were favoured even less and in most instances were rigorously banned from forests. It was maintained that they tainted pastures, causing deer to desert them. On the other hand, geese seem to have been allowed reasonably free access to the forest.

Turbary was the right to dig turf or peat for fuel in the forest. Quantities per holding were exactly defined. *Estovers* was the right to gather or cut wood for fuel. Again defined with some precision, rights to firewood were divided into those concerned with *rotefallen* wood, and *wyndfallen* wood. The former, as its name implies, was the small wood from uprooted trees; the latter, the branches blown off standing trees. The trunks of uprooted trees were not included in estover rights but were the property of the Crown or the person to whom they were granted. Such trees were known as *cablish*.

The right to cut bracken and the right to dig marl for dressing arable land were other concessions frequently attached to woodland farms. Charcoal-burning, mining and quarrying were not normal forest rights but were subject to licences granted by the Crown. *Piscary*, the right to fish, occurred in certain well-watered forests but was not generally enjoyed.

All the forest regulations, with their multitudinous rights and duties, were a fruitful source of dispute and litigation. Medieval records are filled with accounts of court cases. Encroachment, too, was a constant menace to the king's interests. In an attempt to keep it under control, to each forest was appointed a number of knights, known as *Regarders*, whose duty it was to inspect the area thoroughly once every three years and to report on any illicit enclosures. Offenders were brought before one of several courts, according to the gravity of their offence. Minor offences were tried before an *Attachment Court*, held once every 42 days. The *Swainmote*, which had similar functions, was originally held three times a year—15 days before Midsummer, Michaelmas and Martinmas respectively—but later became synonymous with the Attachment Court. The supreme forest court was the *Eyre*, which not only dealt with major offenders but surveyed virtually everything that had happened since the last eyre. Officially an eyre was held for each forest once every seven years, but in practice the intervals became very irregular, in an extreme instance amounting to 50 years.

The Warden or Chief Man of the forest was the official who presided over the Attachment Court or Swainmote, though he could appoint a deputy. He was assisted and supported by the Verderers. The case against offenders was presented by the Foresters. Woodwards, agisters and regarders were required to report any offences that came to their notice and to attend the court to give evidence. At the great eyre everyone of any consequence had to attend, including all the forest officials, all the forest freeholders, representatives of any town adjoining the forest, and all who had committed any offence since the last eyre. An eyre was thus such a vast, complex and expensive undertaking that the temptation to postpone holding one as long as possible was great.

The Attachment Court derived its name from a medieval legal term 'to attach'. It resembled arrest in most respects. For the less serious offences a man might have some of his goods and chattels 'attached', that is, forfeited until the case was tried. More often he was arrested and required to find pledges or sponsors who would vouch for his appearance at the next court. He was then, in effect, released on bail. For serious offences he was 'attached by the body', in other words, put into prison

Fallow deer, though not indigenous, are much more numerous than Red deer in England to await trial. Where he was committed for trial at the next eyre he might thus be faced with a very long term of imprisonment. In practice, the term of imprisonment in later times was usually limited to a year and a day and, in fact, a fine was often substituted for imprisonment. Whether in prison or not, the lengthy interval that so often occurred between eyres meant that many men died while awaiting trial. One of the first items of business at an eyre was to enquire about absentees, and frequently a high proportion of those had died.

Forest offences fell into two main categories, those of *vension* and those of *vert*. Vension referred, of course, to offences concerning deer; vert dealt with damage to trees and underwood. In later centuries the offence of *assart*, meaning the uprooting of trees and bushes in order to cultivate the ground, also became common, as did *purpresture*, meaning encroachment by unlawful enclosure. Penalties changed with the centuries. William the Conqueror decreed, according to the *Anglo-Saxon Chronicle*, that 'whoever killed a hart or a hind should be blinded', and under William Rufus many forest offences were punishable by death. Much depended on the status of the offender, the common distinction being between (a) a freeman, (b) a villein, or peasant farmer tied to his holding, and (c) a bondsman or serf. Thus, if a freeman were caught chasing a stag 'until it panted for breath' he was, at one period, imprisoned for a year. For the same offence a villein was imprisoned for two years, while a serf was made an outlaw. For killing a stag, a freeman lost his freedom, presumably by being downgraded to the status of villein or bondsman; a villein was put in prison, but a bondsman was executed. Penalties were always more severe on strangers than on residents in the forest.

Considerable ameliorations of the harsh forest laws were granted by the Charter of the Forest in 1217, which followed the signing of Magna Carta in 1215. One of the clauses of Magna Carta was that King John should relinquish vast areas which he had made subject to forest law. He failed to do so, but the barons quickly made sure that his heir, Henry III, who was then a minor, would honour the undertaking. It was this Forest Charter which limited the period of imprisonment to a year and a day and extended the rights of forest freeholders.

The Eyre justices of Sherwood Forest in 1287 devised a forest code of their own, in which the following were some of the clauses:

That anyone dwelling in the forest found felling a green oak be attached for the next attachment court, there to find pledges till the next eyre, and to pay the price to the verderers; a second offence to be dealt with in like manner; but for a third offence to be imprisoned at Nottingham and there kept till he be delivered by the king or justice of the forests.

That anyone dwelling outside the forest committing any trespass against the vert, his body is to be committed to prison till he be delivered by the king or justice; for a third offence he is also to lose his horses and cart or his oxen and wagon, or their price, and that price is to be paid at the next attachment to the verderers for the king's use.

That those dwelling in the forest caught cutting saplings, branches or dry-

Hazel flowers, opening in January, are the earliest woodland flowers of the year

wood from oaks or hazels or thorns or limes or alders or hollies or suchlike trees without warrant are to be attached by two good pledges to come to the next attachment court, there to be amerced for the king . . . .

That escapes of beasts of the plough into the forest be pleaded in attachment, and amends taken for the use of the king.

That no man carry bows or arrows in the forest, outside the king's highway, save a sworn forester; and on the king's highway only in accordance with the assize of the forest.

That no man save a sworn forester or other sworn officer attach (arrest) anyone in the future.

That any dweller outside the forest agisting his animals therein is to have such animals taken before the verderers, and the price paid, and to make answer before the justices in eyre.

In all probability this represents an attempt to codify what was general practice.

After the Middle Ages

The previous chapter has demonstrated what a complex entity of rights, privileges, vested interests and obligations a medieval forest was. Far from being an amorphous waste it was mapped, administered and controlled as effectively as any farmland. It was a source of livelihood to many people and a source of revenue to many more.

It used to be thought that the coppicing of woodland dates from the first attempt to legislate about it, in 1483, but a more thorough examination of the evidence shows that coppicing was practised at least as early as the reign of William the Conqueror. Underwood was in strong demand for fencing, faggots, wattle-and-daub in houses, hurdles for farm use and many other minor purposes. As in more recent times the hazel, ash and other underwood of a forest were cut at regular intervals, according to the custom of the district. Once in eight years is a fair average, but in some localities the interval was as little as four years. After cutting, at just above ground level, the stubs or stools would send up new, straight shoots which at the age of from four to eight years were ideal for most purposes. The snag was that deer, cattle, sheep and other animals love to nibble at the young shoots. The problem did not become acute while the waste or wild wood seemed limitless and inexhaustible. As the Middle Ages unfolded, however, the woodlands shrank before human settlement and the remaining forest areas had to support an increasing stock of both wild and domestic beasts. The severe depopulation caused by the Black Death in the middle of the fourteenth century gave a respite, but by the end of the fifteenth century the human population had recovered and the Act of 1483 seemed urgent.

Other forces were at work. The forests, as was well established, were royal property, and therefore any revenue they produced belonged to the king. William I and his successors were so fond of hunting that they were happy to give it priority in the forests, even to the extent of foregoing other income. By the fifteenth century a change had occurred. Though hunting was still popular, the monarchy had become more and more interested in ready cash, and underwood in the royal forests was a source of revenue. So the 1483 Act, fortified by a stronger one in 1543, required woods to be fenced after cutting in order to give the underwood time to recover and young forest trees a chance to get started. Although private landowners, including freeholders with enclosures in the royal forests, must long have practised this measure of control, the law met with strenuous opposition and was widely disregarded. Forest officials responsible for the deer saw the animals' browsing curtailed; commoners resisted any attempt to diminish their rights to graze domestic animals in the forest. Rendering the law ineffective presented no difficulties to an ingenious peasantry. Delaying tactics in the erection of fences were employed; when constructed the fences tended to develop mysterious holes, or the gates were surreptitiously left open. Some forest officials even turned their own livestock into the enclosures to graze. Anyone caught felling trees would plausibly plead that the trees were dying anyway.

The forests took another knock with the dissolution of monastic houses in the 1530s. Medieval monks were not only expert agriculturists but efficient foresters and always had a keen eye for sources of income. With the break-up of the old monastic estates many time-honoured customs went by the board, among them in many instances the practice of the art of forestry.

In similar troubled times 100 years later, during the Civil War, the forests again suffered a period of neglect. Encroachment proceeded rapidly and local residents helped themselves freely to underwood and timber. James I and Charles I, in dealing with the royal forests as in other matters, exercised their disastrous instinct for trying to put the clock back and succeeded only in arousing opposition. When soon after his accession James attempted to shut a section of Windsor Park to the public, 'squires and better sort made private keys and entered like gentlemen of the highest quality; the locks were exchanged and they broke the fences with as little scruple as the tramps'.

Following the same misguided pattern of conduct, Charles I revived the old forest courts of Windsor,

Every old formality was strictly observed; at the opening each forester had to present his horn on bended knee to the chief justice in eyre, and each woodward his hatchet; and these insignia of office were not returned until a fine of half a mark had been rendered. The revival of forest pleas in Surrey was bitterly resented ... many of the gentlemen of Surrey encouraged rather than checked outbreaks of daylight poaching, hunting in companies of eighty or a hundred.

The situation deteriorated further until in 1641 'the people round New Lodge, in a riotous fashion, killed a hundred fallow deer, in addition to some red deer, and threatened to pull down the pales of that park'. Legal proceedings against the offenders were initiated but were naturally abandoned at the outbreak of civil war.

In the New Forest the emphasis had been shifted from deer to timber since Henry VII made Portsmouth the new headquarters of his Navy. Under the Tudors the value of the forests of Hampshire as a source of ship-building material was clearly recognised. The policy was at first continued under the Stuarts, and James I commisssioned a detailed survey of a number of forests. That for the New Forest in 1608 reported 300,000 loads of timber available, of which almost two-thirds were suitable for ship-building. Modern authorities have interpreted that as between 60,000 and 100,000 mature oaks.

Under Charles administration was neglected. Forest officials were not paid and naturally helped themselves to whatever perquisites they could grab. Charles, desperate for money, made over almost the whole of the Forest of Dean, with its timber and mines, to Sir John Winter for a huge capital advance. He offered the New Forest and Sherwood Forest to some of his creditors as security for loans. Yet despite these manœuvrings he still looked to the forests as a source of venison for banquets on special occasions. For Christmas, 1640, for instance, he required 104 does to be sent, some from forests as far away as Rockingham and Clarendon, to Whitehall.

If the forest officials found their stipends falling into arrears during the reign of Charles they certainly did not get paid during the Civil War and the period of the Commonwealth. Acting according to the dictates of human nature, they doubtless made arrangements to pay themselves, and both the forests and their denizens suffered. Although Windsor Forest, for example, was under the nominal control of Sir Bulstrode Whitelocke, an enlightened and reasonable man who made it his business to compile a record of the ancient customs of the forest, the area was nevertheless divided among a number of owners, each of whom did more or less as he pleased with his allocation.

After the Restoration Charles II, though beset with numerous more urgent problems, did what he could to repair some of the devastation. In the Forest of Dean, for instance, he rescued some of the woodlands from his loyal but misguided supporter, Sir John Winter, who within the space of six years had felled 30,000 trees. Charles also re-stocked several of the royal forests with deer, even importing some from Germany. In 1670 he appointed a Royal Commission to survey the New Forest and report on encroachments and other changes that had occurred since the time of King James. On the other hand he made grants in this particular forest in a capricious manner. To a Mrs Winifred Wells, a maid-of-honour at his court concerning whom certain lively scandals circulated, he granted two New Forest coppices in spite of the disapproval of his Lord Treasurer.

Nevertheless, it was in Tudor and Stuart times that the practice of making new forests or plantations was first established. One of the earliest plantations of which any record exists concerns 13 acres in Cranbourne Walk, an enclosed portion of Windsor Park, which in 1580 Lord Burleigh caused to be planted with acorns and afterwards fenced to keep out deer and cattle. In 1625 an enthusiastic forester, in urging Charles I to sow acorns elsewhere in Windsor Forest, quoted the success of this plantation, stating that it had now become 'a wood of some thousands of tall young oaks, bearing acorns, and giving shelter to cattle, and likely to prove as good timber as any in the kingdom'.

The first book on forestry ever published in English was *New Directions of Experience for the Increasing of Timber and Firewood*, by Arthur Standish, which appeared in 1613. In 1664 John Evelyn, the diarist, popularised the new art of silviculture in a book verbosely entitled *Silva, or a Discourse of Forest Trees, and the Propagation of Timber in his Majesty's Dominions*. Evelyn was primarily concerned with producing enough timber for the

Navy, but rightly argued that 'all arts and artisans whatsoever must fail and cease if there were no timber and wood in a nation, . . . we had better be without gold than without timber'. His theories and admonitions were soon being translated into action both by the Crown and by the landed gentry. Inspired by Evelyn, Charles II set aside 300 acres in the New Forest as a forest nursery, devoted to the production of oak seedlings.

The enclosures, which had been increasing in volume during the troubled years of the seventeenth century, developed into a flood in the eighteenth. The success of mercantile ventures such as the East India Company (founded by a charter of Queen Elizabeth I in 1600) was making England a country of capitalists. Country gentry, tired of political adventures and determined to hold what they now possessed, took stock of their assets in the form of land and found them intriguing. New ideas in agriculture held out promises of a vastly increased income if properly exploited. Almost every manor, however, was hopelessly fragmented. Open-field cultivation, in which individuals held one-acre strips all devoted to the same crop, was the norm. The three great fields into which the arable land of the average parish was divided were surrounded by a zone of forest or waste, where each parishioner had certain rights sanctified by centuries of custom. There cattle, horses, sheep and pigs roamed unhindered, multiplying by indiscriminate mating. Any attempt at experimenting with new crops or improved methods of stock-breeding required the consent of all freeholders whose rights were involved, and almost always there was at least one stubborn die-hard who was against innovations of any kind.

The principle of arranging parish enclosures was therefore evolved. In theory it was fair and equitable. The parish was carefully surveyed and each common right and other interest recorded. The land was then divided out on that basis. Naturally the lord of the manor collected the lion's share, but everyone had his allocation. In practice enclosures worked out harshly for the smaller householders, who had been able to eke out a living from their home pasture supplemented by grazing rights, firewood rights and other perquisites on the common land, but who found the few acres allotted to them quite inadequate. Often enough they had to sell out to their bigger neighbours to pay legal costs. And there were many abuses and much sharp practice. Nevertheless the enclosures were a necessary prelude to agricultural progress. Confirmed in possession now of a compact estate in a ring fence, rural landowners and large farmers were in a position to exploit and develop profitably the new ideas of cropping and stock-breeding that were now circulating. The industrial revolution which created the new manufacturing towns and laid the foundations of urban England was matched by the agricultural revolution in the countryside. Between 1702 and 1844 some 6,000,000 acres were enclosed by Acts of Parliament, and most of the land passed into the hands of big rural landowners.

The estates created by these landed gentry were usually masterpieces of landscape artistry. In most instances they were deliberately planned,

A mixture of pine and deciduous trees provide a stark silhouette against the March sky

often with the assistance of a recognised expert such as Lancelot ('Capability') Brown (1715–1783), who earned his nickname by his habit of remarking, when shown an expanse of unimproved countryside, that he could 'see its capabilities'. The familiar rural landscape of today is largely the creation of the first generation of landlords after the enclosures. Magnificent mansions were erected, quite frequently at the cost of existing villages which were moved to other sites at the landowner's whim. Pleasure grounds and parks, with artificial lakes, waterfalls, grottoes and follies of every description, were laid out. The farmland was divided into compact farms equipped with adequate and solid buildings and usually let to tenants. And, above all from our point of view, trees were planted.

While still retaining an interest in deer, the new type of landowner was mainly concerned with smaller game, notably pheasants, partridges, hares and foxes. His efforts at landscape planning were made largely with that in mind. Shelter-belts were designed to afford good shooting and to keep game on the estate. Woods were managed in the interests of pheasants, and such monstrosities as spring-guns and man-traps were set to catch poachers. On the other hand, hill-top clumps of trees, notably beeches, were planted purely for their scenic effect.

Once a parish was enclosed, encroachment virtually ended. Certain commons remained, from which it was sometimes possible to filch small plots, but individual owners naturally fenced their lands and kept out trespassers. The boundaries of the woodland were now fixed and immutable, except for deliberate change by the owners. Within the enclosed forests, open deciduous woodland was standard. Typical oak woodland in southern England had a well-tended undergrowth of hazel with a canopy of trees at the rate of 12 to 20 per acre. Beeches, especially in shelter-belts, hill-top clumps and on hillsides, were more plentiful than in the Middle Ages, as also were sycamores, which were introduced probably as late as the sixteenth century but which were planted extensively by eighteenth-century landowners. One of the chief features of woodland forestry in the eighteenth and nineteenth centuries, however, was the spread of conifers, notably the Scots pine.

Although pines had flourished in England a few thousand years ago, by historic times they had retreated to the Scottish Highlands, where they were the dominant tree in the old Caledonian Forest. The move southward seems to have been started by John Evelyn, who in the late 1630s had a consignment of seed sent to him in Surrey by the Marquis of Argyll. On the English estates it became popular, largely because its value as a nurse crop for deciduous trees. Being of more rapid growth it formed a protective shield around the oaks and beeches with which it was interplanted, and was ripe for felling while the broad-leaved trees were still immature. Two timber crops could thus be taken from the same ground. Spruce and larch had a similar history, though spruce was introduced from northern and central Europe rather earlier, being well established by the seventeenth century. Both were valued for their suitability for fencing stakes and gates.

Most of the other now familiar conifers, such as the Sitka spruce, silver fir, Douglas fir and Lawson cypress, were not introduced until the nineteenth century was well advanced. The cedar of Lebanon was brought in perhaps 200 years earlier and became very popular as a park tree on the new estates. It grows to an impressive size, but most of the great cedars now admired are probably less than two centuries old.

As has been noted, from medieval times onwards the utilitarian aspect of forests, meaning the timber as against sporting rights, has been uppermost. As the size and number of ships increased so did the demand for trees, until in Nelson's day 1,000 first-class oaks were needed to build a ship of the line. One reason why Henry VII moved the headquarters of the Navy from the Cinque Ports and the Thames to Portsmouth was the threatened exhaustion, through iron-working and smelting as well as through the demand for building timber, of the ancient forest of the Weald. England's enemies were fully aware of her dependence on her timber, for in the reign of Elizabeth I the Spanish ambassador to London was in-

structed to look into the possibilities of destroying the Forest of Dean by fire! Although for ship-building there was an obvious advantage of having good oak forest behind the shipyard, many timbers were fetched from distant forests. Today beams can be shaped at will, but for trusses and curved timbers medieval and later craftsmen preferred wood which had grown that way, and merchants used to tour the country searching for great timbers with the desired shapes and angles.

In Nelson's day 1,000 first-class oaks were needed to build a ship of the line like the Victory

As already mentioned, King James I's survey of the New Forest revealed an available stock of 300,000 loads of timber from mature and sound oaks. A hundred years later, with the turbulent years of the Civil War and the Commonwealth intervening, the reserves had sunk to about 19,500 loads. After the Restoration, however, some large-scale re-planting was undertaken—1,400 acres in the New Forest and 11,000 acres in the denuded Forest of Dean. In 1783 another survey of the New Forest showed the reserves there at much the same level as in 1707. Individual landowners made patriotic efforts to help. Improvements of their estates were effected as much by intelligent and consistent management as by new plantations. Timber was now cut at regular intervals and according to predetermined policy rather than haphazardly, and on many estates all trees felled were made good by planting or by natural regeneration. On the other hand, many other estates cleared their forests to make new arable fields, so the net result was a considerable loss.

Recent research has indicated that the demands for timber for shipbuilding may have been exaggerated. It has been calculated that at the beginning of the nineteenth century, with the Napoleonic Wars raging, 100,000 acres of oak woodland would have been ample to provide for ever all the timber required by the Navy, even at that inflated level of demand. And England then had over 1,000,000 acres of forests. Less than 20 years later large consignments of excellent oak began to be imported from Mediterranean countries. However, the tradition that England needed plenty of good oaks for her ships continued to flourish and patriotic estate-owners continued to grow them.

Throughout the nineteenth century private estate-owners were chiefly responsible for such progress as was made. Prizes were offered and grants made for new plantings by several learned societies, such as the London Society of Arts and the Royal Dublin Society. Exotic species of trees were introduced, and towards the end of the century the switch from deciduous trees to softwoods became intensified. Subsequent generations of landowners have, however, deplored the introduction by the Victorians of the rhododendron. Its amenity value, especially when the shrubs are in blossom, is high, but from every other point of view, and especially that of the efficient forester, it is an unmitigated nuisance.

During the century the boundaries of woodland and farmland became more or less static. By the 1870s most landowners considered they had the ratio of the several departments of their estates just about right. Many of them straightened out the boundary-fences and laid out a network of rides through the woodlands, to give easy access and to assist sporting arrangements. It was an age of high farming, and woodland management was on a similar prosperous plane. In the 1870s cheap grain started to pour in from America, followed by shiploads of refrigerated meat from America, Australia and New Zealand. The long agricultural depression had begun. For the next 70 years or so only periods of war gave brief respites from the prevailing rural poverty, in which the country estates inevitably shared.

Pencil drawing of fir trees by John Constable, R.A. (1815)

Farmland lay derelict through the impossibility of finding tenants and, with land a liability rather than an asset, estates sold off as much as they could. Neither they nor the new owners could afford proper forest maintenance, and innumerable acres of woodland lapsed into dereliction.

Men of the Forest

Apart from what may be termed amenity forests, in which efforts are made to cater for holiday-makers, forests today are lonely places. Especially in private woodlands it is possible to wander all day without seeing a soul. Woods are synonymous with solitude. The royal forests of medieval England must have been very different. As can be gathered from numerous examples already quoted, they were alive with people. Consider, for instance, the attendance at that forest court of the Forest of Rutland—by no means one of the largest forests—in 1490 of 250 forest *officials*. And these were officials only, the upper echelons of the population of the Forest. Other ranks always outnumber officers, and there is no reason to suppose that the forests provided an exception.

The implications of an overwhelmingly rural population are worth considering. In the thirteenth and fourteenth centuries, which may be regarded as the middle of the Middle Ages, the population of England was probably between two and three millions. Nine-tenths of these lived in the countryside. London was the only town of any size, with Bristol, Norwich and York perhaps approaching a population of 20,000 each, but most country or market towns gave a home to no more than about 5,000 souls and would thus be classified, by our present standards, as largish villages. Most of the two or three millions of Englishmen at that date therefore derived their living more or less directly from the land. That is more than twice as many as present. Twice as many people but less space for them. Forests, including many moors, mountains and wastes, occupied vast areas, in some instances whole counties. And virtually every manor had its own waste or common, never yet touched by plough. Unless the cultivated fields supported an extremely dense population, it follows that the waste, the commons and the forests must have absorbed their share. And so the records confirm.

Could we step back seven centuries into history we would stand amazed at the crowds of people working in the fields. It is early October and the harvest is just ending. Most of the corn has been cut, though here and there a few peasants are belatedly busy with their reap-hooks on their private acre-strips. The great arable fields, one devoted to wheat and the other to barley, are, of course, divided into long ribbon-like strips, so arranged that no man has two contiguous ones. Inevitably there is much movement between strips and between fields, as the peasant and his family finish work on one and trudge off to the next. When reaping, he has his wife and older children behind him, gathering up the cut stalks and tying them into sheaves, which are then stood in stooks to dry.

Other peasants are transporting the sheaves to their yard in the village.

The more prosperous use an ox-cart, the poorer families carry the sheaves on their backs. The parson is there, collecting the tenth sheaf from every acre and carting them off to his tithe barn. In the great fields the lord of the manor has many strips, in addition to his enclosed demense, and his foreman and serfs and those freeholders who owe him time are clearing away the last sheaves and raking the stubble. The poor widows of the village, stooping over the coarse sacks tied around their waists, are gleaning the fallen ears of corn; nothing must be wasted.

On the third great field, left fallow during the past summer and mown for what hay it managed to produce, some ploughs are already busy, preparing the land for wheat. Each plough is drawn by six or eight slow-moving oxen or cows, one man guiding the plough and two or three more either leading the oxen or prodding them to keep them moving. Cattle in the charge of the village cowherd and sheep watched by the village shepherd still graze on the uncultivated strips of this field. The swineherd with his pigs are in the neighbouring woods, for it is the season of acorns, on which pigs can grow fat, but the village goose-girl is controlling her flock on the stubble-fields, where the geese peck up the loose grains that even the gleaners cannot retrieve. Down in the village clankings and hammerings indicate that the blacksmith and carpenter are busy at work. The clatter of the mill-sails show that some of the harvest has found its way to the village miller. Everywhere there are people—noisy, industrious but somewhat drab, for all are clothed in dull, earth-coloured cloth or, usually, rags.

Such is the scene in the open country around the houses, but in the woods there is almost as much activity. Our first impression is that here, in the woods nearest the village, all except a few great trees are either coppiced or pollarded—that is, they are cut off periodically at either ground level or head-height in order to secure regular crops of poles of brushwood. The woodlands are divided into fenced sections, in which the coppiced or pollarded trees are in various stages of growth. Some were cut in the previous winter, and these (and all those cut within the past two or three years) are protected by a fence of wattled hurdle-work six or eight feet high. Men are repairing gaps in the fences or renewing the gates. Others are cutting the wood in sections of the forest ripe for harvesting and stacking it in heaps, while some have already begun splitting hazel rods and weaving them into the hurdles of which the fences are composed.

Trees were blown down by a recent gale, and gangs of men are dismembering them. The trunks belong to the king, but other men have the right to the branches. Here is a peasant with a cart whose rights only extend to an occasional load of thorn-bushes, and a woodward is checking with him to make sure that he is not exceeding his customary quota. The sound of axes ringing through the forest testify to the presence of woodmen, felling mature trees in accordance with the lord's instructions. Are the timbers for use in ships or houses or as scaffolding for the building of a great cathedral?

We meet the village swineherd with his herd of pigs—ugly, bristly,

This 540-year-old oak in Wiltshire had reached a height of 70 ft when it was felled in 1978

razor-backed beasts, busily shovelling in acorns. They are so like wild pigs that we wonder whether the latter were ever exterminated or simply absorbed into the domestic population. An agister is checking, suspicious that there are more than are entitled to enter the forest.

As we penetrate farther we encounter charcoal-burners, the smoke from whose fires spirals gently up through the tree canopy. There are half-a-dozen grimy men tending a series of smouldering heaps, and from time to time a cart, drawn by a forest pony, arrives to collect a load of processed charcoal. As we watch we are joined by a forester, clad in green cloth, bearing bow and arrows and accompanied by three dogs of greyhound or lurcher type. These are not pet dogs but suspicious brutes who bare their teeth and snarl at us. The forester is one of the few persons allowed to take unimpeded dogs into the forest. Several of the forest workers, we noticed, also had dogs with them, but these animals hobbled or limped, having had their toes cut off so that they should not chase deer.

So far we have not seen any deer, but we now come across a gang of men making a *buckstall* for them. This buckstall is a woodland enclosure surrounded by a fence of wattle hurdles, inside which is a broad, deep ditch known as a *deer-leap*. The fence is sufficiently low to allow a deer to leap over it into the enclosure but sufficiently high to prevent it, hampered as it is by the deer-leap, from getting out again. Here the deer will be fed on ivy, holly, oak twigs and other browsings in hard weather, and here too they can be snared if ever any are required without the trouble of hunting. The one we see is an official buckstall, but some have at times been made illegally, for the catching of deer by people not entitled to them.

At this season, the bracken is tall enough to hide a deer, but soon frost will turn it brown. Then the villagers will be here, cutting it for winter bedding for the livestock and perhaps for themselves: bracken-cutting is a valued right of forest commoners. Hazel-nuts are becoming ripe and will soon be slipping from their husks. They too are a valued forest crop, soon to be gathered by the villagers, who often have them ground and mixed with wheaten flour for making bread.

The tamed forest gradually gives place to the wild wood, though by the end of the thirteenth century that had almost completely vanished from some of the southern forests. Wolves and wild boars were growing scarce, as the entire extensive woodland, from one side to the other, became subject to enclosure and exploitation. We are unlikely to see any of these animals or indeed any others that a twentieth-century rambler in the woods would not see, except perhaps the red squirrel and the marten. The forests, however, are very large, often covering, as noted in Chapter two, scores of thousands of acres, so some of them harbour strange fauna, even outlaws. Robin Hood and his merry men, though their memory is perpetuated in idealised form, were not entirely imaginary.

Let us look a little more closely at some of the human denizens of the forest. The *King* and his *Huntsmen* logically have pride of place. An invitation to a day's hunting with the king was probably very similar to a modern invitation to a house-party including a day's pheasant shooting. The guests would be high-ranking nobles or visiting monarchs; on one occasion in the fourteenth century the king, Edward III, went hunting in Clarendon Forest with two other kings, John of France and David of Scotland, who had been captured in battle and were awaiting ransom. Sir Walter Tyrell, who accompanied William II on that fatal August day in the New Forest, was a visiting knight from Normandy, just possibly invited along so that he could be framed for the murder. The guests would not be numerous—perhaps five or six—but each would be accompanied by a personal retainer, much as pheasant guns have their loaders. The king would be accompanied by his chief huntsman. Concerning the organisation of the hunt there is much conflicting evidence. A study of the events in the New Forest on the day that William Rufus was killed shows that, having arrived near the scene of the hunt, the king and his guests dismounted and took up stations that had been carefully chosen for them. These were just inside the edge of the wood, facing a forest clearing, on the far side of which lay another wood from which the deer were to be driven. Beaters in a curving line guided the stags in the desired direction, allowing the hinds to double back and escape. The huntsmen shot at the deer as they broke cover and bounded across the clearing. On this occasion the king loosed his arrow at a stag and grazed it. It was while he was standing for a few seconds, watching the stag and shading his eyes from the setting sun, that he was shot through the heart.

However, that was not the only method of hunting. Often, it seems, the deer were chased by men on horseback. A series of fifteenth-century pictures illustrate the sequence of events during a royal hunt. The king is out hawking, a falcon on his wrist, when he spies a fine stag and a hind grazing among the trees. In the next picture the hawk has disappeared, having no doubt been handed to an attendant falconer, and the king, blowing his hunting horn and accompanied by a dog which appears to be a greyhound, is starting the chase. In the third picture, urging his horse to a gallop, he is about to loose his second arrow, his first having penetrated right through the deer's neck (*see* plate I). The stag, evidently a powerful and vigorous animal, still keeps going, so the king continued the chase and eventually despatches his quarry with a sword-thrust. The fifth picture depicts the king showing off his trophy, the stag's head held on a pole by a retainer, to the queen, who seems suitably impressed. In the sixth, in an entirely utilitarian manner, the king, having cut the carcase into four quarters, is hanging the quarters from trees, while the greyhound laps up the dripping blood. That method of hunting must have been fashionable at least five hundred years earlier, when in the tenth century King Edmund had his memorable escape from death on the edge of Cheddar Gorge (see p. 110). And other medieval pictures depict kings on horseback dispatching wild boars by the sword.

As might be expected with such a popular sport, hunting had its literature, even in medieval times. The earliest book on hunting concerned primarily with England is *Le Art de Venerie*, written about 1325 by William Twici, who was chief huntsman to Edward II. This book is in Norman-French. Somewhere around the year of 1410 Edward Duke of York, a grandson of King Edward III, translated into English a French treatise, *Livre de Chasse*, and then added a few chapters of his own, calling the entire work *The Master of Game*. In 1486 Dame Julyana Bernes used both of these works in compiling *The Boke of St Albans*. A sixteenth-century book, quoted in a few instances in previous chapters, is *The Noble Art of Venerie or Hunting*, by George Turberville, who, however, translated it from the French. In 1591 Sir Thomas Cockayne wrote his *Short Treatise of Hunting*, mostly personal experiences. And in the seventeenth and eighteenth century the literature of the subject gradually became profuse.

From the early writings one gathers that the usual procedure when hunting stags was to put them up by a dog which corresponded to a bloodhound and then to pursue them with a pack of smaller hounds, known as raches, corresponding to our beagles. Fallow deer and roe deer, on the other hand, needed no starting by greyhounds but had the raches loosed after them immediately.

A word on medieval types of dog will not be out of place. The *Greyhound*, also known as the Gazehound because it hunted by sight, was described by a writer in 1576 as

a spare and bare kinde of dogge (of fleshe but not of bone); some are of a greater sorte, and some of a lesser; some are smooth skynned, and some are curled; the bigger thereof are appointed to hunt the bigger beasts, and the smaller serve to hunt the smaller accordingly.

It was probably rather larger and stronger than our greyhound, perhaps more like a deerhound. Its colour was very variable.

The *Lymer* or *Limehound* seems to have been the medieval counterpart of our bloodhound; it, too, hunted by sight. The *Mastiff* was a huge,

powerful beast, much larger than a modern mastiff and evidently with a reputation for fierceness, for it is often depicted muzzled. In hunting it was employed for running down and killing wolves and wild boars, and it could tackle a red deer stag. That mastiffs belonging to commoners could not be allowed to roam freely in the royal forests but had to be expeditated is understandable.

The *Rache* or *Brache* appears from its pictures to have been a rather jolly little dog, usually black and tan in colour. It hunted in packs, by scent. The *Bercelet* was a smaller edition of the brache.

Such were the common hounds of the forest. In addition, several other types are mentioned in medieval documents. The *Hart-hound* was a kind of stag-hound, used only for hunting the red deer. The king kept a pack in the fifteenth century. The *Buckhound* was similarly reserved for hunting fallow deer, and the *Roehound* the roe deer. Then there were *Boar-hounds*, *Otterhounds* and *Harriers*, though the last-named were used in hunting deer as well as hares. No detailed descriptions survive of any of these dogs. Occasional mentions are also made of *Velters*, which were apparently mongrels, though related to greyhounds, and were used in hunting wild boars. *Strakurs* were also mongrels, more frequently used by poachers than by anyone else.

Predictably, the men in charge of the various kinds of hounds had their own special titles. The man who looked after the greyhounds was the *Ventrer*, or sometimes the *Fewterer*. The huntsman in charge of the raches or bercelets was the *Berceletter*. He who controlled the 'running hounds' was the *Berner*.

The forest officials have already been introduced in Chapter 3. The hierarchy comprised a *Warden*, or *Chief Man of the Forest*, usually a nobleman, and under him *Verderers*, *Foresters*, *Woodwards*, *Rangers*, *Agisters* and in some instances *Parkers*, *Regarders* and *Warreners*. Their numbers varied from forest to forest. A forest court for Clarendon, a large and important forest, was in 1469 attended by the Forest Warden or keeper, his lieutenant, the lieutenant's deputy, a ranger and his deputy, a launder (in charge of the forest lawns) and his deputy, four foresters, two verderers, four woodwards and 12 regarders. In 1490 the smaller Forest of Bere, in Hampshire, had as its chief officials a warden or keeper, his lieutenant, a forester and his deputy, a ranger, and two verderers. At a forest court for the Forest of Pickering in 1334 the warden or keeper had under him seven foresters, one of whom was a woman and was therefore represented by her deputy, 13 regarders, four verderers and four agisters. At a similar court for the Forest of Rockingham in 1490 the head forester, Viscount John Welles, had under him four lieutenants, and under them 'woodwards, parkers, palesters, launders, constables and four-men and other ministers' to the total of 221. In addition, juries of 12 men each from the five Hundreds in which the Forest was included were required to be present. As already mentioned, the attendance at an eyre for the Forest of Rutland in the same year totalled no fewer than 250.

Berners of the fourteenth century. They 'controlled running hounds'

Forest officials had recognised symbols of authority, examples of which are depicted on monumental slabs in Derbyshire and elsewhere. A verderer's symbol was an axe; a woodward's, a kind of bill-hook and sometimes a sword; foresters' symbols varied considerably but included bow and arrows, a sling and a sword.

All the forest officials were important men—knights and esquires holding their positions by being men of substance and having considerable properties in or around the forest. Each would be accompanied by servants and retainers; in the northern forests the records show that the warden normally had a 'bow-bearer' as companion. All had considerable authority, which many of them would exceed, given a chance. Thus, as already noted, Roger Gernet, keeper of the Forest of Lonsdale in about 1220, a wealthy man who should have known better, attempted to take away the rights of a colony of lepers within his domain, charging the lepers an ox for the privilege of turning their cattle into the forest to graze in winter and a cow for the same privilege in summer, whereas a royal charter had declared that they were to exercise those rights freely. It is good to know that Roger was firmly put in his place. In the early fifteenth century the foresters of the Forest of West Derby, in Lancashire, made themselves so obnoxious by 'divers displeasures and annoyances against the tenants, theire wyfes and servants in sundrywise by theire coming to theire houses for theire meat and drink' that the tenants agreed to pay an annual contribution towards the foresters' salaries in order to be rid of the nuisance. A forester of Inglewood in the fourteenth century claimed to be entitled to a meal at the table of the staff of St Mary's Abbey, York, which had interests in the forest, and also the right to take away, whenever he wished, 'a flagon of the best ale, two tallow candles, a bushel of oats for his horse, and a loaf of black bread for his dog'.

From these and similar records it can be gathered that the forest officials were in general an arrogant and officious lot. An encounter with one of them (and they must have been fairly thick on the ground) on our incursion into a medieval forest would probably have been an unpleasant one.

Under the somewhat top-heavy administration, the forest *Peasant* came to the best terms he could with life. He had the one advantage that at times he was needed. His royal master required *Beaters* when hunting and he needed the products of forest crafts. There must have been a demand for *Woodmen* who understood how to fell a tree; for *Sawyers* and *Carpenters*; for *Charcoal-burners*; for men who could make wattle hurdles or cleft palings; for *Bee-wards* who collected the forest honey; for men to take charge of hounds, horses and hawks; for *Bowyers* (bow-makers) and *Fletchers* (arrow-makers); and for the farm produce from the little forest holdings. Also, as enclosures increased and woodland areas diminished, useful rents could be collected from forest holdings. A depopulated forest was of little use to anyone.

In all probability, most medieval forest holdings were very similar to those which survive in the New Forest today. They consisted of a thatched

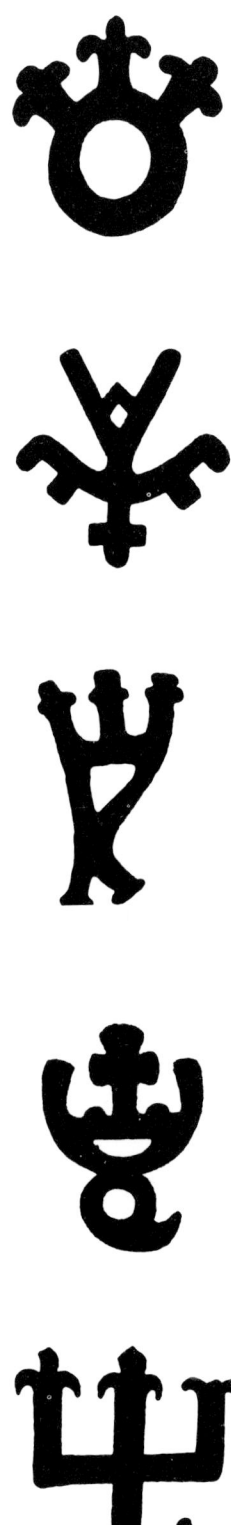

'A forest holding would consist of a thatched house and outbuildings and a few acres of enclosed land' with the right to turn loose in the forest a specified number of livestock. This photograph of a typical New Forest holding was taken in the 1950s

Medieval cattle-brands as used in Epping Forest

house with yard, outbuildings and a few small enclosed fields. Each holding would have specified rights in the forest, such as the right to pasture a stated number of cattle or horses, to turn loose a stated number of pigs at certain seasons, to gather nuts, to collect dead wood for fuel, to turn out geese to forage, to cut turf, even sometimes to fish. It was farming based on livestock, for growing crops was always a hazardous business. In early times it was forbidden not only to fence a field but also to chase away deer which came to feed on the crop.

As noted in Chapter 3, the forest rights concerning livestock were controlled by *agisters*. One common method of ensuring that only permitted animals were loose in the forest was to arrange a system of branding. Our illustration shows a collection of medieval cattle brands from the Forest of Essex. Although at first sight they seem complex each simply consists of a letter of the alphabet (sometimes on its side) surmounted by a crown.

Agisters still operate in the New Forest. There are, I believe, three of them, each of whom supervises the stock of a certain section of the forest. Formerly they rode horseback on their rounds, dressed in the approved uniform, with bright-buttoned waistcoats and broad-brimmed hats, not unlike American cowboys; now they operate by car.

Verderers, too, are still very much a feature of the New Forest life. The Verderers' Court, as constituted by the New Forest Act of 1877, comprises six members elected by the commoners and one member officially appointed: each must own not less than 75 acres within the forest. They meet in the Verderers' Hall at Lyndhurst and their duties include appointing and paying the salaries of officials and employees, preventing unlawful enclosures, collecting dues for pasturage, pannage and other forest rights, and the holding of swainmote courts.

Reverting, then, to our expedition into a forest on an October day in about the year 1300 we shall be sure to meet numerous forest folk busy at their work. Now, for instance, is the season of nutting and of collecting acorns and beech-mast. The pigs are out in strength, shovelling up acorns greedily under the eye of the swineherd, but parties of peasants, mostly women and children, are also collecting them. As late as 1868 in the Log-book of a village school—Landford, on the northern edge of the New Forest—the schoolmaster records:

November 2nd. Am rejoiced to find the Acorning has ended for this Season and that nearly the whole of those absenting themselves on that account have returned to School this morning; having had a most bountiful harvest, such as one as the oldest inhabitants have no recollection.

In 1826 William Cobbett met a party of unemployed weavers from the woollen towns in west Wiltshire far from home in the Wylye valley, where they were gathering hazel-nuts. And William Chafin, writing of life in Cranborne Chase in 1818, notes:

The woods consist chiefly of hazel, which produce nuts in great profusion, to the relief and benefit of all the hamlets and villages for miles around it. It is their second harvest; for when all the corn hath been got in, and the leasing in the fields at an end, the inhabitants betake themselves to the woods; whole families from distant places flock to the Chase; bring their little cots, provisions, utensils and every necessary for their comfort that they can provide themselves with, and make their abode there for whole weeks at a time if the weather will permit.

Chafin adds that most of those collected in the Chase were sold in the towns 'particularly the sea-ports, and the price is generally on a par with wheat'.

The underwood workers meantime had conducted their annual negotiations with the appropriate forest official, had been allocated their section of ripe underwood and were preparing for their winter work. One of their first tasks was to erect a shelter, open to the south, of hurdles and thatched with straw, in which they could sit and work on rainy days. The first wood faggots they cut would be built in a barrier around this hut, leaving a small courtyard in which they could stack a supply of hazel wands. There they could sit snugly in foul weather, splitting their wands and weaving their hurdles.

In an adjoining wood felled timber would be being sawn into logs or planks and then hauled off to various destinations. In addition to the wandering cattle, pigs and perhaps sheep, therefore we would encounter teams of horses, straining against the dead weight of massive logs.

Charcoal-burning was, and to a very minor extent still is, an autumn and winter activity in the woods, and the charcoal-burners were even more permanent residents in the forest than the other peasants. Underwood workers—nut-gatherers, cowherds, swineherds, shepherds, goose-girls,

Deep in the forest lived the charcoal-burners, grimy men whose smouldering heaps sent gentle spirals of smoke up through the canopy of trees (photographs c. 1900)

woodmen, forest officials—all went home at night, but the charcoal-burners must needs stay by their hearths. Each circular hearth, carefully built according to a traditional pattern using logs of level size, took about a week to burn out and had to be watched day and night so that it should never burst into flame. Charcoal-burners erected little huts by a group of dome-shaped hearths and presumably kept watch by rota or else trained themselves to wake at short intervals throughout the night. The medieval demand for charcoal, before coal came into general use, was virtually insatiable. Charcoal was used particularly for all metal-work, including the making of armour and armaments, as well as, in somewhat later times, for gunpowder. Where iron was found in proximity to extensive woodlands and hence to plentiful supplies of charcoal, as in the Weald and the Forest of Dean, smelting furnaces and forges proliferated, and the woods resounded to the clank of hammers and the huffing of bellows.

Autumn was the season for collecting honey. Bees were often kept in straw skeps, but many swarms of wild bees lived in hollow trees in the forest, and doubtless bee-keeping experts knew how to provide artificially hollowed logs for them. Honey was in great demand in medieval times before sugar was available. Not only was it used as a sweetener but was highly regarded as the basic ingredient of mead. It is not easy, too, to appreciate the enormous quantities of beeswax used by a pious Catholic population for wax candles. In Russia, where the subject has been studied in depth, bee-keeping in the forests was highly organised. A forest would be divided into bee-walks, which could be treated as property independent of the land or indeed of the trees in which the hives were situated. Like the charcoal-burner, the *Bee-ward* had a hut in the woods from which he worked. It seems quite likely that a somewhat similar organisation existed in the forests of early England.

Collecting oak-bark (for use in tanning) at the turn of the century

A forest crop harvested in spring rather than in autumn was tree-bark. This was stripped off, by a process known as *Rining* for which a special tool was used, in early May when the sap was rising. Oak was the tree most widely subjected to the treatment, its bark being used for tanning, but, as noted earlier, lime bark was also in demand. At Cricklade, in north Wiltshire, a special celebration was held at the beginning of June to mark the end of the 'bark harvest' in the neighbouring Forest of Braden. It was conducted along the lines of a Harvest Home Supper, and a play written for the occasion was performed by the tanyard workers. 'Rining' was also carried on in late Victorian times in woodlands along the northern edge of the New Forest.

Yet another incidental and minor forest industry which survived in certain southern woods, especially those included in earlier times in the Forest of Clarendon, until well into the present century was truffle-hunting.

Truffles are, of course, underground fungi found in autumn under woodland trees, notably beeches and oaks. Of the several methods of locating them that by using specially trained and specially bred dogs is traditional. Several families of *Truffle-hunters* lived in the village of Winterslow, near Salisbury, and worked in woods over a wide area, using a breed of small dogs which they claimed, perhaps correctly, had originated in France. In 1860 they petitioned Parliament to be excused the annual tax of 12 shillings recently imposed on dogs on the grounds that they were poor labouring men

> living in a woody district of the country where there is a great many English truffles grow, which we cannot find without dogs, we do therefore keep and use a small pudle, sort of dog wholy and solely for that and no other. . . . It has been carried on by our ancestors for generations without paying tax for the dogs.

A character of frequent occurrence in medieval forests was the *outlaw*. The tales of Robin Hood are accurate to the extent that sometimes outlaws operated singly and sometimes combined to form bands. Not all were altruistic enough to rob the rich to help the poor, unless by 'the poor' they meant themselves. And, pleasant though life in the greenwood may have been in high summer, it must have been far otherwise in winter. As F. E. Kenchington, in *The Commoners' New Forest*, observes,

> In real life Maid Marian must have become very shrewish, and dug her toes in for a dry house when the autumn rains set in and as each year brought its addition to the family.

Whatever may have been the custom in early times, outlawry in the thirteenth, fourteenth and fifteenth century was usually imposed only on fugitives from justice. If a man answered a summons to appear at court and was found guilty of a forest offence, he might be fined or forfeit some of his possessions or confined to prison for a time, but he was not normally outlawed; but if he ran away, he was. And an outlaw, being outside the range of the law, forfeited all his possessions. Theoretically there seemed no alternatives beyond journeying to some far-off place or taking to the woods. The punishment would seem to have been irrevocable, but ways around it were evidently found. Robert de Milner, who held the important post of forester of Longdendale in the Forest of the High Peak, 'took over twenty head of game and carried them to his father's house; not appearing at the eyre, he was outlawed'. It can be imagined however, that after he had disappeared for a discreet period, his family had him back and started him in business again. A case from the reign of Henry VII records the misdeeds of one, John Bromall, 'a myschiefes man and *outlawed* for divers murdores and fellones', who was nevertheless employed as a strong-arm retainer by the deputy steward of the same forest.

Another vanished figure of forest life was the *Hermit*. A man of religious convictions, with a liking for solitude and a contempt for the pleasures of this world, the hermit would retire to the depths of the forest, build himself a little hut and there live a life of meditation. At least, that was the theory, and hermits were generally regarded as holy men. Some were probably deformed or handicapped, some were misanthropes, but some seem to have worked out a decidedly pleasant way of life. A fourteenth-century engraving depicts a hermit, apparently lame, who has constructed a neat, well-thatched little house behind a well-made hurdle fence. He is doffing his hat and presumably begging from a passing knight in armour. When staying at Pickering in 1323 Edward II was presented with a petition from a hermit known as 'William, the hermit of Dalby'. At an earlier date William had obtained a royal permit to pasture two cows in the forest. Now, his herd having grown, he asked for permission to keep three cows. It was granted 'for so long as he remained a hermit'. The thought may have crossed the king's mind that this holy man was not doing too badly out of his vocation.

A class of people *not* found in medieval forests was the *gipsies*. The origin and early movements of the gipsies remain veiled, but they seem to have arrived in eastern Europe in the fourteenth century, in central Europe early in the fifteenth, and probably in England early in the sixteenth. An Act of 1530 made it a capital offence simply to be a gipsy; many were hanged and many more deported, but more filtered in, and by the reign of Elizabeth I there were an estimated 10,000 in the country. It was not until that time, however, that they became familiar denizens of the forest. Now traditional forests such as the New Forest and Forest of Dean have their resident, or semi-nomadic, population of gipsies, mostly belonging to well-known families and loosely organised in a matriarchal society, a 'Queen of the Gipsies' making headlines from time to time in the Press. Their attractive horse-drawn vehicles have, however, now given way to luxury motor-caravans, and few now practise their traditional craft of peg-making.

Even a picnic area of a national park forest, then, is not more alive with human beings than our autumn forest of long ago. The picnicking holiday-makers, their children playing around the trees, are not dissimilar, save in dress and affluence, with the picnicking nut-gatherers. Only in a factory are we likely to find so many men at work as in the medieval forest.

Most of the crafts and professions they represented have vanished. A forester today is a man who works in a forest—a skilled and trained man, it is true, but a manual worker, not a knight or a lord. Woodward is now known only as a surname. Verderers and agisters survive only in the few forests, notably the New Forest, where the old customs and administration still function. Warreners and parkers have long since been forgotten. Most of the old craftsmen, too, have disappeared. The chestnut-paling industry still flourishes in Kent and east Sussex, but the old crafts of the hazel underwood have now only a few surviving practitioners, most of them middle-aged or elderly, even though the demand for wattle hurdles for gardens is extremely buoyant. 'Rining' is a dead art; no-one now searches for truffles, and the breed of little 'pudle' dogs trained for the purpose

The king hunting (Royal ms. 10 E iv, ff. 253, 254, 255, reproduced by permission of the British Library Board)

is extinct; nor do bee-keepers exploit the nectar of the forest trees, though lime honey is more expensive than ever it has been. Gipsies, though still addicted to trading in horses and ponies, are more inclined to engage in transactions involving scrap metal than clothes-pegs. The autumn fruits of the forest, such as hazel-nuts, beech-mast, acorns and sloes, have lost their commercial value. Outlaws or their modern counterparts take refuge in great cities rather than in the forest. A man can live the life of a hermit quite as effectively though less pleasantly in a high-rise flat as ever was possible in the depths of a wood.

So, apart from the forests open for recreation, the woods have become lonely places. There must be many woodland hollows deep in bracken and brambles and rhododendrons where a man, dying suddenly, might lie undiscovered till only his bleached skeleton remained. The only human feet that ever penetrate into these secluded places are those of gamekeepers. The modern gamekeeper is a very different character from the medieval keeper of the forest, who was an official of wealth and authority. The gamekeeper is an employee of a great estate, charged with one duty only, that of attending to the welfare of his master's game. In that respect, of course, he is the direct descendant of all those medieval forest officers whose prime concern was with the king's deer, though pheasants have now taken the place of the deer.

The change occurred with the wholesale enclosures of the eighteenth and early nineteenth centuries. As early chapters illustrate, enclosures and encroachments of forests and commons were always going on, but the process became a tidal wave from about 1740 onwards. In the succeeding century thousands of private members' bills sanctioning the enclosure of manors and villages were passed by a complacent Parliament. It was the age of the great estate. Wealthy landowners built magnificent mansions, laid out parks and engaged in large-scale landscape planning under the guidance of such gifted artists as 'Capability' Brown. Villages were unceremoniously moved to new sites, follies and clumps of trees were set on hill-tops, streams were dammed to create ornamental lakes, and in many instances the formerly open forest was enclosed by a high wall. Within the estate precincts the game which afforded sport to the owner was jealously guarded. Deer had become scarcer, but the cult of the pheasant was becoming dominant. For a time any villager daring to set foot in woodlands where in former days he had possessed common rights ran the hazards of man-traps and spring-guns.

For him the situation had deteriorated. Throughout the centuries he had been tolerated in the forest, though hedged about with restrictions and given clearly to understand that he took second place to the deer. Now his status was inferior to that of the pheasant, and the forest was out of bounds. Otherwise things were much the same as before. Poaching offences continued to occupy most of the time of rural courts. For example, in the Forest of Rockingham in 1249 'Simon, the parson of Old, took a roe deer'. When the case was brought before the forest court, Simon did

Aerial view
of the Forest of Dean
Photo. J. E. Hancock

not appear. An order was therefore made on the Bishop of Lincoln, requiring him to make Simon attend, and in due course he was fined £5. To give some idea of the severity of the fine the price of wheat in 1247, a year of great scarcity, was 53s. 8d. per ton, so Simon had to pay the equivalent of two tons of wheat (by 1979 values that would be about £170). Compare this with the case of George—who, 600 years later, in 1848, was convicted of using a gun to kill pheasants in what had formerly been the Forest of Clarendon. He too was fined £5, or, in default of payment, was to be imprisoned for three months. Wheat that year averaged about £10 a ton, so his fine was the equivalent of half-a-ton of wheat (£85 or so of our money).

In the Middle Ages the numerous officers charged with the duty of protecting the royal deer waged a guerilla war not only against human marauders but against any beasts that seemed to offer a threat. Thus wolves were finally exterminated in most of lowland England by the end of the fourteenth century, and other carnivorous animals, notably foxes, wildcats and often badgers, were mercilessly harried. When gamekeepers took over on the rural estates the persecution was extended to smaller mammals, such as stoats, weasels, polecats, martens and even hedgehogs, and to any bird with sharp talons and curved beak. Guns made them now far more efficient at destruction than their predecessors, armed only with bows, slings and traps, could ever have been. Polecats and martens were virtually eradicated, while owls, hawks of every species, jays, crows and magpies were common exhibits on keepers' gibbets, which now became familiar features of the forest.

This chronicle should now switch to the present tense. Mindful of legislation against gin-traps and for the protection of many species of birds, keepers less frequently display their victims' carcases on gibbets, though on private estates such grisly collections are still quite common. The slaughter goes on with little abatement. Laws are effective only insofar as it is possible to enforce them, and who can supervise what goes on in the lonely, secluded woodlands of today? The modern cult of natural history has certainly created an enlightened public, but the places where these things happen are out of bounds to them.

Big money dictates policy in game preservation. Most woodland shoots are now run as syndicates. The members, often wealthy businessmen, pay very considerable sums for the right to several days' shooting each year, and a member may entertain a valued overseas colleague to a week-ends' shoot. For his large investment the man expects a satisfactory return. When he and his guests come down to the country for a shoot they expect to find plenty of pheasants to aim at. They are prepared to reward keepers who provide a good day's sport and to clamp down severely on inefficiency. Knowing this, keepers are inclined to take no chances. Anything that seems to threaten their cosseted pheasants has to go, and it is futile for conservationists to argue for tawny owls, kestrels, buzzards and the rest. These birds have been known to take pheasant chicks, and that is enough. The

Cross-section of an ancient tree-trunk. In the relatively new science of dendrochronology, the tree-rings are used in dating archaeological material.

conservationists are not there to see what happens and, in any case, they do not pay the wages.

Nor should criticism be confined to private estates. Outside of amenity and recreation areas the Forestry Commission lets the shooting of its woodlands to syndicates, just as private landowners do, and gamekeepers employed by the syndicates operate in exactly the same way. In spite of a widespread belief that ours is a more enlightened age, the law of tooth, claw and gun dominates the forest much as it did in Victorian times, nor, apart from the weaponry available, has it changed much since the time of William the Conqueror.

In another respect, too, developments in forestry parallel quite closely those in agriculture. Just as today the superfluity of peasants performing sundry manual tasks has been replaced by powerful machines, so forestry, too, has been mechanised. In agriculture operations on the land are now confined chiefly to seedtime and harvest, leaving the fields at other seasons lonely and uninhabited. So it is with modern forests, except that the intervals between the periods of activity are much longer. The young trees of the new plantations are left to grow for many years before they are ready for the first thinning. Then men equipped with machinery arrive and for a brief period the forest again hums with activity. The forest still provides work for an élite of skilled foresters, but their numbers are necessarily much lower than those of the old woodland workers.

Outside the game preserves forests are becoming more and more the shrines of the cult of holiday. Several decades earlier than the English, the Dutch, with more sea than is sometimes comfortable, tended to gravitate on holiday to their woodlands in preference to the seaside. Now we are following their example. In national parks and Forestry Commision plantations more and more facilities, in the shape of picnic-areas, camping-sites, forest and nature trails, forest museums and car trails, are being provided. A splendid example has been set by H.M. the Queen, who has opened some 1,780 acres of Sandringham Park to the public.

(LEFT) making a hay-crib for sheep—once a common underwood craft; note the gate-hurdles in the background. (RIGHT) a craftsman in Wiltshire making hurdles with split hazel rods

We still have some little way to go before we use our forests as fully as is the case in, for instance, Canada and the U.S.A. In western Canada, with which the author happens to be familiar, forest camping-sites and lodges, equipped with piped water, sanitation, barbecue equipment and piles of logs (ready-cut by convicts!), are thick on the ground. Many Canadians take up residence in the forests for the summer, commuting to work daily from their woodland retreat. Some, where the forest camp happens to be by a convenient lake, commute by sea-plane.

So they rediscover what our ancestors knew well—that the woods are a wonderful and magic place to be in when summer comes. From early English minstrels (*Summer is icumen in, Llude sing cuccu*) to Shakespeare and later poets, English poetry bubbles over with the joy of life in the greenwood. The family parties of nut-gatherers thoroughly enjoyed their autumn holiday in Cranborne Chase. And even in winter 'Forth to the woods did the merry men go, to gather in the mistletoe'.

What, originally, were the inhabitants of Wishford (see p. 118) really up to in the woods so early on the morning of Oak Apple Day? Why is the maypole regarded by many as a phallic symbol? What was the function of the May Queen? Beyond much doubt, May Day, or Oak Apple Day, or whatever date has inherited the old spring customs, was the day when young people participated in the renewal of life that came with the spring: off to the woods, where the trees were bursting into leaf, flowers were blooming and birds were singing and mating, there to join in the general ecstasy. The May Queen originally had a May King as partner. They personified the ancient god and goddess of the forest, who sometimes also masqueraded under the alias of Robin Hood and Maid Marian—the mysterious powers that each spring were responsible for the renewal of life in the greenwood. Even today their influence has not quite departed. We can, like Bismarck and like the Red Indians of North America, stand firmly with our back to an oak when the sap is rising and feel some of its life and energy surging through us. There is still magic in the forest.

Wild Life in the Forests

Much more light penetrates to the floor of the forest in broad-leaved woodland than in dense conifer woods. Sunlight falling through the leaves of deciduous trees creates a dappled pattern beneath, a fact which makes the dappling on a fallow deer perfect camouflage.

Open, broad-leaved forests have three or four vertical zones: (a) the upper canopy, (b) the underwood zone, (c) a layer of brambles, bracken, nettles and other tallish plants, and (d) the woodland floor. Each has its characteristic flora and fauna. In dense conifer forests the intermediate layers are missing. In commercial plantations the trees are planted so thickly that any plants trying to grow under the trees are starved of light and smothered by competition. Even when the trees are thinned the dense clothing of needles on their upper branches so effectively excludes the sunlight that only a few hardy and shade-loving plants can survive beneath.

In its early stages, however, a coniferous forest offers an attractive habitat to certain species of animal and bird. Unhampered by grazing sheep, rabbits and other large herbivorous animals, coarse grasses grow vigorously, forming a dense mat and often almost concealing the young trees. They provide ideal cover for mice and voles, which are encouraged to multiply at a prodigious rate. Predatory birds and animals, such as foxes, stoats, hawks and owls, increase in response to this abundant food supply. As the trees grow tall the wild life population either sinks back to a lower level or moves to any new plantations in the vicinity.

The wild life population of deciduous woodlands is more stable, though subject to cycles to a certain extent. In open, broad-leaved woodland with hazel underwood, for instance, in the year after the hazel is cut primroses, wood violets, wood anemones and other flowers of the woodland floor bloom profusely. As the hazel grows tall in subsequent years so do brambles, woodland thistles, honeysuckle, St John's wort and other tall plants, crowding out the lowlier ones. When the hazel is cut again at the end of seven or eight years the coarse undergrowth is also cleared and the cycle starts again. Each set of plants is probably the better for an enforced rest of a year or two.

In both deciduous and coniferous woodlands the deep forest is intersected by broad rides, and these, with the margins of the woods, form a much more varied and interesting habitat than the heart of the forest. Here, where the natural vegetation of the locality has a chance to flourish, are bluebells and pink campions, bracken and foxgloves, cow parsley and dogroses, and such shrubs and bushes as wayfaring tree, dogwood, guelder rose, blackthorn and gorse. The fauna is equally varied. The woodland rides in particular provide an ideal environment for the display flights of nightjar, woodcock and a number of species of butterfly and are good places for observation, for sooner or later almost every animal and bird which lives in the wood is almost sure to cross them.

A reminder that in the ancient forests of England all forest land is not woodland may be in place here. Visitors to the New Forest, which of all forests is the one that most fully retains its medieval characteristics, will note that heath and scrub are at least as extensive as the woods. Yet the fauna and flora of that very different type of country cannot be ignored in a survey of the forest, for the proximity of trees may well be a factor in making the habitat attractive to some of the rare and interesting creatures, such as the smooth snake, sand lizard, Dartford warbler and certain butterflies and moths, which make their homes there.

The Trees of the Forest

The most numerous deciduous tree in English forests is the OAK. In the primeval forest it must have been largely dominant, and even now it is foremost among the relatively small numbers of broad-leaved trees planted by the Forestry Commission each year. Throughout the nineteenth century the commonest type of oak wood was the open coppice, in which the trees were just thick enough to provide a continuous canopy, under which grew coppiced hazel cut, as already noted, about once every eight years. Oaks themselves have been sometimes coppiced; that is, they have been cut down to ground level at regular intervals to produce crops of strong young saplings—and even more have been pollarded. The great Knightwood Oak in the New Forest was once pollarded, though that happened so long ago that the pollarding is difficult to detect.

In old mixed forests many huge ancient oaks still survive. Some have been allowed to stand in parkland and even built-up areas after the forest around them has been destroyed. In spite of their appearance of great age, it is likely that most of these venerable trees are not more than about 500 years old. Forest lore says that an oak takes 100 years to grow, 100 years to live and 100 years to decay, but some oaks greatly prolong the decaying process. The *Guinness Book of Records* states that the British oak with the largest girth is at Borothorpe Farm, near Bourne, Lincolnshire, with a circumference (in 1973) of 39 ft 1 in.; this tree, however, was once pollarded. The largest one unpollarded is the Majesty Oak at Tredville, Kent, with a girth of 37 ft 5 in. The tallest oak is at Whitfield House, in Hereford and Worcester, which has a height of 138 ft.

There are two native species of oak, the Sessile Oak and the Pedunculate Oak. The main points of difference are that the flowers and acorns of the Sessile Oak have no stalks while the leaves are stalked; in the Pedunculate Oak the leaves are stalkless but the flowers and acorns are carried on stalks. In practice the distinctions have not overmuch value, for very many oaks seem intermediate between the two and are probably hybrids. As a generalisation, which implies there are many exceptions, sessile oaks seem to have

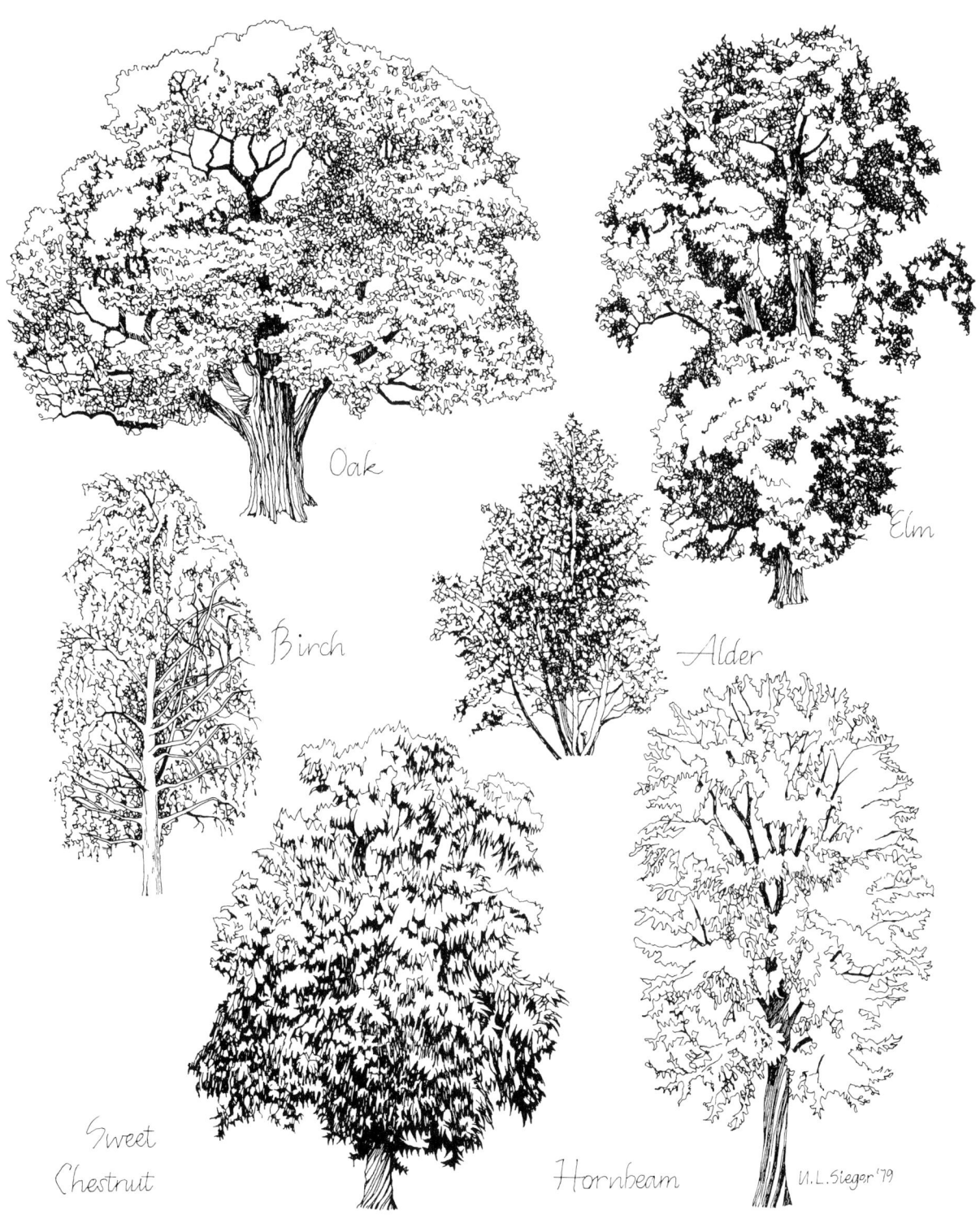

Common trees of the forest

been predominant in the old forests of lowland England, with pedunculate oaks replacing them in the North and in Scotland. But the situation is complicated by the fact that foresters have tended to favour the pedunculate oak in new plantings. In addition to these two native forms, several exotic species have been introduced. Chief among them are the *Holm Oak* or *Ilex*, the *Turkey Oak* and the *Red Oak*. The Holm Oak, sometimes known as the Evergreen Oak because its leaves last for two years, is not uncommon but is usually found in gardens and parks rather than in forests. The Turkey Oak is a handsome tree with long leaves that have serrated edges and acorns that appear to have their cups covered in moss. It grows well on poor soil but produces timber of indifferent quality. The Red Oak, of which there are several species, is of American origin and has in the present century been planted on a fairly large scale.

The BEECH was a latecomer to Britain and managed to spread only as far north as the Midlands before Man started to reshape the landscape. It has been the subject of some curiously misleading statements, as for example Julius Caesar, in reporting his campaign in south-eastern Britain in A.D. 43, says that the Beech was unknown there. Over the past few centuries beeches have been planted in most parts of Britain but are still most plentiful in the south and east, where they thrive best on chalk and limestone soils. Among the best known are Burnham Beeches, on the Chilterns in Buckinghamshire, where many trees are 300 to 400 years old. In many instances the older trees were once pollarded. Our ancestors followed the practice with many tree species, taking, in the case of the beech, a crop of poles and firewood once in about 20 years. Many of the weirdly shaped beeches still to be found in old forests are specimens once subjected to the treatment.

The canopy of a beech wood is denser than that of the oak, and, as the trees usually grow sufficiently close together to leave no space between them, there is normally no growth of underwood and few other plants will flourish in the shade. The tree itself, though, is one of the loveliest of English trees.

Mature specimens of the ASH are generally found as isolated trees in hedgerows, gardens and parks rather than in woodlands. Where ash woods do exist, they have usually been coppiced or pollarded to produce regular crops of ash-poles. As the wood splits easily, these are used for cleft hurdles, for tool-handles and for furniture. The normal life of an ash tree seems to be about 200 years, but coppicing or pollarding tend to prolong it. Professor Oliver Rackham suggests that an ash stool $18\frac{1}{2}$ ft across in West Suffolk, the largest he has seen, may be at least 1,000 years old.

BIRCH is one of the first colonisers to appear when forest begins to take over former grassland or tundra. Pollen deposits reveal that it pioneered the movement of the forest northwards over Britain which started in about 8200 B.C. It is also found on the margins of ancient woodlands, such as those of the New Forest, and it frequently takes over devastated areas where the timber has been felled and which have then been left derelict. For birch requires an open site, with plenty of space and air. Often called 'the lady of the woods', it needs room to grow gracefully. Lovely though it is, the birch is not an especially useful tree. It used to be regarded as a good wood for charcoal and for turnery but cannot compare with softwoods, oak and beech as a commercial crop. Its life-span is seldom more than 50 or 60 years, and its height seldom exceeds 50 to 60 ft.

Although ALDER is sometimes considered to be one of the five main broad-leaved forest trees of Britain, it is usually found on forest margins or along the banks of a forest stream. Essentially a denizen of damp situations, often growing on heavy soil with its roots in the water, the alder is seldom planted but establishes itself where conditions are right. To see a mature, well-grown alder is rare, for most alders have been coppiced in the past. When efficiently exploited the poles were cut every 15 years or so, but most of them are now neglected.

Abundant though it was before the visitation of Dutch elm disease in the 1970s, the ELM is now hardly ever found in woodlands. Botanical archaeologists have found that, once widespread in lowland Britain, the Elm began to decline quite suddenly between 3100 and 2900 B.C., at the time when Neolithic men were starting to engage extensively in farming. The inference is that the elms were mostly on forest fringes and in park-like country which lent itself to cultivation, where it was very vulnerable to human interference. Once the trees were felled, the nibbling of the shoots by domestic livestock prevented natural regeneration. Much the same probably happened in later times, with deer as well as sheep and cattle taking a toll, until eventually the much-harassed elms could survive only where they could find some protection, as in hedgerows. Fortunately the common elm can propagate itself by suckers, which can run along hedges and send up shoots, so the result was an abundance of hedgerow elms without the trouble of planting. A considerable increase probably occurred after the enclosures of the eighteenth and early nineteenth centuries vastly increased the numbers of hedgerows. In many instances a clump of elms will be found to have originated by suckers from one parent plant. Elms thrive best in fertile lowland soils, especially near rivers. They are handsome, useful trees, the wholesale destruction of which by Dutch elm disease is greatly deplored. In the past many were either coppiced or pollarded, treatment from which they readily recovered.

While the common elm often has a dense growth of brushwood around the base of the trunk, the *Wych Elm* does not. It is a smaller tree than the common elm, with a larger leaf, and it does not send out suckers. The common elm is most plentiful in the south and midlands, whereas the wych elm is commoner in the north, where it sometimes forms sizeable woods on the slopes of glens and dales. The incidence of the element 'Wych' in field and other place-names in the south suggests that the species was more widely distributed than at present.

It is probable that the SYCAMORE was introduced to Britain from the Mediterranean at some time in the Middle Ages. A handsome, sturdy tree producing useful timber, it occupied a few decades ago nearly 90,000 acres, besides which it is often found in mixed woods or in isolated stands around farmyards. It likes fertile soil but does well on limestone and chalk. Reaching maturity at 80 years or so, a well-grown tree can then attain a height of 70 to 80 ft and, if allowed, will last another 70 or 80 years.

The HORNBEAM, although an indigenous tree for at least the past 6,000 years, has a much more limited distribution, being confined mainly to heavy soils in the south-eastern counties. Epping Forest and Enfield Chase may be considered its headquarters. Traditionally hornbeam trees were lopped and pollarded, the right to the young shoots being jealously maintained by the commoners of the forest parishes. The rights were exercised until about 100 years ago, and the gnarled and grossly mis-shapen trees now characteristic of the district are the result of that practice. When left untrimmed the hornbeam will grow into an attractive spreading tree from 50 to 80 ft high.

Surprisingly, recent archaeological research based on pollen grains establishes that LIME around 3000 B.C. was probably the dominant tree over much of lowland Britain. It was one of the later arrivals as the tree zone spread northwards following the last Ice Age, first appearing about the middle of the fifth millennium B.C., but it seems to have thoroughly established itself in the south-east, replacing the oak. The frequency of the element 'lin' or 'lynd', an abbreviation of 'linden', in Anglo-Saxon place-names reflects its familiarity to the Saxons, and even now it is commoner than is perhaps generally supposed. Woods entirely of lime are rare, but lime trees are to be found in many mixed broad-leaved woodlands, and lime is, of course, a favourite species in parks and avenues.

The decrease in numbers of limes within historical times is probably due partly to the tree's preference for good, fertile soils, from which it was eliminated for cultivation, and partly to the liking of cattle, sheep and deer for its young leaves. Until about 100 years ago it was frequently coppiced or pollarded. Most limes now growing in Britain are hybrids between the native small-leaved lime and the introduced large-leaved lime, which comes from southern and central Europe.

Of the several species of Poplar now grown in Britain four are reckoned to be indigenous or long naturalised. They are the ASPEN, the WHITE POPLAR, the BLACK POPLAR and the GREY POPLAR.

The quivering Aspen, its circular leaves incessantly a-flutter, though an interesting feature of the woodland scene, has no commercial significance and so is not at all common.

Common trees of the forest

The White Poplar has been grown in England for some 300 years but was originally introduced from the Netherlands. Growing quickly, sometimes to a height of 50 to 70 ft, it attains maturity within 50 to 60 years. Its wood is known as *abele* and had in times past several specialist uses, including the making of roof-joists for thatched roofs. Today, however, it has little commercial value.

The true Black Poplar is an enormous tree, often 100 ft high with a massive, knobbly trunk and huge curving branches. A genuine native, it is now quite rare, and as it almost always grows by itself by streams in meadows it is only of passing interest here. However, the familiar Lombardy Poplar is in reality a variety of the Black Poplar, although so unlike it in appearance. And other varieties of Black Poplar, notably *Robusta*, have since the war been planted extensively to produce a quick-growing crop. Encouraged by grants, farmers have been planting them and other hybrid varieties on odd blocks of land, especially in damp situations. Growing at the rate often of three feet a year, they can be ready for harvesting within 30 years and produce a heavy volume of timber.

The Grey Poplar, once thought to be a distinct species, is now known to have derived from a cross between the White Poplar and the Aspen. Several other species of poplar have been introduced from America but none has become common.

WILLOWS, too, belong to river banks and other damp localities rather than the forest. Some of them produce useful timber, but their commercial value has rested chiefly on (a) the pollarding of trees to produce regular crops of supple rods for sundry rural crafts, and (b) coppicing them to produce thin osiers or withies for basket-making. A specialist use, for which a distinct variety has been developed, is the making of cricket bats. Most cricket-bat willows are cultivated in the eastern counties; they grow so quickly that it is said that a man may harvest five successive willows of marketable size from the same site in his lifetime. Pollarded willows, often leaning over streams, usually have their great pollarded topknot about six feet above ground. This is to ensure that the young shoots are produced out of reach of cattle.

Willows are a numerous race. Britain has 12 or 13 distinct species and perhaps as many as 70 or 80 varieties. The Common Willow, of which the *Cricket-Bat Willow* is a variety, is also known as the *White Willow*. Other common species are the *Crack Willow*, the *Sallow*, the *Osier* and the *Weeping Willow*. Although the osier is generally visible only as a plantation of slender rods, it will, if it is allowed to, grow into a tree 20 or 30 ft high. So will the sallow, though more often it occurs as a shrub or bush of considerable nuisance value in wet woodlands.

Although the SWEET CHESTNUT produces a crop of nuts, edible in a favourable year, they are not normally the plump nuts that are roasted on braziers or on the bars of a glowing fire. Those are imported from the Mediterranean, from which region the tree itself was brought to Britain, probably

Leaf-shapes of the common trees

in Roman times. In England the species is grown primarily for its coppiced wood which, cut at intervals of 12 years or so, is utilised for making chestnut fencing pales, hop-poles, gates and similar purposes. Probably some 60,000 acres of sweet chestnut, most of it coppiced, are still to be found in Britain, by far the largest concentration being in the Weald and the adjacent areas of Kent, Sussex and Hampshire, where the old underwood industries still flourish. There are also uncoppiced chestnut woods in the Forest of Dean, Norfolk, Wiltshire and other counties.

The HORSE CHESTNUT merits a mention only because of its spectacular appearance, which has earned it a place in innumerable parks, both in public and private. Though its 'conkers' make it popular with small boys, its commercial value is virtually nil.

WILD CHERRY. A. E. Housman's lovely poem reminds us that this is a woodland tree. It occurs singly or in small numbers in mixed deciduous woods, where it often grows to an impressive size. Specimens 100 ft or more high are known. The timber is a beautifully grained quality wood, valued by furniture-makers. The BIRD CHERRY is common by brooks and lakes in the north, rarer in the south, but seldom attains more than shrub proportions.

In the mixed woodlands of medieval times the HOLLY was an important tree, though in oak and mixed broad-leaved forests it occurred, and still occurs, more frequently as a shrub than as a tree. In many instances it was specifically protected by forest laws, as providing useful deer-browse in hard winters. In the New Forest it is the commonest of all the intermediate vegetation beneath the tree canopy. Holly grows to tree stature usually on the edge of or outside the forests. Well-grown trees are frequent in old hedges, where they have been left untrimmed because of the superstition that they are witches' trees and so unlucky to cut. The wood is hard, smooth and pure white.

During the past two centuries HAWTHORN has become known as the chief ingredient of well-made hedges. Through neglect it often sprawls into a considerable bush, buried in sweet-scented may-flowers in spring and bearing prolific crops of haws in autumn. Full-grown hawthorn trees are not so common but may be found in parks and open woodland. They were a familiar feature of medieval forests, valued perhaps for the protection they gave to timber trees. The young shoots produced after cutting are palatable to most grazing animals.

Several other medium-sized trees are, like the hawthorn, members of the Rose family. They include the CRAB APPLE, WILD PEAR, ROWAN, WHITEBEAM and WILD SERVICE TREE. All occur on the fringes rather than in the heart of broad-leaved forests. Though attractive in appearance and enhancing the woodland scenery they are of little economic importance. The Rowan, or Mountain Ash, is a mountain and northern species which has in the present century become more familiar in the south through having been introduced as an ornamental tree. The Whitebeam and Wild Service Tree resemble each other in many respects, but whereas the leaves of the whitebeam are elliptical those of the wild service tree are toothed like those of the maple. Both species occur sparingly in chalk and limestone districts.

The MAPLE occurs most frequently in south-eastern England where it is widely distributed but not very common. Though usually a hedgerow shrub, it can under favourable conditions develop into a tree 50 to 60 ft high. It is found in meadows and on the margins of forests.

CONIFEROUS TREES

The history of the *Scots Pine* has already been briefly referred to. As the glaciers of the Ice Age retreated, the tundra they left behind was colonised first by birch scrub and then by pine in about the seventh millennium B.C. For many hundreds of years pines were predominant over most of Britain, but with climatic changes retreated northwards. In historic times they were confined mainly to Scotland, and especially to the great Caledonian Forest. Unexploited there for centuries, they were 'discovered' about the year 1600. In the eighteenth century landowners began to bring seed south for planting on their newly enclosed estates, a practice which soon became a popular cult. To take the New Forest, where it is now a prominent feature of the scenery, as an example, the first plantings are said to have occurred in 1776, though some had been made on private estates in the area a few decades earlier. At first it was used to provide windbreaks for young oak plantations, but soon pure stands were being planted and by the beginning of the present century had extended over at least 5,000 acres.

The development of commercial forestry under the Forestry Commission has naturally increased to an enormous extent the importance of conifers. Policy was dictated by the law of supply and demand, and the demand was preponderantly for softwoods. In the first decade of the Commission's operations, of 138,279 acres of woodland planted or replanted, 130,768 were to conifers and only 7,511 to hardwoods. As our only indigenous conifer, apart from the yew and the shrubby juniper, the Scots pine naturally had to play a leading part and was used very extensively in some of the earliest of the Commission's new forests, as at Thetford, in Norfolk. Since the second world war the Commssion has been planting about 25,000,000 Scots pines a year, and the total acreage of pines (though this includes Scotland) is well over 400,000. The Scots pine is extremely hardy but grows quickly. Under favourable conditions it can attain a height of more than 100 ft.

Although all other coniferous trees found in Britain, with the exception of the yew, are exotic, some of them have been here for a long time and are very numerous. One of the most abundant is the NORWAY SPRUCE, the familiar Christmas tree, of which the Forestry Commission's plantations are measured in hundreds of thousands of acres. When it was first introduced no-one knows, though it is known to have been grown in England before the middle of the sixteenth century, but it was planted extensively on private estates in Victorian times. A handsome tree, producing a tall, straight trunk, it often grows to a height of 80–100 ft in Britain, though considerably higher in Scandinavia and parts of central Europe.

Another European conifer now grown on a large scale is the EUROPEAN LARCH, a tree which, unlike most conifers, sheds its leaves in winter. It was probably introduced to Britain from the Alps early in the seventeenth century and became popular as an estate tree in the nineteenth. An enormous boost was given to its cultivation by the Duke of Atholl, who planted some 10,000 acres of it on his Perthshire estate between 1764 and 1826. Landowners soon discovered that not only would it grow well and was very hardy but that its timber made very durable fencing stakes. As a matter of fact, it is so attuned to a harsh climate that the mild English winters give it an insufficient rest period, with the result that English timber is of lower quality than of that of central Europe. For all that, extensive areas, amounting to hundreds of thousands of acres, are now grown here. The larch is a stately, straight-trunked tree, reaching a height of 80 to 120 ft.

JAPANESE LARCH, the foliage of which is bluish green instead of the bright emerald of the European larch, and which has twigs of reddish brown which show up well in winter, was introduced in 1861 and now features prominently in our new forests. It succeeds on soils too poor for European larch and in northern and mountainous regions. Even more successful in the north is the *Hybrid Larch*, resulting from a cross between the European and the Japanese. Several millions of the Japanese and the Hybrid larches are planted every year.

Many of the most important species in British coniferous forests originated in America. One of the most successful has been the SITKA SPRUCE, which is now planted at a rate of about 20,000 acres a year. It is an attractive tree, its blue-green needles having silvery-grey undersides, and does well on peat soils, sometimes growing to a height of 200 ft or more. Originating in Alaska and British Columbia, it can tolerate anything a British winter can throw at it, even in an exposed situation.

The DOUGLAS FIR is another tree from British Columbia, where it produces gigantic specimens, some of them over 300 ft tall. In Britain none is yet old enough to have attained such dimensions, for the species was introduced only just over 100 years ago, but already some are 200 ft high and have a girth of 15–20 ft. Though more exacting than some species in its soil and climatic requirements it is being grown fairly extensively.

LAWSON CYPRESS, another giant conifer from western America, is better known as an ornamental tree in parks and gardens than as a forest species. As with many other ornamental conifers it has fernlike foliage, and its attractive appearance has prompted nurserymen to evolve a wide range

of varieties, in different colours, shapes and habits of growth. As a timber tree in Oregon and northern California it often grows to a height of 200 ft, but England has none that has reached that height so far. The Lawson cypress is nowadays often planted along the edges of forests, for amenity reasons, but there are some pure stands.

The WESTERN HEMLOCK and CANADIAN HEMLOCK, or HEMLOCK-SPRUCE, are trees of Canada and the United States that resemble the Norway spruce in general appearance but have flattened foliage like that of the yew. The Western Hemlock has proved the more successful in Britain and is grown on a modest scale, the Forestry Commission planting several hundred thousand trees a year. Already trees have reached a height of more than 100 ft, though that is only half the height attained in British Columbia. A characteristic of the hemlock is that the leading shoot always droops over.

Yet another British Columbian conifer of impressive proportions is the WESTERN RED CEDAR, also known as the AMERICAN ARBOR VITAE or the THUJA. It resembles the Lawson cypress, though rather coarser in growth and with yellower leaves. Like the other western giants it often exceeds a height of 200 ft in its native land, but in Britain it has not yet been planted extensively, and we have few large specimens. Here it takes its place with Lawson cypress as primarily an ornamental plant for parks and gardens, but its time may yet come.

Two other conifers from western America are better known in Britain from pictures than from life. Both the CALIFORNIAN REDWOOD and the WELLINGTONIA, or CALIFORNIAN BIG TREE, were introduced as park trees in the 1840s and the 1850s, and some of the specimens planted early have already achieved a truly impressive stature. These two species are, of course, the two which share most of the world's records for the largest and oldest trees in the world. A Californian wellingtonia known as 'General Sherman' in the Sequoia National Park, California, stands 274 ft 4 in. tall, has a girth of 79.1 ft at five feet above ground and is estimated to be between 3,500 and 4,000 years old. A Californian redwood also growing in its native country is considered to be the world's tallest tree, with a height of 366.2 ft. Despite these impressive records, neither tree is being grown commercially on any large scale in Britain.

A less spectacular but very useful conifer from the western coast of America as far north as Alaska is the LODGEPOLE PINE, which has foliage of a brighter green than that of the Scots pine and prickly cones. It has proved successful on poor, peaty soils in exposed districts and so is now being planted on a substantial scale by the Forestry Commission.

The catalogue of magnificent species of conifers which have evolved in western America testifies to the suitability of the humid climate there to their development, and as the British climate is not unlike that of, say, Vancouver Island it is not surprising that British forestry has derived so many of its most promising forest species from that source. However, the

Lightning strike on a great oak

whole world has been pretty thoroughly combed for new material, as the following list demonstrates.

The CORSICAN PINE, a variety of the Black Pine of Mediterranean countries, has proved eminently suitable for sandy soils in Britain and now covers scores of thousands of acres. It is one of the predominant species in the vast new forest of Thetford Chase.

The SERBIAN SPRUCE, first found about 100 years ago growing in thin limestone soil on a Yugoslavian hillside, has met with surprising success in Britain and is now planted commercially.

The SILVER FIR was once held to be one of the most promising and reliable of exotic conifers and was extensively planted by Victorian landowners. Then it was so badly attacked by aphids that it lost its commercial value. Today it survives chiefly as an ornamental tree in parks, though some of the surviving individuals are very large.

The GRAND SILVER FIR, another British Columbian species, has begun to replace the European Silver Fir, though so far grown on only a small scale commercially. The aphids that devaste the European species seem not to worry it.

Four species of Cedar, namely, the CEDAR OF LEBANON, the ATLAS CEDAR, the INDIAN CEDAR, and the INCENSE CEDAR, are found fairly frequently in Britain, but nearly all are in parks and arboreta. Though they grow quickly and are highly ornamental, their commercial possibilities in this country have not been exploited. The JAPANESE CEDAR is not a cedar at all but a near relation of the Wellingtonia.

Differing in many respects from all the other conifers under consideration, the YEW is an undoubted native—one of the oldest inhabitants of the British Isles. Although not now planted for any commercial purpose, the yew is found in many mixed woodlands and sometimes in pure stands of several acres. Whether it was ever planted in these places or sprang up naturally from seeds dropped by birds cannot be determined, but the yews that adorn many churchyards were certainly planted by man. The once widely held theory that they were grown there to provide woods for long-bows has now been discarded. Probably the real explanation lies in now forgotten pagan associations, and some yew trees may indeed span the centuries back to pagan times. The yew grows very slowly, producing exceedingly hard wood, and it is generally conceded that some of the ancient yews locally reputed to be more than a 1,000 years old may indeed be that age. The *Guinness Book of Records* agrees that the Fortingall Yew, near Aberfeldy, in Perthshire, must be somewhere near 1,500 years old.

Yews would undoubtedly be more numerous if it were not for their reputation for being toxic. Many a horse, cow or sheep has dropped dead after nibbling a few sprigs of wilting yew, though the fresh green foliage from growing yews may, it seems, be eaten safely. Instances both of sudden fatalities and of yew being taken with impunity have come to the author's notice, but the former are sufficiently numerous to prompt farmers to destroy if possible any yew trees on land where livestock are to graze. Yews usually produce a spreading canopy which effectively inhibits the growth of any other vegetation beneath it, but sometimes one will thrust straight upwards to produce a tall, noble tree. The wood is generally employed for farm and estate purposes, yew gateposts, for instance, being virtually indestructible, and any craftsmen prepared to take the trouble find it a wonderful material for fine carving.

FOREST UNDERWOOD

Of the several species of forest underwood exploited commercially the most important is undoubtedly the HAZEL. Few people have ever seen a natural hazel tree. Even those specimens that have now attained an impressive size have had their beginnings in shoots from a coppiced stump, have had to share both space and roots with other shoots from the same stump and are consequently mis-shapen. When not interfered with, however, hazel can grow into a small tree, 30 or so feet high, though even then its natural tendency is to spread and straggle. Hazel arrived in Britain between 7500 and 5500 B.C. and spread to every part of the islands. It is a natural underwood, growing as a rule in association with taller broad-leaved trees, its branches and foliage occupying the intermediate vertical zone in woodlands. Over most of England it was in early and medieval times a companion of the oak.

The practice of coppicing was evidently known in Saxon times and is referred to in the Domesday Book. As already noted, it consists of cutting a young tree or bush just above ground level at regular intervals. The stub or stool which is left promptly sends up more shoots in the following spring, and these are in due course harvested after the elapse of the recognised term of years, which for hazel is about eight. Hazel lends itself perfectly to the treatment, which can be continued indefinitely. The hazel stools in many woods must be hundreds of years old and are still alive and healthy though now completely neglected.

Much of the popularity of hazel was due to the ease with which it can be split. A skilled craftsman can take a slender hazel rod five or six feet long and less than an inch in diameter at its thickest end, and with a billhook can split it neatly from end to end. The split hazel, very supple and very durable, can then be used for weaving hurdle-work. Apart from the agricultural applications of pens for sheep and of hedges, such hurdle-work was once used very extensively for wattle-and-daub, the common material for internal walls of houses in early and medieval times. Covered with limewash and then plastered, the hazel wattle will last for centuries and may still be found quite often in old houses.

Other woods which split easily and were therefore in high demand are *Ash, Sweet Chestnut* and *Willow*. As already noted, the sweet chestnut underwood industry still flourishes, there being still some 40,000 or 50,000 acres of chestnut coppices in and around The Weald. The interval between cuttings is rather longer for sweet chestnut than for hazel, averaging 12

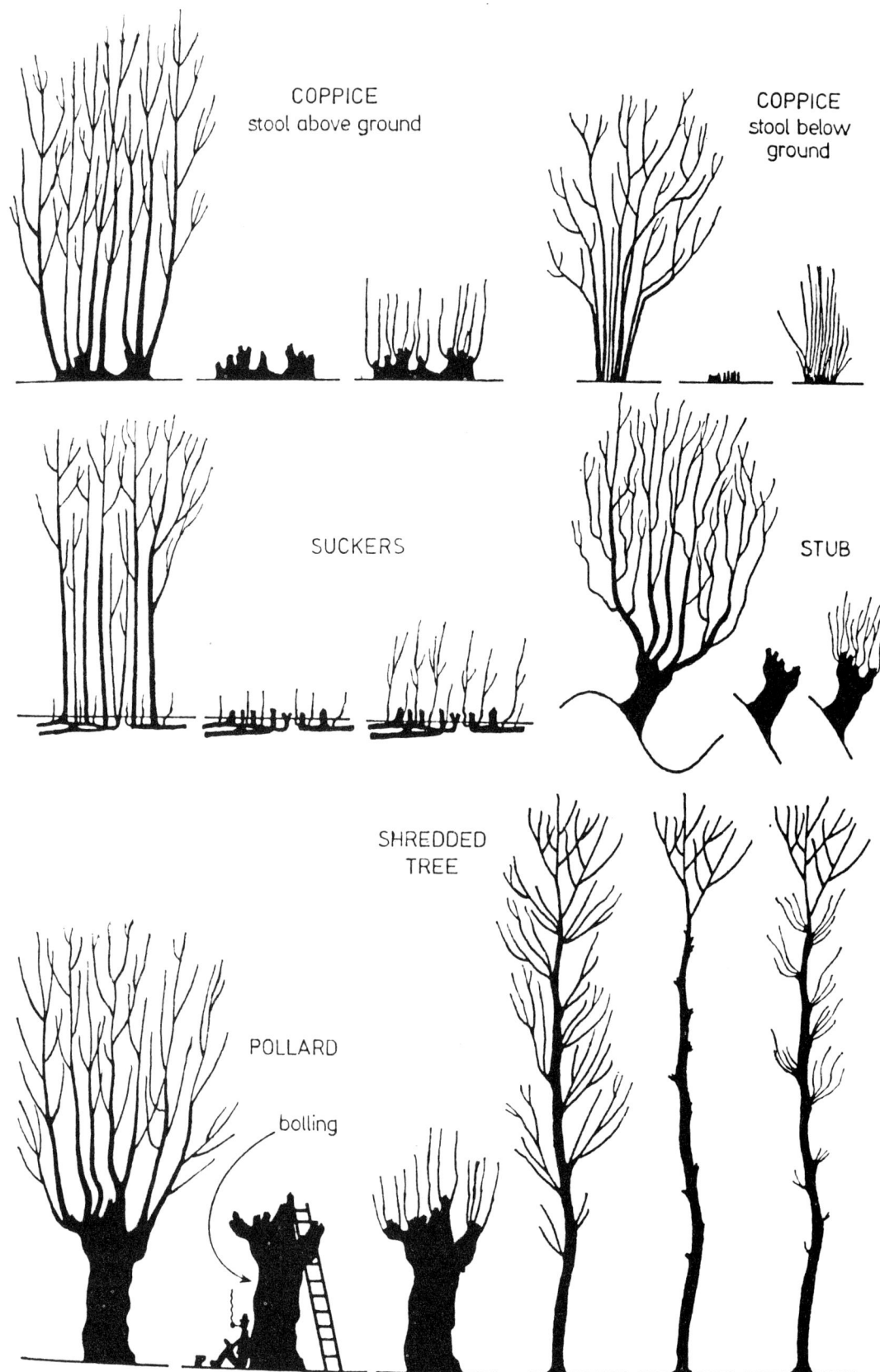

years. Willow coppicing or pollarding is still practised for specialist purposes, especially to provide withies for basket-making. It will be gathered, too, that until about 100 years ago virtually every species of broad-leaved tree was pollarded. *Lime*, *Elm*, *Hornbeam*, *Willow*, *Ash*, *Beech*, *Sycamore* and even *Oak* were all induced to produce a regular crop of rods and brushwood wherever possible. With most of these species, which when undisturbed grow into large trees, pollarding and coppicing was a peasant practice, indulged in when no forestry-minded landowner was able to impose a veto.

A rule, strictly observed in most districts, was that when underwood was cut the site had to be completely cleared and tidied. All brambles, briars and the dead stalks of tall herbaceous plants had to be demolished whether they were useful or not. As a matter of fact, there was little for which a use could not be found. After the best underwood, of hazel, chestnut or whatever, had been selected and cut to suitable lengths, the twiggy tops were tied into bundles for use as pea-sticks or faggots. Almost any type of brushwood would serve for faggots. There was also a special type of faggot, known as a bavin, for use in cottage bread-ovens, into which it was thrust whole and the door shut until it was entirely consumed. Such a faggot would be composed of largely thin twigs and rods which would burn easily and might contain even a few thorns and brambles. Large bundles of brushwood, resembling gigantic saugage-rolls, were sent to ports for use as ships' fenders.

Holly and ivy were reserved for cutting as famine rations for deer and cattle in winter, and oak trees often had their twigs and outer branches trimmed for the same purpose. Wood of small diameter, such as ash might produce in eight to twelve years, was in strong demand for ladders, tool-handles, posts and other craft purposes. Charcoal-burners were often around, seeking suitable wood. Medieval records contain references to grants of even loads of thorns, purpose unspecified. All in all, the management of the underwood was highly organised, reducing waste to a minimum.

Although this ancient woodland economy has become more or less obsolete, most of the old crafts are still alive, though with few practitioners. In secluded woodland districts men still make hurdles, wood faggots, bean-rods, spar-gads for thatching and tool-handles. During the past two or three decades they have found the demand exceeding the supply, and some of their products, such as wattle hurdles for the adornment of gardens, have become luxury items. The exploitation of the sweet-chestnut coppices, for chestnut paling and hop-poles, is of course as flourishing as ever.

Among the underwood shrubs and bushes so far not mentioned individually are *Wayfaring Tree*, *Dogwood*, *Spindlewood*, *Guelder Rose*, *Wild Service Tree*, *Buckthorn*, *Wild Plum* and *Blackthorn*. Most were cut during the normal clearing operations and bundled into faggots, few having any particular value. Spindle was in former times in some demand for making such items as spindles for spinning and for accessories for other home crafts

Different ways of managing wood-producing trees

which required small sections of very hard wood. Blackthorn is too thorny for most purposes, but in Victorian times participated in a vogue for knobbly walking-sticks. *Box*, which is found in some woodlands, had and has a considerable value for making rulers, small boxes, certain musical instruments, blocks for wood-engraving and similar specialist purposes. Only *Elder*, which grows fast and freely wherever it can obtain a foothold, was almost universally shunned for superstitious reasons. So persistent have been the associations of bad luck that even today many householders refuse to burn elder wood or to allow it into the house.

It would be interesting to have seen what use our ingenious ancestors would have found for that now familiar and troublesome feature of the underwood, the *Rhododendron*, which was introduced from Asia Minor only in Victorian times. Beautiful but useless, it quickly becomes established in all but alkaline (lime-rich) soils and forms thickets as impenetrable as tropical mangrove jungle. The flowers are magnificent in June but, apart from that, the best that can be said of the rhododendron is that it provides dense cover for pheasants, roe deer and other woodland fauna.

FLOWERS OF THE FOREST

One result of the regular clearance of underwood from broad-leaved forest was that it gave a chance for the lowly flowers of the woodland floor to flourish for a few years. When coppicing was extensively practised the woodlands in spring were a picture-book of delicate colour. In March and early April the newly cleared ground around the hazel was studded with pincushions of sulphur-yellow Primroses. Around them the Wild Anemones or Wind-flowers tossed their heads in the little breezes that found their way into the woods, while Wood Violets gazed down demurely at the scampering black spiders. Cinquefoil, Wild Strawberry and Bugle added their modest contribution to the cheerful scene.

As the year advanced the place of these early blossoms was taken by massed Bluebells, interspersed with a sprinkling of early Purple Orchids. Sweet Woodruff, Wood Spurge, Avens and Solomon's Seal found the environment much to their liking, and favoured woodlands harboured in secret glades plantations of Lilies-of-the-valley. Dog's Mercury, Wood Sage, Ground Ivy and Herb Robert (or Wild Geranium) were abundant, and in some woods Oxlips and Wild Columbines were to be found. In dry, shaded corners the rare Bird's-nest Orchid might push its way through the dead hazel leaves.

Still later, towards midsummer, Wood Vetches, Wood Sorrel, Yellow Archangel, Bell-flowers, Wood Sanicle and Foxgloves took over, while clumps of Nettles grew tall; then the golden St John's-wort and the numerous tall, spiky woodland Thistles, with Enchanter's Nightshade in the shadier places, while Stinking Iris unfolded its undistinguished purplish flowers and later flaunted its bright orange berries.

All that happened in the first year and the second. But by the end of the second summer the coarser and more vigorous vegetation was becom-

Thomas Gainsborough: 'Gainsborough's Forest', 1748 (detail) *Crown copyright, The National Gallery, London*

ing more dominant. The Thistles, Wood Spurge, Hemp Agrimony, Nettles and the rough-leaved woodland grasses were combining with creeping Brambles, sharp-clawed Briars and the insidious Honeysuckle to smother the lowly and more delicate flowers. The Primroses which in the first year after coppicing formed spreading rosettes set against a few small leaves, now lifted their flowers on long stems and grew tall and straggly in an attempt to keep ahead of the vigorous weeds. As the hazel, too, increased its growth and shrouded them in shade, they tended to give up the struggle and produce few flowers but plenty of large, flimsy leaves. So the cycle unfolded, until in the eighth or ninth year the victorious undergrowth was swept away, the hazel trimmed back to the bare stool, and the primroses, anemones and violets, all the better for their enforced rest from flowering, came into their own again.

Now that few woods are coppiced, this attractive sequence has unhappily become almost obsolete. The larger and coarser herbaceous plants dominate the woodland floor for a few years until they too are suppressed by the increasing shade thrown by the unchecked hazels. After a time little grows beneath them except certain shade-loving weeds, such as Mercury, Nettle, and Enchanter's Nightshade and the ubiquitous Bramble and Briar.

Similar cycles, with the species varying according to soil and climate, occur in most woods; immunity from human interference has almost always the same result. Another factor is the density of the wood. Obviously open woodland, in which the trees are sparse enough to allow light to penetrate between them, supports more species than a wood in perpetual shadow, though often the open spaces quickly become choked by shrubs and bushes such as the Wayfaring-tree, Hawthorn and, again, Honeysuckle. In suitable areas the glades are filled with Bracken; in others the Bluebells have to share with the powerfully scented Ransoms or Wild Garlic. Where open woods grow on a grassy floor the explanation is that sheep, cattle or deer have been allowed access and have destroyed all the herbaceous vegetation except grass. Oak woods on wet soils sometimes have a floor layer that includes Creeping Jenny, Ragged Robin, Figwort and Meadowsweet, with often a subsidiary growth of Sallow.

The dense canopy of beech woods allows few plants to flourish beneath it. Where the beeches are full-grown and planted close together the woodland floor is often bare earth carpeted by a layer of dead beech leaves, with here and there a patch of Mercury or Nettles. In such an environment certain uncommon orchids, including the Greater and Lesser Butterfly Orchids and the Red Helleborine, find a congenial habitat. Where the trees are more widely spaced, allowing light to penetrate, the vegetation of the woodland floor is often very similar to that beneath oak trees. Primroses, Wood Anemones, Wild Strawberry, Wood Violets and Lilies-of-the-valley unfold their petals in spring, and no sylvan scene is lovelier than millions of Bluebells under beech trees.

Beeches are most abundant in chalk country and there they are often

Oak Tree
Drawing by Kevin J. Dean

found in association with yews, sometimes sharing the same wood and sometimes occupying separate stands side by side. Yew trees are even more inhibitive of the woodland-floor vegetation than are the beeches. In a mature, thickly planted yew grove nothing else grows, and there is not even a covering of dead leaves to hide the chalk. The atmosphere is eerie, even sinister.

The new coniferous woods eventually arrive at a similar state, though the intermediate stages have more interest. The attraction of newly planted conifers for mice and other wild creatures has already been mentioned. Fenced or otherwise protected against grazing animals, including rabbits where possible, the grasses that clothe the ground of a new plantation grow tall and coarse, often hiding the young firs and pines for the first few years. In winter the herbage, notably of Molinia grass, dies off and is blown about by the wind, creating a dangerous fire hazard in a dry spring. As the trees grow taller, the grass is naturally suppressed until it entirely disappears from most of the forest floor, leaving only a layer of needles in deep shade.

The margins of woodlands, of whatever composition, have the most varied population of shrubs and herbaceous plants. Here tall trees have their trunks hidden by a luxuriant growth of lesser ones, including some of the loveliest of woodland species such as Hawthorn, Guelder Rose, Wild Cherry and Rowan. Around them cluster the herbaceous plants—Foxgloves, Scabious, Wild Raspberry, Water Dropwort, Bracken—while Traveller's Joy and Ivy creep about, searching for support. The inhabitants of these forest fringes are too numerous to enumerate, comprising the greater part of the British flora.

Woods provide a favourable environment for many of the lower forms of plant life, including ferns, mosses, lichens and fungi. The oak has a quite remarkable attraction for epiphytes, the trunk and branches of older specimens often being blanketed with mosses and polypody ferns. In forests on the edge of western moorlands the mosses and ferns are sometimes replaced by lichens, which festoon the trees with luxuriant, shaggy grey whiskers.

Carrying home bundles of faggot wood, c. 1900.

Polypody Fern (wood engraving by Marcus Beaven)

Fungi of many species proliferate in autumn, in woods where they feed on decaying leaves and other vegetable debris. Among them are most of the most spectacular and vividly coloured British species such as the Wood Agaric, Hygrophorus, Russula, Peziza and Cortinarius. In several instances only minor differences distinguish between the edible and the deadly poisonous varieties—so, unless one is an expert, it is best to leave them all alone. Fungi are naturally more plentiful in broad-leaved forests than in conifer woods, but even gloomy pine plantations have their quota, of such species as the Blusher (*Amanita rubescens*) and the Sickener (*Russula emetica*). Certain species are confined to or are most often found on certain species of tree; thus the Razor-strap Fungus (*Polyporus betulinus*) grows only on birch, a rather similar fungus (*Ganoderma applanatum*) on beech, *Coprinus picacens* on the floor of beech woods, *Collybia dryophila* mostly under oaks, *Polyporus radiatus* usually on the trunks of alder. Some species of fungus flourish only on rotting stumps and logs, while others attach themselves to living trees.

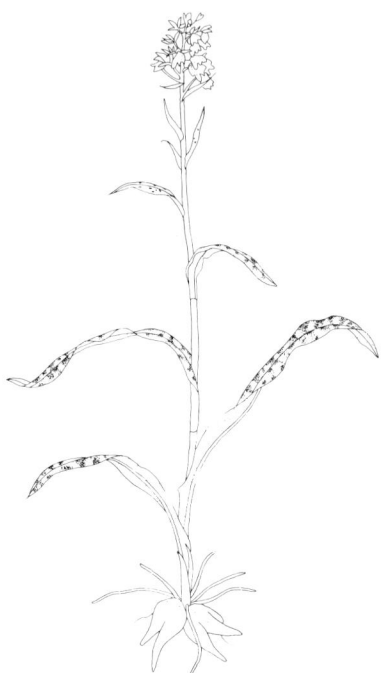

The Animals of the Forest

DEER

To say that the forests were made for deer is no exaggeration. Only successive royal decrees for protecting deer, backed by severe laws, prevented the plough from claiming all but the poorest forests. And medieval forests were so meticulously controlled and manipulated for the benefit of deer that to some extent their very nature must have been altered. Two species of deer, the *Red Deer*, and the *Roe Deer*, are indigenous to Britain. A third, the *Fallow Deer*, was introduced in ancient times, possibly by the Romans, possibly by the Normans. All three were throughout the Middle Ages included in the category 'beasts of the chase'.

The RED DEER is fundamentally a woodland animal. That it is now common on many Highland moors and mountains is simply due to the destruction of the forests which were its natural habitat. The mountain deer of Scotland do not attain such a large size or grow such large antlers as those of the forests of central Europe. Park deer in England, however, do reach greater weights, though they have lived in their restricted environment for so long and have enjoyed artificial feeding in hard weather that they may be regarded as semi-domesticated. All British red deer have the same ancestors: they are descended from large and splendid animals which roamed the primeval forests in Mesolithic times. In such a specialised business as the preservation and hunting of deer became in the Middle Ages it is not surprising that special terms were devised for identifying the animals at the several periods of their lives. For the Red Deer the technical terms were as follow:

A male Red Deer in its first year was a *Calf*.

Red deer about six months of age. In their first year they are technically calves.

A male Red Deer in its second year was a *Brocket or Knobber*.
A male Red Deer in its third year was a *Spayard*.
A male Red Deer in its fourth year was a *Staggard*.
A male Red Deer in its fifth year was a *Stag*.
A male Red Deer in its sixth year was a *Hart*.
A male Red Deer in its seventh year was a *Great Hart*.
A female Red Deer in its first year was a *Hind Calf*.
A female Red Deer in its second year was a *Hyrsel or Hearse*.
A female Red Deer in its third year and thenceforward was a *Hind*.

The Spotted Orchid

The Red Deer was the prime Beast of the Forest and was in medieval times found in all the royal forests and chases. Today it survives on Exmoor and in the neighbouring Quantock Hills, in the Lake District, in the New Forest and, of course, in the Scottish Highlands. Occasionally individuals wander to other districts; for example, in the mid-1970s a solitary stag spent a year or so roaming about the countryside of the Wiltshire/Hampshire border north-east of Salisbury, in what was once the vanished

Forest of Melchet. It was eventually shot for the incessant worrying of a herd of heifers with which it was consorting.

The rutting season for Red Deer is autumn, which brings the calving time to around Midsummer. Two weeks on either side of Midsummer were in the Middle Ages known as the 'Fence Month', when the deer had to be kept quiet and undisturbed at all costs. Fences were erected at key points and roads giving access to a forest were manned by keepers or foresters who collected tolls from the driver of any vehicle seeking to pass, theoretically as compensation for any disturbance its presence might cause to the hinds.

The forest laws applied equally to FALLOW DEER, though, of course, medieval forest-folk could readily distinguish between the two. As with the Red Deer they applied technical names to the animals at the several stages of their lives. Both a male and a female Fallow Deer in its first year was known as a *Fawn*.

> A male Fallow Deer in its second year was a *Prickett*.
> A male Fallow Deer in its third year was a *Sorrel*.
> A male Fallow Deer in its fourth year was a *Soar*.
> A male Fallow Deer in its fifth year was a *Buck*.
> A male Fallow Deer in its sixth year was a *Great Buck*.
> A female Fallow Deer in its second year was a *Tegg*.
> A female Fallow Deer in its third and subsequent years was a *Doe*.

Whatever the date of their introduction, by the Middle Ages Fallow Deer had become abundant in almost every forest, and even more so later. In Cranborne Chase, for example, the estimated stock in the reign of James I was about 2,000, but by 1828 it was considered to be between 12,000 and 20,000. That was gross overstocking, and it is no wonder that the deer sustained heavy casualties in severe winters and also made themselves a thorough nuisance to the local farmers. In 1825 in one walk alone of Cranborne Chase, near the village of Ashmore, more than 500 carcases were counted, the victims of 'murrain', a term which included any disease, including starvation, to which a more precise description could not be applied. Similar statistics exist for a number of medieval forests, as, for instance, 350 head of both red and fallow deer in Sherwood in 1286, and the enormous total of 2,209 in Clarendon Forest in 1470.

In this Chase in the eighteenth and nineteenth century the hunting season for bucks traditionally began on 1 July, but a special hunt for young bucks took place on Oak Apple Day, 29 May. The season ended on 25 September when the fox-hunting season started. The hunting of dry does was from Martinmas to Candlemas, though how the hunters differentiated between dry and pregnant does is not clear. Contemporary chronicles state that buck-hunting began at 4 p.m. and was thus an evening sport. Stag-hunting, on the contrary, began in the morning, so that the whole day would be available for the chase. For the country as a whole the buck-hunting and stag-hunting season was from 24 June to 14 September and was known as *Pinguedo*. The season for hunting does and hinds,

A doe fallow deer with young

extending from 11 November to 2 February, was known as *Fermisone*.

Henry VIII had an interesting survey made in 1538–39 of the deer in royal forests north of the river Trent. The count revealed 6,352 Fallow Deer and 2,067 Red Deer, a total of 8,419.

Fallow Deer are still much more numerous than Red Deer in England. They are widely distributed in woodland country but are even more plentiful in parks, in many of which they can be considered semi-domesticated. Their breeding cycle is much the same as that of the Red Deer, the rut taking place in October and the fawns born around midsummer. White fallow deer, which are not albinoes, occur from time to time.

The ROE DEER, once widespread, became scarce during the seventeenth and eighteenth centuries, retreating to the northernmost counties of England. At some time around the beginning of the nineteenth century Lord Portarlington re-introduced a stock to his estate at Milton Abbas, Dorset, where they settled down and flourished. By the 1890s some had moved across country to colonise the New Forest, where in 1976–77 there were thought to be some 400–500 head; the number is almost certainly increasing all the time. In most southern counties the species is now common wherever adequate woodland exists, and it has spread to nearly every part of England. It has thus regained the status which it seems to have enjoyed in the Middle Ages, for Roe Deer are mentioned in the records of forest courts in counties from Yorkshire to Devonshire. They were apparently not as common as the other two species, however. In 1344, for instance, a keeper in Pickering Forest was accused before a forest court of making free with the forest deer. During his period of office it was alleged that he took 134 harts, 158 hinds, bucks and does, and two roe deer. The last-named, he pleaded, were taken accidentally by his hounds and killed before he could rescue them. Similar tallies of red and fallow deer fail to mention roe deer at all.

The breeding cycle of the Roe Deer is rather earlier than those of the Red and Fallow. July and August are the rutting months, and the fawns are dropped in May. The Roe Deer, however, is one of the animals in which the phenomenon of delayed implantation occurs. After the egg cells have been fertilised the embryo remains undeveloped till about the end of December. It then starts to grow, making the actual gestation period about five months though the period between mating and the birth of the fawn is nine months.

Several other species of deer have in recent years escaped from collections in parks and have become acclimatised. SIKA or JAPANESE DEER, a few of which were liberated in the southern counties around the beginning of the twentieth century, are now fairly widespread throughout the south, and some have spread to the Midlands and north. There are estimated to be about 80 in the New Forest. This species resembles a small Red Deer.

Specimens of the MUNTJAC, sometimes called the CHINESE BARKING DEER, escaped from Woburn Park, in Bedfordshire, at about the same time and are now well established in the Chilterns and adjacent areas. These are very small deer, no more than 18 in. high and, being essentially a woodland species, are easily overlooked. There are also a few of the allied INDIAN MUNTJAC at large.

Another species spreading outwards from Woburn is the SIBERIAN ROE DEER, which is similar to the native species but rather larger and with bigger antlers. And a third species, also originating from Woburn, is the tiny CHINESE WATER DEER.

A young Scots pine damaged by deer

The fourth of the traditional Beasts of the Chase was the WILD BOAR, now extinct in Britain. Throughout the Middle Ages boar-hunting was a favourite royal sport, and boar's head was a traditional Christmas dish for the aristocracy. A special breed of dog, the boar-hound, was evolved for hunting the wild pigs. When the last boar was killed is not known, but they were still being hunted as near to London as Windsor in the early seventeenth century, James I engaging in a hunt there in 1617. Probably they became extinct during the Commonwealth or soon afterwards.

The WOLF disappeared from most of England at an earlier date. Place-names indicate that it was common and ubiquitous in Saxon times, and it continued to be so in much of England and Wales until at least the thirteenth century. The last wolf in Clarendon Forest was killed in the fourteenth century, and for the same century there are numerous records of wolves in the Peak Forest in Derbyshire. At a court in Derby in 1285 two foresters were found to hold land in return for dealing with wolves in the Peak Forest. On being asked to define their duties, they replied that

Each year, in March and September, we ought to go through the midst of the forest to set traps to take the wolves in the places where they had been found by the hounds: and if the scent was not good because of the upturned earth, then we should go at other times in the summer (as on St Barnabas' Day), when the wolves had whelps, to take and destroy them, but at no other times; and we might take with us a sworn servant to carry the traps; we are allowed to carry a bill-hook and spear, and a hunting-knife at our belt, but neither bows nor arrows; and we can have with us an unclawed mastiff trained to the work. All this we are to do at our own charges; but we have no other duties to discharge in the forest.

One of the foresters who so testified rejoiced in the name of John le Wolfhunte.

It seems probable that the Peak district was one of the last strongholds of the Wolf in England. The species may have become extinct about the end of the fifteenth century.

The former status of the WILD OX, or AUROCHS, of the forest is doubtful. A huge, fierce beast that inhabited the northern forests of Europe in primeval times, it was familiar to Julius Caesar in Gaul and therefore probably still found in Britain in the first century B.C. References to wild bulls in medieval documents are, however, of dubious validity. It was common practice to turn all the cattle of a parish or manor to graze together on the surrounding waste land under the care of the village cowherd. Bulls were seldom castrated, so mating was indiscriminate. Fights between bulls normally result in the loser going off on his own to sulk or to recuperate. That must often have happened in Anglo-Saxon and medieval England. So when we find William FitzStephen writing in 1174 'of stags, of fallow deer, of boars and of forest bulls' roaming in 'an immense forest, woody ranges' in the immediate vicinity of London we suspect that these were domestic bulls escaped to the wild—though they may not have been. Another writer in 1603 mentions the hunting and killing of wild bulls in Pembrokeshire, but he also implies that the bulls had owners.

On the other hand, the Chillingham cattle of Northumberland, still wholly undomesticated, are genuinely descended from primitive wild stock. The park in which they still live was enclosed in 1220, and the containing stone wall has been maintained ever since. Very similar but with small points of difference are the Chartley Park white cattle which were there when the park, in Staffordshire, was enclosed in 1248, and small numbers of other wild herds survive here and there in Britain.

In medieval times the FOX was regarded as a decidedly inferior animal of the chase. For most of the period it was indeed classed as vermin, and men were employed to destroy it. Records of the Forest of Rockingham in Northamptonshire, in the fifteenth century refer to 'fox-trees' and 'fox-stubbes'. Study of the context reveals that these were trees or stools (which could be cut for coppice-wood) granted to certain foresters as a reward for killing foxes. The foxes were normally trapped or snared in the royal forests, on the grounds that hunting by chase would disturb the deer. Outside these royal domains they were freely hunted by the gentry except in the Fence Month, though a sixteenth-century writer thought little of the sport. Apparently, the procedure was to chase it to earth and then dig it out, but the fox usually forestalled the hunters by bolting as soon as the terriers got near it, and the chase had to begin all over again. By the beginning of the nineteenth century fox-hunting had so increased in social esteem that, as has been noted, the buck-hunting season in Cranborne Chase was brought to a close on 25 September in order to allow fox-hunting to begin.

Today hunting the fox is as popular as ever, and foxes are probably more plentiful than they have been for centuries. Their local status depends largely on whether an estate-owner puts the greater value on foxes or on pheasants, but some foxes are to be found in most woods. In the past few decades many of them have deserted forests to move into suburbs, where they act as scavengers and are safe from hounds.

BADGERS were in general regarded as incidental denizens of medieval royal forests. There are a few records of grants to hunt badgers being made by kings in the thirteenth century, but in general the animals seem to have attracted little attention. Badgers are still plentiful in suitable districts, which means places with soil easy for digging yet fairly dry. In such localities setts centuries old are still occupied.

The OTTER ranked rather higher in the hierarchy of game animals, for it merited a special breed of hound to hunt it. They are mentioned in proceedings of the thirteenth and fifteenth centuries. Otters are not necessarily forest animals but are creatures of lake and river, the existence of woodland on the banks being quite incidental. However, many forests were and are well watered, and otters are great travellers, so their occurrence in the forests must have been quite frequent. They are now a strictly protected animal and have become rare.

The MARTEN, now extinct in much of Britain though it survives in a few remote places, was in the Middle Ages classified as a Beast of the Chase, as distinct from the nobler Beasts of the Forest. On the other hand, a document of 1271 includes Martens with foxes and cats as vermin. It seems that the Forestry Commission's new forests in Scotland and the north may be giving the Marten a chance to increase, though these are early days. The Marten is essentially a woodland animal, spending most of its time in trees.

The POLECAT is another animal persecuted to the verge of extinction which has now staged a recovery, especially in central Wales, where it is no longer uncommon. A near relation of the smaller domestic Ferret, with which it can interbreed, it is a bloodthirsty animal, taking a heavy toll of ground-nesting birds and domestic poultry if it gets a chance, but it likes a wood as a base for its expeditions into the surrounding farmland.

The cover provided by the Forestry Commission's new forests in Scotland is certainly proving a boon to the WILD CAT, which is now increasing in numbers after sinking to a very low ebb. The last Wild Cat in England is said to have been killed in 1853 in Northumberland. In earlier centuries the Wild Cat was classified both as vermin and as a Beast of the Chase. It was once found in most English forests. A charter of Henry II, in the twelfth century, grants permission to hunt wild cats in Windsor Forest. A sixteenth-century writer, Turberville, in a book entitled *Noble Art of Venerie or Hunting*, implies that at that time the Cat was not deliberately sought out for hunting but was chased by hounds when they chanced to find it. Describing a hunt he writes,

At last, when they may no more, they will take a tree, and therein seek to beguile the hounds. But if the hounds hold into them and will not so give it over, then they leap from one tree to another and make great shift for their lives, with no less pastime to the huntsmen.

In favourable localities badgers occupy setts many centuries old

Any wild cats found in England now are feral cats—domestic cats which have taken to the wild. They are quite distinct from the authentic WILD CAT and are evidently descended from a different species.

HARES are not usually considered forest animals. They prefer open places to dense woodland, though the author has seen individuals in glades in the middle of extensive forests. In medieval times the Hare was classified as a Beast of the Warren, indeed, as the chief Beast of the Warren (for an explanation of 'Warren', see p. 21). In one of the best organised and most important warrens in the kingdom, that of Somerton, in Somerset, the Hare was evidently given the status of a Beast of the Forest, especially reserved for the king's hunting: accordingly, killing Hares at Somerton became a serious offence. Preservation was even taken to the length of calling together the representatives of four neighbouring villages, at Christmas 1256, to hold an inquest on a hare found dead by a verderer. The jury tactfully found that the hare died of 'murrain'.

A special breed of hound was developed for the hunting of otter early in the Middle Ages

On the other hand, in 1288 the freemen of Cranborne Chase complained at an eyre at Sherborne, not very far from Somerton, about attempts to deprive them of their dogs, which they needed to maintain their traditional right to hunt the Hare and the Fox. In the Forest of Pickering, Yorkshire, there are records of fairly numerous cases of poaching hares, though the real offence seems to have been disturbing the deer while chasing the hares. Hares were usually hunted by greyhounds but were also often dispatched by arrows.

Until myxomatosis decimated them in the 1950s RABBITS were present almost everywhere in the countryside in such prodigious numbers that to appreciate that in the early Middle Ages they were uncommon and carefully preserved animals requires an effort of the imagination. Although

In the medieval period the fox was regarded as a decidedly inferior animal of the chase

The hedgehog was once considered a delicacy among the gipsies

they were probably brought to Britain by the Romans they seem to have died out subsequently and to have been reintroduced by the Normans, who confined them to protected warrens. Medieval records contain frequent references to poachers taking rabbits, or 'conies' as they were then called. The rabbit warrens in the Forest of Clarendon, Wiltshire, seem to have been especially large and important. In 1495 they contributed no less than £100 towards the king's household expenses, and in the reign of Charles I they were assessed at more than £200 annually.

SQUIRRELS, which must have been abundant in the primeval forests of England, are sometimes mentioned in forest documents, usually in lists of animals, including the Fox and the Wild Cat, which foresters or freeholders had permission to hunt. These were, of course, Red Squirrels, the now familiar Grey Squirrels having been introduced from America at the end of the nineteenth and the early years of the twentieth centuries. The Red Squirrel now survives in some of the remoter parts of the country but is vastly outnumbered by its stronger and more vigorous cousin. Squirrel-hunting, incidentally, survived as a rural sport until within living memory.

The smaller mammals of the forests were beneath the notice of medieval chroniclers. STOATS, WEASELS, HEDGEHOGS, SHREWS, RATS, MICE and VOLES are all forest creatures, interlocking parts of the ecology of the woods. Stoats, Weasels and Rats have been the objects of incessant persecution on the great woodland estates for several centuries, chiefly because of the toll they take of ground-nesting birds, but still manage to survive. All of them, together with Hedgehogs, feature as vermin on which bounties were payable in eighteenth-century churchwardens' accounts.

Of the lesser rodents, who compensate for their small size by their prodigious numbers, the SHORT-TAILED VOLE and the FIELD MOUSE are the most important. The long, coarse grass of the new conifer plantations of the Forestry Commission and private landowners provide them with an ideal environment, and they breed so enthusiastically that at times their population reaches plague proportions. Fortunately a corresponding increase in the numbers of predators usually restores the balance after a few years.

This woodmouse is not easy to distinguish from the background.

An interesting denizen of the woodlands, the DORMOUSE, is seldom seen but by no means rare in the southern counties. It prefers oak-and-hazel coppices with a southern slope. In about 1890 some specimens of the EDIBLE DORMOUSE or FAT DORMOUSE, were released near Tring, in Hertfordshire. They subsequently established themselves in the beech woods of the Chilterns and have more recently spread to other parts of the country, the presence of a colony in north Dorset having not long ago been brought to the author's attention. They tend to make their home in the roofs of forest houses where, being nocturnal, they are exceedingly noisy in the late evenings.

Birds of the Forest

The birds of most interest to the kings for whom the historic forests of England were created and maintained were (a) hawks and falcons and (b) any other birds which hawks and falcons could catch. The exception was the *Swan*, most of which were royal property, though some were at various times granted to the sovereign's subjects. It seems to have been regarded as a 'Fowl of the Forest', of more or less equal status to a Beast of the Forest. In many instances protecting the king's swans was part of the duties of forest wardens or foresters. The birds were rounded up annually for the 'upping' or 'hopping', which consisted of marking each swan by a nick in the beak. Through their propensity for straying, Swans were continually getting lost, and medieval accounts hold many records of birds missing or stolen.

The falcons and hawks commonly used in falconry and nesting in the wild in England in medieval times were the PEREGRINE FALCON, SPARROW-HAWK and MERLIN. The KITE, common in the Middle Ages, was regarded as a scavenger and so beneath the notice of the nobility, while the KESTREL'S mode of hunting, consisting as it does of hovering, did not commend itself to falconers. The BUZZARD is too slow and lethargic, though sometimes used for catching rabbits. GOSHAWKS were greatly esteemed by medieval falconers but probably bred in England only rarely. The HOBBY was considered a valuable falcon but was probably never more than an uncommon summer visitor to southern and midland England, as it is now, England being at the northern limit of its range.

The Peregrine is a bird of cliffs and crags though in former times, when it was much commoner than now, it probably nested in woodlands as well. Regarded as the king of falcons, it must always have been in great demand. Birds of the western and northern moors, Merlins are dashing little falcons but are too small to be used against birds larger than the blackbird and skylark. Sparrow-hawks have the right approach to commend them to a falconer—a sudden dash, a flurry of feathers, and the unsuspecting victim is knocked into oblivion. They are essentially birds of the forest, especially of woodland margins.

A great rarity today is the HONEY BUZZARD, which occasionally nests in the New Forest and which may have been more widespread in the Middle Ages. The three Harriers, the MARSH HARRIER, the HEN HARRIER and the MONTAGU'S HARRIER, may also have bred more frequently and more widely than at present. All are birds of marshland and heath but, as noted, many of the ancient forests included a great deal of such terrain.

Of the birds taken by falcons, those regarded as most important in medieval times seem to have been the PHEASANT, the PARTRIDGE, the WOODCOCK, the HERON and most of the *Ducks*. All are mentioned occasionally in medieval documents, generally in connection with poaching and trespass. The Heron, not now considered to be a palatable table fowl, was certainly eaten in the Middle Ages; there are even records of orders for Herons to be sent from several forests to London for the king's table. One can appreciate that the sight of a falcon stooping at a killing of a large, slow-moving Heron would be exciting for a medieval falconer.

Woodcock were more often taken in nets than killed by falcons. Special nets, known as Cockshuts and used at twilight on the edge of forest glades, were commonly employed. The incidence of place-names which include the word 'Cock', such as 'Cock-road', 'Cockshoot' and 'Cockleys', indicates that Woodcock were much commoner than they are at present. However, they still breed quite plentifully in woodland areas, and their numbers are reinforced in autumn by migrants from across the North Sea. Duck, too, were often netted, after having been coaxed into decoy ponds, though they were also considered good targets for falconry.

The Pheasant is not an indigenous British species. The earliest documentary reference to it is in the eleventh century, a few years before the

Young tawny owls

Norman Conquest. Those who think that it was introduced by the Romans may well be right. Two races, or sub-species, of Pheasant are involved, one originating in the Caucasus, the other in China. The Chinese or Ring-necked Pheasant is generally supposed to have been brought to Europe at a relatively late date, but perhaps sufficient attention has not been given to the fact that a pheasant depicted on a mosaic floor in a Roman villa at Woodchester, in Gloucestershire, has a definite white ring to its neck. In the medieval forest pheasant were incidental game, ranking far below the royal deer and the wild boar. By the eighteenth century their status had shot up, and from the nineteenth onwards they were and are supreme on private woodland estates. Pheasant-rearing and shooting have become a fashionable cult, to which almost all other considerations are subsidiary. Woods have been laid out and new woods and shelter-belts planted for the benefit of the pheasants and the guns. Predatory animals and birds have been ruthlessly trapped, shot and poisoned by zealous keepers intent on preserving a maximum stock of pheasants for their employers. In rural England the past 200 years have been the Age of the Pheasant, and the pampered birds are still exceedingly plentiful.

A game-bird about which little information is available from earlier centuries is the BLACK GROUSE, though it must have been much more widely distributed than at present. It now survives, though in small numbers, in the northern counties, on Exmoor and in a few places in mid-Wales and north Wales; odd birds occasionally wander to their former haunts, such as the New Forest. Unlike the Red Grouse, the Black Grouse is a forest bird, though preferring the edge of the woods. Moors with scattered trees and occasional plantations provide an ideal habitat.

Of the larger birds now resident in woodlands the commonest is undoubtedly the WOOD-PIGEON, which breeds in enormous numbers in both broad-leaved and coniferous forests. The paucity of early records suggest that either it was little regarded or was much scarcer in medieval times. One would suspect the latter, for a strong-flying wood-pigeon would seem to be a worthy target for even the noble Peregrine.

The smaller woodland species which attract the modern naturalist were of little interest to the medieval sportsman. A thickly planted wood is not the easiest of places for bird-watching, though a coppiced wood is much better. The best season for observing the bird-life of a wood is in winter and early spring, when the deciduous trees are bare. Observation is aided by the fact that the birds circulate through the wood in a loose group and according to a fairly consistent timetable. All the observer has to do is to find a convenient station and sit still. In time the entire avian population of the forest will pass by.

The species likely to be seen include five species of Tits, namely the GREAT TIT, BLUE TIT, MARSH TIT, COAL TIT and LONG-TAILED TIT (in certain districts the rarer WILLOW TIT), NUTHATCH, TREE-CREEPER, WREN, ROBIN, GOLDCREST, HEDGE-SPARROW, CHAFFINCH and BULLFINCH. In spring and autumn there will also usually be WILLOW WARBLERS and CHIFFCHAFFS and

When feeding the nuthatch taps gently at the bark of trees like a miniature woodpecker

perhaps BLACKCAPS. Sometimes GREATER and LESSER SPOTTED WOODPECKERS accompany the gipsy throng. It is instructive to note how thoroughly this peripatetic assembly exploits their environment. The Tree-Creepers, Nuthatches, Woodpeckers and some of the Tits concentrate on the tree-trunks; the Wrens, Hedge-Sparrows, Robins and Chaffinches forage on the forest floor (though the Chaffinches alternate between the floor and the tree-tops); the Long-tailed Tits, Bullfinches and several other species work the intermediate zone. For five to ten minutes the woods around the sedentary observer will be filled with birds; then all will have passed on and the forest will seem silent and empty.

In summer, when birds are nesting, the fauna of broad-leaved woods in southern England includes the NIGHTINGALE, the WOOD-WARBLER, the SPOTTED FLYCATCHER (in open woodland), the GARDEN WARBLER, and, in some western and northern woodlands, the REDSTART and the PIED FLYCATCHER. On June nights woodland glades will be alive with the whirring clatter of NIGHTJARS, which may quite often be seen engaging in their eerie display flight. The 'roding' flight of the WOODCOCK, which occurs in similar glades and rides, takes place rather earlier in the year.

JAYS, noisy except in the breeding season, are common in most woods, though less so in those rigidly preserved for pheasants, for Jays are nest-robbers. TURTLE-DOVES and STOCK-DOVES nest along forest margins, where too CUCKOOS call throughout May and June. BLACKBIRDS, SONG-THRUSHES, MISTLE-THRUSHES and GREEN WOODPECKERS are reasonably common and well distributed. The woodland Owls are the TAWNY OWL and the much rarer LONG-EARED OWL. The Tawny or Wood Owl may often be heard hooting at night though, once again, in pheasant preserves it has suffered because of its hooked beak and sharp claws.

Nightjar displaying. Unlike every other British bird, when sitting on a branch the nightjar perches *along* instead of across it

Other Forest Wildlife

Open glades and the margins of forests, especially on sandy soil, are frequently infested by ADDERS, which come out to sun themselves on sunny summer days. GRASS SNAKES are also plentiful, and the New Forest with certain heaths and woodlands in the neighbouring counties of Dorset, Surrey and Berkshire are the only British habitats of the rare SMOOTH SNAKE or CORONELLA.

The same localities, together with sand dunes on the Lancashire coast, are the only British haunts of the otherwise rare SAND LIZARD, which is the chief food of the Smooth Snake. Both the COMMON LIZARD and the SLOW-WORM are quite plentiful though in different types of terrain, the Lizard preferring warm sandy heaths with scattered trees whereas the Slow-worm likes damp places.

All three British species of NEWT, the CRESTED, SMOOTH and PALMATE, may be found in woodland ponds. Broad rivers were often included within

the boundaries of medieval forests, but most forest waters today are no more than brooks and streams. Their fish therefore are minor species such as BULLHEAD, LOACH, MINNOW and STICKLEBACK, though there may well be EELS, especially in lowland streams, and BROWN TROUT occur even in high moorland waters.

The insect life of forests is so varied and prolific as to need a book for even a cursory mention of all the species. Most insects are confined to localities in which the food-plants of their larvae are found, and woodlands abound in the food-plants of butterflies, moths, solitary wasps, gall-flies, plant-bugs, beetles and others. Surveying butterflies alone, the HIGH BROWN FRITILLARY, RINGLET, SPECKLED WOOD, PURPLE EMPEROR, WHITE ADMIRAL, DUKE OF BURGUNDY FRITILLARY, PURPLE HAIRSTREAK, WHITE-LETTER HAIRSTREAK and CHEQUERED SKIPPER are essentially woodland species and may be found flitting around forest rides at the appropriate seasons. That magnificent rarity, the Purple Emperor, has a damp woodland (Blackmore Copse, Farley, near Salisbury) devoted exclusively to its preservation.

Some of our most handsome moths, such as several species of UNDERWING, the OAK EGGAR, the OAK BEAUTY and the PUSS MOTH, are woodland species, while smaller ones, such as the GREEN TORTRIX, compensate by sheer numbers for their small size and are able, in the larval stage, to do considerable damage to oak trees. Large acreages of pines have at times been devastated by the caterpillars of the PINE BEAUTY MOTH.

Under the trees of both broad-leaved and conifer forests the WOOD ANT of formidable appearance creates its imposing nests, often two or three feet high and 20 or 30 ft in circumferences. The great ants swarm on the

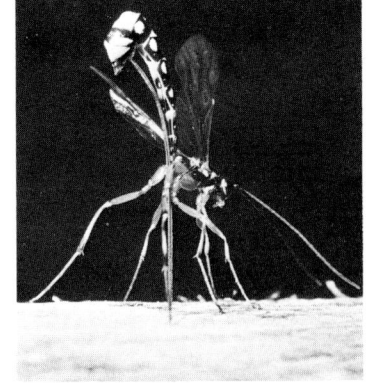

Ichneumon fly: a friend of the forester, since it parasitises forest pests.

Open glades and the margins of forests are frequently infested by adders

A dramatic shot of stag-beetles fighting

woodland floor and are an effective deterrent to trespassers. In early times HIVE BEES seem to have been regarded as a forest asset, for there are medieval instances of foresters and other forest officials claiming bees and honey as a perquisite. However, the 1217 Charter of the Forest, as quoted in a case heard at an eyre of Pickering Forest in 1337, stated that every forest freeholder should be entitled to honey found in his own woods. It is said that the lord of the manor of Minstead, in the New Forest, claimed the honey from his woods as late as 1852. In general the honey referred to in old records seems to have been 'wild honey', that is, honey made by ownerless bees, usually in hollow trees. Probably, however, peasants often assisted the process by suspending hollowed tree-trunks high in trees for bees to colonise, as happens in Africa today.

Beetles of the forests are known chiefly by the damage which the larvae of certain wood-boring species perpetrate. Most tree species have their own parasitic beetle, such as the PINE WEEVIL, the ELM-BARK BEETLE (vector of Dutch elm disease) and the ASH-BARK BEETLE. Pine forests are often infested by the large and impressive SIREX wood-wasps, whose larvae eat tunnels 10 or 12 in. long in the heart of the timber.

The New Commercial Forests

The U-boat campaign of the first world war convinced the Government of the need for promoting the production of home-grown timber. Forestry had dwindled to a very low ebb. Surviving woodlands were less than 5 per cent. of the total land area—virtually the lowest of any country in Europe—and most of them were in a shocking state of neglect. Moreover, in spite of considerable planting of conifers in mid-Victorian times, the old forests were predominantly of hardwoods, whereas the current need was for softwoods, especially for the making of pulp and paper. The authorities had discovered that while in time of peace softwoods could be bought cheaply overseas, in wartime they required inordinate shipping-space.

Although there existed at the beginning of the century an Office of Woods, Forests and Land Revenues which had become involved in a few small afforestation schemes, in 1914 no national survey of timber resources had been undertaken and the Government had little idea of what was available. Nor was it especially interested during the first two years of the war. In 1916, however, it at last became aware that woodlands were disappearing at an alarming rate (it was later estimated that during the war some 450,000 acres of woods were lost), and panic measures by the Government were only prevented by the consideration that 80 years are needed to produce a mature pine tree and 120 years an oak.

What the Government did in this emergency was to appoint a Forestry Sub-Committee of the Ministry of Reconstruction, to advise on what should be done to avert any future calamity. Its Report, known as the Acland Report, after Sir Francis Acland, its chairman, recommended the formation of a Forestry Commission, which was duly established in 1919. The Commission was to have a target of 1,770,000 acres of new woodland but was given 80 years to achieve it. Its immediate task was to afforest 200,000 acres within the next ten years, 150,000 acres by direct action and 50,000 acres by collaboration with private owners. In addition it was estimated that a further 50,000 acres of woodland felled during the war would be replanted by private owners of their own volition, thus completing a total of 250,000 acres of new forests by 1929.

The target was not reached, for two main reasons. One was that the activities of the Commission were bedevilled by frequent policy vacillations on the part of the Government. The other that, following the repeal of the wartime Corn Production Act in 1921, agriculture relapsed into its former depression and with it the entire countryside. Little incentive

The Great Spotted Woodpecker *Drawing by Kevin J. Dean*

existed to do anything, and vast areas of felled woodland on private estates remained unplanted, a wilderness of brambles and scrub. In the early 1920s the Commission only just escaped falling victim to a Government economy campaign. Surviving, it gradually got down to work and by 1929, the end of the first ten years of its career, it had acquired 310,000 acres of land for new plantations and had planted 138,279 of those acres. In addition, it had, in 1923, taken over responsibility for the forests on the Crown lands —the ancient royal forests—amounting to about 121,000 acres. The task before the Forestry Commission was thus complex. Its prime function was to produce timber commercially, and the demand was overwhelmingly for softwoods, alias conifers. At the same time it had control of the ancient royal forests which were producing mainly hardwoods and which were, in any case, mostly on heavy soils considered ideal for growing oaks. At various times it was also required to make a contribution towards alleviating the persistent unemployment problem, which it did by establishing forest camps. Very low on its list of priorities were amenity considerations; the era of forest parks had not yet come.

During the 1930s the Commission pressed ahead with its acquisition of new land for planting, of which there was no scarcity in that period of depression. As the Commission itself acknowledged, it was often looked upon as mugs who would buy up poor land that nobody else wanted. Much of this was hill land in the north and in Wales, which local people were confident would never grow trees: in that they were wrong. With unemployment continuing rife, much consideration was given to schemes for combining the new plantations with agriculture. Forest holdings were set up, of a size manageable as part-time units by men primarily employed in the forests. In the new Forest of Kielder and in other northern forests an arrangement was devised whereby afforestation could be combined with sheep-farming of the traditional pattern. The new forests, of conifers, were planted on the hillsides, leaving the tops of the moors and the valley lands free from trees. A farm would thus consist of a group of lowland pastures around the farmstead and grazing rights on the uplands above the trees, with broad, fenced rides linking the two. Not only did the scheme work, but as the trees grew they tended to soften the climate of the valleys, rendering them more suitable for dairying.

On the other hand, in some regions the Commission encountered intense opposition, and nowhere more than in the Lake District. An organisation known as The Friends of the Lake District was founded in 1935 to oppose the Commission's plans, which it did very vociferously. The Commission did nothing to help matters by making the mistake of planting its first woodlands of conifers in rigid, rectangular blocks. A mountainside divided vertically by a straight line from base to summit, the dark green of a dense growth of firs on the one side contrasting harshly with the bare rocks and coarse grass on the other, was certainly unsightly. It was the Commission's first major brush with amenity interests, and the lesson was soon learned. Ironically, when 30 or so years later the time came

Purple Emperor
Butterflies (m/f)
Drawing by Kevin J. Dean

for the early plantations to be felled there was a similar public outcry against such vandalism.

By 1939, the end of the Forestry Commission's second decade, 359,000 acres of new plantations had been made, and nearly 300,000 further acres had been acquired for future planting; 230 new forests had been created, and several thousand men were regularly employed, in addition to many casual workers. Satisfactory progress was thus being made, but the second world war, with its enormous demands for timber, came too soon for the Commission's new plantations to make much of a contribution. Once again the burden fell on the older forests, both those in private hands and the former Crown forests for which the Commission now had responsibility. Between 1939 and 1945 it is estimated that 373,000 acres of woodland were completely cleared and a further 151,000 acres temporarily destroyed by the felling of all mature and useful trees: one-third of the nation's resources in standing timber had been used up in six years. The task of rehabilitation was therefore immense. A document entitled *Post-War Forest Policy*, prepared by the Forestry Commission immediately after the war, recommended a target of 5,000,000 acres of new plantations within the next 50 years, and broadly this was accepted by the Government. Ever since, the Commission has been working towards that goal.

As already noted, the mid-1930s saw the Forestry Commission in conflict with amenity interests in the Lake District. A compromise was reached whereby the Commission agreed to keep its operations outside a central zone of some 300 square miles, to which a few years later adjoining Eskdale, where controversial schemes had been visualised, was added. Criticism was also voiced concerning the New Forest, Snowdonia, the Wye valley and elsewhere. Much of it was met by a more imaginative policy over plantations. Instead of ruler-straight lines, the new forests now had wavy or irregular edges, often planted with a fringe of deciduous trees. Scenic beauty became an important consideration when planning new plantings.

Amenity includes recreation, which in the decades after the war more and more people were seeking in the forests. Following the example set in other northern countries, the Forestry Commission began the creation of a series of forest parks, the first of which was opened in Argyllshire in 1936. Most of the early ones were in Scotland (while this book is concerned primarily with England) but parks in Snowdonia and the Wye valley were established before 1950. The contemporary ones include the Border Forest Park, extending on both sides of the Cheviots, the New Forest and the Dean Forest Park, also three more in Scotland.

Early in 1971 there were in the whole of Britain 124 forest trails open to the public, 14 forest information centres, nine fully equipped campsites and a large number of picnic-sites, and more have since been added. The forest trails offer attractive opportunities for children in particular to explore the countryside, leading them uphill and downhill and over timber bridges and causeways across marshy ground, with printed guides to identify the trees, flowers, birds and insects they may see en route and, at the end of the ramble, wood benches and tables for picnicking. Nevertheless recreational facilities in British forests have far to go before they reach the prevailing standards in countries such as Canada, the United States and some in Europe, where also forest camps and picnic-sites are far more numerous.

From most points of view the present forest scene is a reasonably healthy one. In 1979 the Forestry Commission, celebrating its sixtieth anniversary, was felling many of the trees it had planted in its early years and thus receiving some return on its long-term investments. It had learned from its early mistakes valuable lessons on landscaping, and people were learning to appreciate the sight of forests growing on what was formerly bare countryside. In general it had achieved an amicable working arrangement with neighbouring farmers, with whom in the early days it was often in conflict. It was responding to the increasing public demand for recreational facilities in its forests.

In the private sector similar developments were occurring, except as far as public access was concerned. Modern motor transport makes access to distant parts so easy that landowners, suffering from the more deplorable results of trespass, are more inclined to put up fences than to take them down. An enlightened attitude towards forestry, however, now prevails, fostered largely by a dedication scheme whereby, in return for an agreement to manage its woodlands efficiently and in accordance with modern commercial practice, an estate is entitled to certain helpful grants, particularly in connection with re-planting. In both Forestry Commission and private woodlands conifers are overwhelmingly predominant. That has given rise to severe criticism from some quarters. Writing in 1976, Professor Oliver Rackham asserts that at least a third of Britain's ancient woodland has been destroyed since the end of the second world war. Commenting in detail on the East Anglian and East Midland areas which he knows best, he estimates that almost half the ancient woodland surviving in mid-Suffolk was lost in that period, 42 per cent. has gone in the Forest of Rockingham (Northamptonshire), 46 per cent. in central Lincolnshire, 36 per cent. in west Cambridgeshire, and so on. He means not that the woods have disappeared in every instance, though in some they have, but that they have lost their ancient character through the replacement of old broad-leaved species of trees by conifers.

Certainly the change drastically affects the ecology of woodlands. Closely-planted conifers create a much denser cover than open broad-leaved forest and effectively smother many of the plant species of the forest-floor. In its turn the fauna of the forest is changed. Some species are squeezed out while others find the new conditions much to their liking. The underwood crafts are another casualty, though in most instances they were dying before the planting of softwoods assumed recent proportions.

Gazetteer

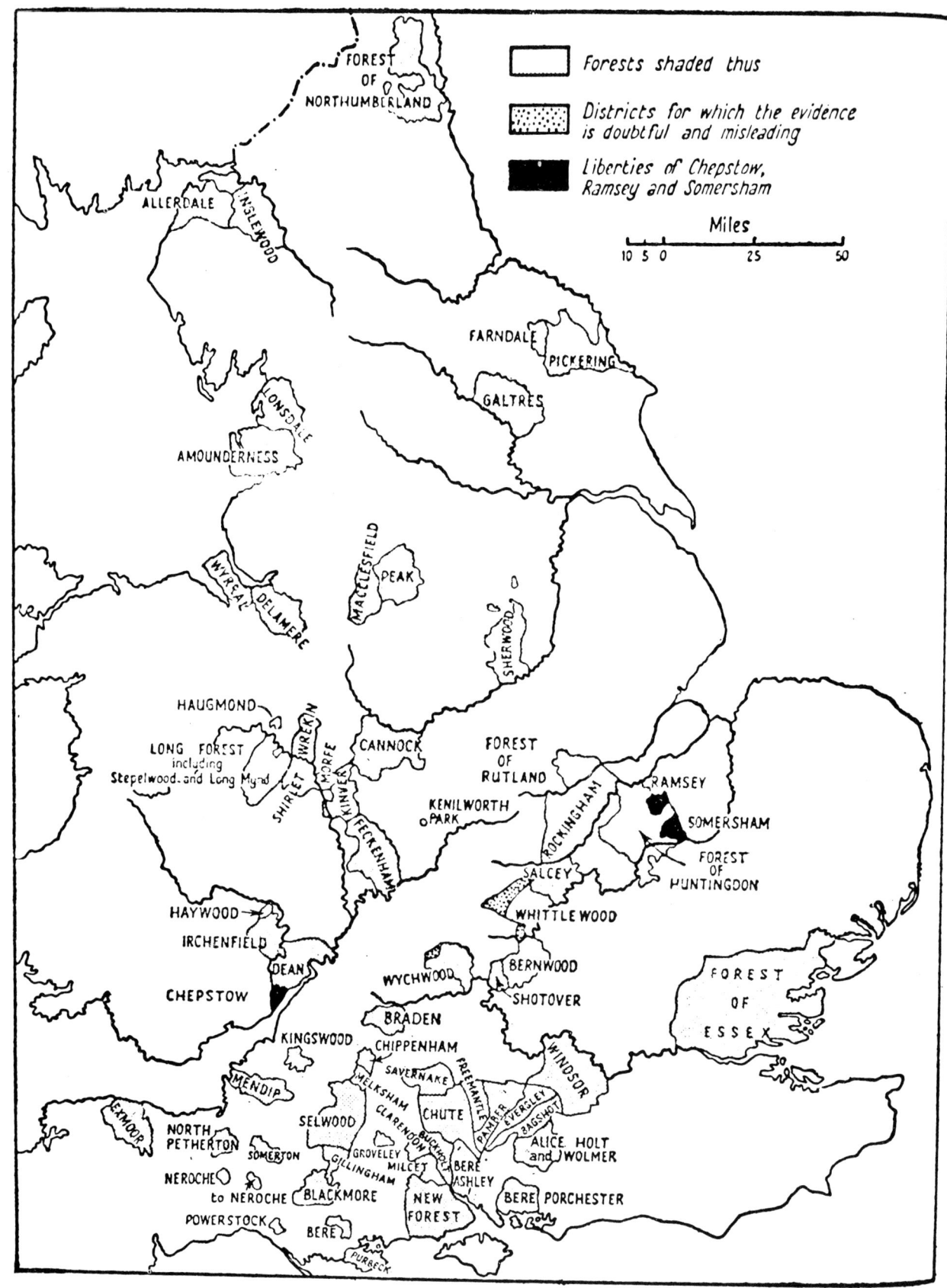

The extent of the royal forests about the middle of the thirteenth century

THE FOREST OF DARTMOOR

Dartmoor is one of those wild regions where the word 'forest' would be better translated as 'chase'. While it seems likely that the woods on the fringes of the moors were once more extensive, there is no evidence that the moors themselves, with their tors and bogs, were ever forested. There is, indeed, little documentary information about Dartmoor until the thirteenth century. Dartmoor as such is not mentioned in Domesday Book, its whole vast extent, some 100,000 acres, being included in the parish of Lydford (making Lydford the largest parish in England).

A number of medieval references imply that the kings of England came hunting here from time to time. Henry III, for instance, made a grant of land locally to Adam Esturmey on condition that he supplied two barbed arrows when the king came to hunt on Dartmoor. The manors of Woodbury and Druscombe were held on similar tenancies—three barbed arrows each. Accounts of the Earl of Cornwall, who then held Dartmoor, for the year 1296–97 show that there were 2,442 cattle agisted on the Moor and also 487 horses. Red deer were present, for there are references to penalties for trespass in the fence month, when the hinds were dropping their calves. On the whole, however, Dartmoor was too far from the capital for the king's visits to be frequent. There were other more productive forests nearer home.

By 1354 the number of cattle had increased to 4,347 and the horses totalled 398. In 1409 cattle numbered 6,380 and horses 370. In 1451, 5,197 cattle and only 129 horses. One gets the impression that the commoners were overstocking the Moor with cattle and that the horses, doubtless Dartmoor ponies, were suffering in consequence. By 1571 sheep begin to appear in the estate accounts and were soon far outnumbering the cattle. Sheep in large numbers were introduced to central Devon in the twelfth century by the Cistercian monks of Buckfast Abbey where, however, they had ample enclosed land for pasture. Probably the upheaval caused by the Dissolution of Monasteries in the 1530s caused the flocks to be more widely dispersed and so to find their way eventually to the high moors. They must have provided strong competition for the red deer.

The medieval records abound in references to peat-cutters, each of whom paid fivepence a year for the privilege; in 1403 there were 21 of them. The peat was apparently needed as fuel for smelting the tin, which had been mined on Dartmoor from very early times. From the thirteenth century onwards the activities of the tin-miners of Cornwall and Devon were controlled by special *stannary* courts, which were not finally abolished till 1896. Medieval charters granted tinners the right to cut peat as well as to mine for tin and exempted them from a wide range of taxes, tolls and other impositions, though they had to pay certain dues to the Crown. The tinners had their own Parliament and own code of laws which were relentlessly enforced, as a seventeenth-century poem illustrates,

> I oft have heard of Lydford law,
> How in the morn they hang and draw,
>   And sit in judgement after;
> At first I wondered at it much,
> But soon I found the matter such
>   As it deserves no laughter.

As Devon became more closely settled other villages and parishes assumed rights in Dartmoor. Twenty-one of them became known as *Venville* parishes. Originally the custom arose because the inhabitants of those villages were continually getting fined for allowing their cattle to stray on the Moor. In the end it proved more practicable to impose an annual fine on every householder in the parish, and this came to be regarded as a rent. In return for the payment the householder was entitled to turn loose on the Moor in summer as many cattle as he could keep on his own holding in winter, and also to cut whatever turf or peat he needed. However, all beasts had to be removed from the Moor between sunset and sunrise—a serious limitation.

With all this agistment and encroachment going on, the red deer must have been increasingly harassed. In the eighteenth century, when land enclosures were proceeding rapidly, farmers and landowners were complaining vociferously about the damage done to their crops in winter by deer. At last in about 1780 the Duke of Bedford's stag-hounds were sent down from Woburn for the purpose of eliminating the deer, which they accomplished thoroughly. A near-contemporary report says that 'Tavistock was so glutted with venison that only the haunches of the animals killed were saved, the rest being given to the hounds'. It must refer to the holocaust when the hounds did their work, but even so, it would seem to be somewhat exaggerated.

Ownership of Dartmoor is still vested in the Duchy of Cornwall, and the commoners of the Venville parishes still maintain their rights of pasturage and turbary. The old rule that animals had to be removed at night has lapsed, so the Moor is heavily populated with sheep, cattle and ponies, the sheep predominating. The only red deer now occurring are a few that wander over from Exmoor.

Dartmoor has since 1951 been a National Park, extending from Okehampton in the north to Ivybridge in the south, and from Tavistock in the west to near Bovey Tracey in the east. Within these broad limits the numerous interests which claim rights on the Moor try to resolve their frequent conflicts. Sheep, ponies, cattle, caravans, the Army, the prison at Princetown, nature conservationists, water authorities, ramblers, huntsmen and the rest make often incompatible bedfellows, but somehow compromise is reached.

The Forestry Commission controls about 5,000 acres of the Moor and has made extensive conifer plantations, especially in the Postbridge sector. Summer visitors will notice the big blocks of dark trees in the vicinity of Princetown. Many of the deep valleys that lead down from the Moor are still cushioned in deciduous trees, including some fine oaks.

An unusual and almost unique segment of the ancient forest is WISTMAN'S WOOD, on the left bank of the West Dart, high on the Moor. Because of the altitude (1,200–1,400 ft) and meagre soil this grove of oaks is stunted, gnarled, twisted and shaggy with ferns, moss and lichen, like something imagined by Walt Disney. Most of the trees have little or no trunks but send out sprawling branches which tangle around the boulders and bog-holes. In spite of the tallest being no more than a few feet high, the trees are estimated to be between 300 and 500 years old. The bizarre and even sinister appearance of the wood has attracted its quota of myths and legends, including a suggestion that it was a grove associated with Druidical worship.

In the same area two other small woods, BLACK TOR BEARE and PILE'S COPSE, are rather similar though their trees are a little larger and less congested.

In addition to the ponies, cattle and sheep, Dartmoor provides a habitat for several of England's rarer birds and animals. The latter include badgers, an occasional otter and perhaps still some red squirrels. Dippers, grey wagtails, pied flycatchers, redstarts, ring ousels, sandpipers and merlins nest, and ravens and buzzards can frequently be seen. Both red grouse and black grouse occur, though in small numbers, and Montagu's harrier nests from time to time. The reservoirs attract numerous waterfowl in winter.

THE FOREST OF EXMOOR

Although an ancient royal forest, Exmoor was never heavily wooded. The Saxons, who came here in the eighth century A.D., probably found the hilltops bare and damp, as they are now, with dense woods and undergrowth in the coombes and vales, creeping in some instances up the steep hillsides. Numerous place-names in and around Exmoor testify to the presence of trees in the valleys. Thus, 'Holnicote' is derived from the Old English word 'holegn', denoting holly; 'Withypool' is 'willow pool'; 'Selworthy' denotes a settlement by a sallow copse; and 'Timberscombe' is self-explanatory.

A detailed examination of relevant entries in the Domesday Book confirms the division of Exmoor between well-wooded slopes and a bare plateau. As settlement advanced up the valleys, so trees in the bottoms and on the lower slopes were cleared, leaving an intermediate zone of timber. All the uncultivated part of Exmoor was, however, naturally appropriated by William the Conqueror as a royal chase, to which his harsh forest laws applied. Thereafter the story of Exmoor is punctuated by frequent summonses for poaching, trespass and suchlike misdemeanours, though from the low fines usually imposed it appears that the offences were not regarded as being of any great gravity. At a forest court in 1270, for example, five of the trespassers were let off because they were considered too poor to pay anything.

In the time of William the Conqueror the Forest of Exmoor is estimated to have comprised about 60,000 acres. Later kings, notably Henry II, Richard I and particularly John, encroached on the neighbouring manors to the extent of about 20,000 additional acres, a confiscation more deeply resented because it was illegal. After John's death all the new acquisitions were disforested.

Exmoor remained royal property right through the Middle Ages and down to the reign of George III, though most monarchs granted it to someone currently in favour. Henry VIII settled it on Catherine of Aragon as part of the marriage settlement, and later gave it to his third wife, Jane Seymour. James I also, in due course, gave it to his queen, Anne. The last lease granted by the Crown was to Sir Thomas Dyke Acland in 1784. In the year of Waterloo an enclosure Act of Parliament for Exmoor allotted one-half of the total area to the king, one-eighth to Sir Thomas and the rest to sundry local landowners. Evidently large sections of the old forest had been carved off or filched at earlier times, because the 1815 survey found only 18,810 acres. The king promptly sold his allocation to a Mr John Knight.

Both the Aclands and the Knights became great names in the subsequent history of Exmoor. The Aclands were keen huntsmen and played a leading part in establishing the tradition of stag-hunting in West Somerset. They also set about reafforesting much of Exmoor, and the family records reveal that no fewer than 800,000 trees were planted in the estate between 1810 and 1826. In 1944 Sir Richard Acland gave 9,848 acres of his estate to the National Trust, a magnificent property which has since been extended to cover some 12,400 acres.

The Knights were more interested in farming, though John Knight began by making some extensive plantations around Simonsbath and establishing a tree nursery. The present Exmoor landscape owes much to the family, for it was they who were mainly responsible for the pattern of large fields with high banks surmounted by beeches which characterises much of the top land. Some mining enterprises launched by the Knights were, however, a failure.

At the beginning of the twentieth century Exmoor was divided among a number of big landowners who, however, found making a profit difficult on the poor hill soil. In 1954 Exmoor was designated a National Park, under the Act of Parliament passed in 1949, the area included extending from the Brendon Hills to Combe Martin in the west. Much of the territory within these boundaries belongs to the National Trust and much to the Forestry Commission. Now, in the last quarter of the century, agriculture, forestry, nature conservation and the cult of holiday are experiencing the problems of co-existence, though on the whole the difficulties that inevitably arise from time to time are usually solved harmoniously. As more and more holiday-makers pour into the south-west along the new motorways, Exmoor is tending to become overcrowded in July, August and September, and the authorities are increasingly worried about its future.

Parts of Exmoor are still well wooded. The National Trust alone maintains about 2,000 acres of forests on the Somerset side of the county boundary. The Forestry Commission's activities, devoted inevitably to conifers, are concentrated chiefly in the eastern part of the area, especially on the outlying massif of the Brendon Hills, where they have 3,000 acres of trees. The valley woods, as in the past, still contain some magnificent trees, many of them deciduous.

Medieval records apparently refer to the red deer and roe deer but not the fallow on Exmoor, which is still, with the neighbouring Quantocks, the chief home of the red deer in England. The red deer range over most of the National Park and probably number between 500 and 700. In 1855 only about 50 were left in the whole of Somerset, but a resumption of hunting then gave them a measure of protection, for the hounds have the support of many farmers who would otherwise probably be after the deer with guns, for they are very destructive of farm crops at times.

Another major feature of the wildlife of Exmoor is the Exmoor pony, whose ancestors have roamed the moor for thousands of years, probably before any human beings trod the upland turf. There are now six herds on Exmoor, three of them of pure-bred animals and three crossbred. They are rounded up annually and the surplus crossbreeds sold at Bampton Fair, held on the last Thursday of October. The pure-breds are usually sold privately or through the agency of the Exmoor Pony Society.

Badgers and foxes are plentiful on and around Exmoor, and there are probably a few otters. Among the birds unusual in lowland England are the dipper, ring-ousel, pied flycatcher, merlin and raven. The moors still hold a few black grouse and red grouse, while buzzards are plentiful.

NORTH PETHERTON (SOMERSET)

The Somerset Forest of North Petherton apparently lay entirely within the boundaries of North Petherton parish. As, however, the parish in the present century comprised over 10,000 acres and was in former times much larger, reaching to and including the town of Bridgwater, the Forest was quite extensive. Surveys or 'perambulations' were made in 1279 and 1298, and many of the place-names mentioned can be identified, including Stathe, Moorland, East and West Lyng, Thurloxton, Shearston, Durston, and Huntworth. Their locations reveal North Petherton as a marshland forest—low-lying land alongside the Parret and the Tone, with probably much more extensive meres and swamps than at present.

Within the limits of the Forest the kings of the late thirteenth century had a Park and presumably a residence. In 1538 the historian Leland says that the Park was surrounded by a ditch, a natural boundary in lowland Somerset. He records that in the Park lived a great number of deer which 'trippe over these dikes and feede al about the Fennes and resort to the Park again'—a very satisfactory arrangement from the point of view of the owner, for while the deer could get out and back easily, cattle and sheep could not get in. Leland adds that there was a pretty moated lodge in the Park. Nearly 50 years later, in 1584, a witness in a lawsuit stated that about 1,800 deer lived in the Park.

In earlier times Robertus de Odburville, appointed by William the Conqueror to be the Forest Baron of Somerset, evidently had his headquarters at North Petherton, which was considered to hold precedence over the other Somerset forests. He was assisted at North Petherton by a royal park-keeper named Anschetil, who evidently had charge of a 'deer-yard' which may be another name for the Park. The deer, from later references to 'harts', certainly included red deer. Although so well stocked with deer, it is likely that North Petherton was valued at least equally for the wildfowling it offered. With so much open water and so many undrained marshes the place must have been a paradise for waterfowl. William the Conqueror was simply following Saxon tradition in confirming North Petherton as a royal forest, and a Saxon charter of the early tenth century refers to lodgings for the king's falconers.

North Petherton Forest has long since been disafforested, and, since the visitation by Dutch elm disease, is not even well wooded. Its pools and marshes, too, have disappeared, except in occasional winter floods.

NEROCHE FOREST

One of the five ancient royal forests of Somerset, Neroche formerly occupied much of the Blackdown Hills, wild border country between Somerset and Devon. Castle Neroche is a prehistoric hill-fort crowning the summit of the eastern end of the hills (870 ft above sea-level) and commanding splendid panoramic views of the Vale of Taunton. The early history of this earthwork is uncertain, but soon after the Norman Conquest it was taken over by Count Robert of Mortain, half-brother to William the Conqueror, and converted into a typical Norman castle. The Norman occupation seems, however, to have been a short one, for after about 20 years the fort was abandoned in favour of Montacute. The name appears to mean 'near the place where the hounds were kept'.

In Saxon and Norman times the Forest of Neroche covered more than 5,000 acres and still embraces some 2,400 acres. In the fifteenth century it was granted to the Portman family, who held it until 1944. It was then purchased by the Crown Lands Commission and leased to the Forestry Commission. Replanting has naturally been mainly with conifers, though

Hauling timber from the forest was once a task exclusively for horses

there are still a number of deciduous copses, but the landscaping is imaginative and an attractive nature trail, starting from the old earthworks, has been laid out. There are badgers and roe deer in the woods, and plenty of tits, warblers, and other woodland birds.

THE FOREST OF MENDIP

The bleak, wind-scoured heights of Mendip strike us now as being anything but forest country, but throughout the Middle Ages Mendip was one of the five royal forests of Somerset. It was among the favourite summer hunting-grounds of Saxon kings, one of whom, Edmund, had a memorable escape from death on the edge of Cheddar Gorge. Chasing a stag, his horse bolted and raced straight towards the brink of the precipice. The events of his life flashed momentarily across his mind, and particularly a quarrel he had just had with his gifted statesman, St Dunstan. He vowed if ever he got safely out of this scrape he would be reconciled with Dunstan. At the last moment the horse swerved and pulled up, panting. Edmund shakily turned its head towards the royal lodge at Cheddar and the coming reconciliation.

Whether the summit of Mendip was ever forested, in the sense that it was covered with trees, is of course open to doubt. It was a vast tract of un-enclosed and mostly waste ground at least 20 miles long and therefore attractive for hunting. The hill-slopes and much of the terrain at their foot would doubtless have been woodland, and it was here that the kings had their hunting lodges. Cheddar was frequently used by the Saxon monarchs but they had another at Axbridge, on the site now occupied by a building known as King John's Hunting Lodge. Although King John and other medieval kings often visited Axbridge, that particular building, in fact, belongs to the early sixteenth century. Chewton Mendip was another royal manor.

Royalty was not oblivious to the mines of Mendip. The mines were presumably worked by local people on payment of certain dues to the king, for at some time in the Middle Ages the revenue was valuable enough to be the subject of a grant to four local magnates known as the Lords Royal. They were the Abbot of Glastonbury, the Bishop of Bath & Wells, the Lord of Chewton and the Lord of the Honour of Richmond in East Harptree. Each in his own division was responsible for maintaining the ancient laws, customs and privileges of the mines and was empowered to hold his own courts and to mete out justice. The Lords Royal evidently owned the smelting works, to which the miners were bound to deliver their ore, paying dues of 10 per cent. Lead was the chief mineral mined; but calamine (from which zinc is produced), manganese and iron were also exploited from quite early times.

POORSTOCK (DORSET)

The Forest of Poorstock or Powerstock in west Dorset, between Beaminster and Bridport, although at one time a royal forest, was always small. Scraps of common land at Powerstock and some woodlands in the quadrangle bounded by Mapperton, Hooke, Toller Porcorum and Powerstock are vestiges of the old Forest.

THE FOREST OF GILLINGHAM

Originally the Forest of Gillingham, in the northern extremity of Dorset, was a division of the great Forest of Selwood (q.v.). A survey of the reign of Henry VIII states that it then measured four miles by one mile, which is not large for a medieval forest. The chief places in the Forest were Gillingham itself and Motcombe, the latter place-name having a significant derivation, for it means 'the valley of the moot, or meeting place'. However, in the fifteenth century the courts for the Forest were held at Shaftesbury.

Saxon kings hunted in this Forest, and Edward the Confessor was offered the throne by a Great Council at Gillingham in 1042. Henry I paid several visits and King John was frequently here. Encroachment seems to have been common during the later Middle Ages, as the pressure of population grew. The Forest was disafforested in 1625, after which most of it was claimed for agriculture. This area is now mostly good dairy land.

THE FOREST OF BLACKMORE

In the Middle Ages much of the country around the headwaters of the river Stour, in Dorset, now known as the Blackmore Vale, was included in the Forest of Blackmore. It adjoined the much smaller Forest of Gillingham and was said by Leland, in the reign of Henry VIII, to stretch from Yeovil to Shaftesbury. That, however, may be an exaggeration to the extent that various lands had been disafforested and enclosed by charters granted by several medieval kings.

The countryside now is rather poorly wooded, being mostly rich meadow land. Probably Duncliff Hill can serve as a sample of what the original forest was like, with Lydlinch Common representing the poor, undrained areas which were devoid of trees.

The medieval Forest was evidently well stocked with red, fallow and roe deer, to judge from royal grants made. It was said at one time to have been known by the name of White Hart Forest, after a white hart which made a place in local history. The story is that Henry III when hunting here saw a white stag which struck him as being so beautiful that he refused to have it killed. One of his subjects, a man named Thomas de la Linde, and some comrades were less merciful and, overtaking the stag at a bridge in the parish of Pulham, slew it. On hearing of this, the angry king sent the offenders to prison, fined them heavily and put an annual tax on all their lands. The bridge was thenceforth known as King's Stag Bridge, and the tax as White Hart Silver. Unfortunately for the authenticity of this romantic tale, etymologists say that 'King's Stag' in its original form was 'King's Stake' and referred to a boundary mark.

THE FOREST OF SELWOOD

The great Forest of Selwood, known even in Celtic times as *Coit Mawr*, 'the great wood', once occupied the entire border zone between Wiltshire and Somerset. Fifteen miles long and at least six miles broad, it constituted for centuries an almost impassable barrier, infested by wild beasts and outlaws. In fact, it held up the Anglo-Saxon advance westwards for nearly 100 years.

An attractive picture of the first Christian mission in these parts is of St Aldhelm, who at the age of seventy had recently been made the first Bishop of Sherborne, trudging through the Forest with his harp and accompanied by a small and nervous band of disciples. When he detected signs of human presence he would settle himself on a log or bridge, strike up a tune and lead the singing. A red-faced old man of imposing appearance, Aldhelm was an accomplished musician who also possessed a vivid turn of language when, a congregation having assembled, he switched to the theme of hell fire. The converts were baptised in shoals.

It was in Selwood that King Alfred, reappearing 'as one risen from the dead', met the Anglo-Saxon levies from Wiltshire, Hampshire and Somerset, prior to his victorious campaign against the Danes in the spring of 878. Much ingenuity has been expended on trying to identify the locality of the rendezvous, called in the *Anglo-Saxon Chronicle* 'Ecgbryhthesstane'. The tall brick building, Alfred's Tower, erected in the nineteenth century on the crest of Kingsettle Hill, right on the county boundary, is probably not on the exact site but near enough to enable one to form a good idea of the terrain.

As with a great number of English forests, Selwood was subjected to a survey in 1298, the background being a promise which Henry III made to restore all land illegally afforested. His son, Edward I, initiated the survey to honour Henry's unfulfilled pledge. Many of the places mentioned as marking the boundaries of the Forest at that time are recognisable. They include South Brewham, Witham, the river Frome, Warminster, Kilmington, Kingsettle Hill, Penselwood, Stavordale and Upton Noble.

Today the general area of Selwood is still one of the best wooded parts of southern England. Most of the ridge of which Kingsettle Hill is the southern section is thick with tall trees. On the Wiltshire side of the county boundary the land rises gradually towards the summit, like a swelling wave, and much of it has been converted to arable farming, but the hills loom over Somerset like an ocean roller about to break. From the foot of the scarp to the crest is a steep, abrupt climb, and Somerset to the west is an exceptionally turbulent countryside, with innumerable little hills, deep coombes and madly meandering streams. One can readily imagine what an ideal haven it must have been for robbers and outlaws when buried in dense forest.

Two splendid estates with appropriate mansions occupy important slices of ancient Selwood and preserve much of the best woodland. One is Stourhead, National Trust property, which glows with colour in May when the rhododendrons and azaleas are in bloom and also with equal beauty but less exuberance at daffodil time. The other is Longleat, which can match Stourhead's rhododendrons but has also more spectacular attractions. A little farther north Woodland Park, Brokerswood, near Westbury, is a 120-acre park catering for those who love woodland walks.

Roe deer are now abundant in Selwood, and there are some fallow deer. Foxes and badger are quite plentiful, as are most species of woodland birds. The hill-slopes and forest glades harbour many interesting insects, including several species of fritillary butterflies, white admirals, purple hairstreaks and dragonflies. The sunken lanes, their banks glowing with massed bluebells and campions, are especially lovely in May. The wildlife of Selwood has, of course, been enhanced dramatically by the lions, camels, chimpanzees and other exotic creatures which attract visitors to Longleat.

KINGSWOOD (BRISTOL)

The Forest of Kingswood in early times covered much of southern Gloucestershire north of Bristol. It was established as a royal hunting-ground by Saxon monarchs (hence its name) and was retained as such by the Norman kings. After its disafforestation in the reign of Henry III the area became notorious as a haunt of outlaws, squatters and criminals. The exploitation of coal here in the seventeenth century resulted in the growth of a class of tough independent miners, who lived in a state of near-anarchy. It was here that John Wesley and George Whitfield began their open-air preaching in 1739, an occasion commemorated by a beacon and memorial on Hanham Mount.

Kingswood has now largely disappeared under bricks and mortar. It is a mainly residential suburb of Bristol with a population of about 30,000, though with some factories. Some vestiges of the old Forest remain, however, including the Panorama Walk, which from an escarpment 250 ft above the river gives spectacular views of the Avon valley.

CRANBORNE CHASE

Archaeological investigations suggest that in immediate pre-Roman times the hilly country along what is now the Dorset/Wiltshire border was quite densely populated. The high plateau and the hillsides are patterned with the outlines of innumerable Celtic fields and villages. The people, who evidently belonged to the tribe of the Durotriges, put up a spirited resistance to Vespasian's legions, and presumably for that reason the region was subsequently much more heavily taxed than most of the rest of Britain.

The local inhabitants also seem to have held out against the invading Saxons, 500 or 600 years later, for what is now upland Dorset was evidently still in British hands for some time after all the neighbouring shires had been occupied by the Saxons. When, however, the region was conquered the population seems to have drifted away. The sequence of events is obscure, but the Saxons were in general valley people who liked to keep near a river. Whether they enslaved or exterminated or absorbed the British population is not known, but when records begin the area had obviously reverted largely to waste, a mixture of open downland, scrub and some extensive woodlands.

Such country was, in the eyes of Saxon and Norman monarchs, clearly designed to be a royal chase, and so it became, under the name of Cranborne Chase, which it still bears. During historic times, however, it was usually in the possession of someone to whom the king had granted it, for services rendered. Thus William II gave it, with the manor of Cranborne, to Robert FitzHamon. Just over 200 years later Edward I granted it to a Richard Lovell. In the reign of Edward III the Earl of March claimed the whole area. In 1544 Henry VIII made it over to Queen Catherine. And so it went on, until in 1714 it passed into the hands of the Rivers family.

The boundaries of the Chase were a cause of many disputes, the confusion being made worse by the existence of an Outer and an Inner Chase. The Inner Chase comprised the watershed that forms the Dorset/Wiltshire border, together with the greater part of the valley of the little river Ebble. The Outer Chase once extended well into the Nadder valley to the north, to the Avon valley in the east, to Blandford and Wimborne in the south and to the Blackmore Vale in the west. Estimates of the actual acreage in medieval times vary from 300,000 to 800,000. Certainly in the thirteenth century, when the new city of Salisbury was being built, the Earls of Gloucester who then held the Chase exercised their right to exact tolls on waggons and pack-horses crossing Harnham Bridge, on the outskirts of Salisbury, in the fence month, when the hinds drop their fawns. The Inner Chase is said to have had a circumference then of about 27 miles and to have comprised about 40,000 acres.

In the course of the centuries, as the countryside became more thickly populated, new farms and estates were carved out of this vast territory.

Deer-hunters of Cranborne Chase, c. 1720. The workmanship of their helmets was much the same as that of a straw bee-hive.

The process was, for the most part, gradual and peaceful, but underneath existed a latent cause of friction. It only needed the current owner of hunting-rights in the Chase to try to exercise them over all the land within the old boundaries, and the sparks began to fly. The earls of Salisbury made an attempt in the reign of James I, and for the next 200 years the conflict simmered, coming occasionally to the boil.

From time to time ill-advised noblemen determined to assert their claim to hunt deer to the limit of the ancient boundaries and to demand the removal of anything that interfered with the free movement of the animals. In short, they called upon all their neighbours to pull down their fences. The reaction of the neighbours to what they considered an outrageous demand was predictable, and, as many of them were not poor peasants but landowning aristocrats equally wealthy and influential, the owners of the hunting-rights quickly had a guerilla war on their hands.

The poaching war of Cranborne Chase is notorious in local annals. It was waged not by labouring men in search of something for the pot but by indignant and hot-headed young members of noble families with well-organised gangs of retainers. Their arms were normally staves and flails, with which they fought many a pitched battle with the Chase keepers. Both keepers and poachers wore armour of padded quilting and protected their heads by wicker helmets, a few examples of which still survive in local museums. When the offenders were caught and hauled before the magistrates they were let off with a fine which they could easily pay, and hostilities went on unchecked. Eventually, a law increasing the maximum penalty to seven years' transportation deterred the gentry from participating directly, but lower down the social scale there were plenty of men willing to take the risk. In fact, the skirmishes became more bitter, and a number of murders occurred. The quarrel was finally resolved by an Act of Parliament of 1828, whereby in return for an annual rent charge of £2,000 a year and a private park the then owner of the hunting rights, Lord Rivers, agreed to relinquish them. Cranborne Chase was thus at last disfranchised.

That the Chase was well populated by deer at all times is clear from surviving records. A survey in the reign of James I put the number of fallow deer at around 2,000. At the time of the disfranchisement it was estimated that in the Chase were not more than 20,000 or less than 12,000 deer. The Chase also harboured considerable numbers of what was known as 'small game', of which rabbits, woodcock, hares, pheasants and partridges seem to have been the most important.

Records of the eighteenth century depict the Inner Chase as being divided into many coppices, intersected by rides, alongside which holly trees were planted. The underwood, chiefly hazel, was cut every 14 to 16 years for the manufacture of hurdles, thatching-spars and other commodities. Immediately after cutting, the coppices had to be enclosed by wattle fences too high for a deer to jump, thus protecting the new hazel growth. The fences remained in position for three years, after which they were lowered in places to allow the deer access. No cattle were allowed into the coppices before the fourth year, or in some instances, the seventh year, when the fences were taken down. Cattle were then entitled to graze in the woods between 12 May (Old May Day) and 23 November (Martinmas) each year. A curious incidental fact is that in measuring the coppices a unique measuring unit was employed. It was called a 'lug', which is a West-country term for the rod, pole or perch standardised at 16 feet, but the Cranborne Chase 'lug' was 18 feet.

Now no longer a forest and divided among many private estates and farms, the Chase retains some of its ancient character. There are coppiced woods, downland half buried in scrub, deep coombes with sides too steep ever to be cultivated, and long panoramic vistas. From one height near the village of Ashmore it is possible, on a clear day, to see the entire length of the Isle of Wight. The old underwood crafts, notably hurdle-making, are still exercised by a remnant of craftsmen, and there are still deer in the woods, though more roe than fallow now. On Wingreen Hill, the highest point of the Chase (altitude 911 ft), the National Trust owns 38 acres, including the clump of trees which are a landmark for miles around.

THE FOREST OF MELCHET

The Forest of Melchet, in south-eastern Wiltshire and western Hampshire, was throughout much of the Middle Ages merged for administrative purposes with the Forest of Clarendon, but earlier it seems to have been regarded as a separate unit. It adjoins Clarendon on the east and extends well over the Hampshire border. Its northern section was known as Buckholt, or 'beech wood', a name which survives as that of a farm, and documents of the fourteenth and fifteenth century refer frequently to grants of Buckholt beeches to various beneficiaries.

In 1442 an order was issued to fell no fewer than 400 beeches in Buckholt Forest, valued at two shillings to two shillings-and-six pence each. Oaks, of which 200 were cut in Melchet in the same year, sold at about three shillings each. The Forest was well staffed by foresters, verderers, keepers, rangers, regarders, woodwards and other persons whose function is obscure, and a fourteenth-century order stipulated that all were to be regarded as on the permanent staff—they were to be paid for 365 days a year, which meant that they collected their wages for Sundays and the numerous holy-days as well as when they were working. The Forest seems to have been well stocked with deer, which were sometimes fed on hay in winter.

Although there is still a Melchet Court in the vicinity of the old forest, the name is no longer applied to the woodland. The countryside is, however, still densely forested, the actual area of continuous woodland being one of the most extensive in southern England. Until recent years these woods have been mostly deciduous, but since the second world war a gradual change has been made to conifers, under the aegis of the Forestry Commission. There are still beeches at Buckholt, and roe deer and fallow deer still roam the woods. The southern part of the woods is rich in wildlife and is one of the haunts of the rare hawfinch. An outlying wood, *Blackmore Copse*, has been designated a nature reserve, primarily for the purpose of preserving the rare and splendid Purple Emperor butterfly.

GROVELEY (WILTSHIRE)

The Forest of Groveley is one of the smaller English forests and has probably been much the same size as at present since the early medieval period. It occupies the hill plateau or watershed between the valleys of the rivers Wylye and Nadder a few miles WNW of Salisbury.

In the fourteenth entury and probably earlier Groveley was apparently regarded as an outlying part of the Forest of Clarendon (q.v.). In the reign of Edward III it supported two foresters, and 100 years later, in the reign of Edward IV, one woodward. It is now, and has been for several hundreds of years, a part of the estate of the Earls of Pembroke, whose seat is Wilton House.

Adjoining Groveley on the north side the village of Wishford keeps alive a greenwood custom probably dating from pagan times. At daybreak on Oak Apple Day, 29 May, the householders, roused from sleep by a noisy band, trudge along the mile or so of sunken lane to Groveley and there cut green boughs, which they carry down to Wishford to decorate their houses. A specially large oak bough is hoisted to the top of the church tower. Prizes are awarded for the best decorated houses and also for the branch bearing most oak-apples. In mid-morning a coach takes a party of villagers, dressed in Victorian costumes, to Salisbury where they carry oak branches into the Cathedral and present them to the Dean before the high altar. Their leader then raises the shout 'Groveley, Groveley and all Groveley!', in which they all join enthusiastically. Afterwards they perform a traditional dance on the lawn outside the west door. Ostensibly all this is to perpetuate their rights to cut wood in Groveley and to celebrate a victory over an Earl of Pembroke who attempted to interfere with it 200 or so years ago. In fact, the custom is very much older than the eighteenth century, for it is set out in some detail in a document entitled, *The Sum of the Ancient Customs belonging to Wishford and Barford out of the Forest of Groveley*, and prepared at the time of the Dissolution of Monasteries in the reign of Henry VIII. The rights then included not only the gathering of wood and the cutting of green boughs but also the agisting of cattle and pigs to graze there and the killing of one fat buck every Whitsuntide. The ritual and social customs attached to the celebrations have their roots far back in prehistory.

THE FOREST OF CLARENDON

The royal Forest of Clarendon in the Middle Ages included not only the present forest country of the Clarendon Estate but large areas of adjacent woodland, including the outlying forests of Melchet and Buckholt. Possibly, too, the 'lost' forest of Penchet may have been incorporated though, alternatively, Penchet may in early times have been a name given to the whole forest. The Forest occupies, or occupied, an extensive block of country due east of the city of Salisbury. Excavations in the 1930s revealed underneath the foundations of the great medieval Palace masonry of an earlier date, suggesting that the Forest had been a royal chase for a long time, perhaps even in the Saxon era.

On the crest of a steep chalk scarp giving a distant view of Salisbury spire, Clarendon Palace, the king's residence when he came hunting here, is reputed to have been once the second largest building in England, surpassed only by the Great Hall of Westminster.

The first king of whose presence at Clarendon there is any record was William the Conqueror. In fact, the first mention of Clarendon is in a writ, issued at Winchester in 1072, summoning Ethelwig, Abbot of Evesham, to attend with his armed followers at Clarendon 'in the octave of pentecost'. William was then probably preparing for his invasion of Scotland. The document thus provides evidence that Clarendon was a royal residence within ten years of the Conquest. In those days, though, it was almost certainly a hunting lodge, for William had a strongly fortified castle only three miles away at Old Sarum, and he could hardly have needed a second.

The great days of Clarendon begin with Henry II, said to be the last king of England to regard Winchester (less than 20 miles away) as his capital. Records begin in the second year of his reign (1155–56) and recur almost annually. Thereafter for three or four centuries it was a favourite country seat of English monarchs. Money was lavished upon it (more than £262 in a single year in the days when a penny was at least the equivalent of a modern pound), and world-famous artists and architects were called in to beautify it (in 1235 a Master Walter, 'notary of the Emperor', spent many days here, apparently painting murals). Although the story, quoted on a plaque on a surviving wall of the Palace, to the effect that King John of France and King David of Scotland resided here with their captor, King Edward III, while plague was raging in London is not entirely accurate, almost every English monarch from William the Conqueror to Henry VI seems to have spent a good deal of time at Clarendon. Henry III was especially fond of his forest lodge.

The Palace has the distinction, unusual in archaeological sites, of being well documented. Preparatory to a royal visit a survey was made, with recommendations about necessary repairs, and many of these records have survived. Excavations were undertaken here in the 1930s with a view to matching the remains and particularly the ground plan of the Palace with the documentary evidence.

In 1273 a survey was also made of Clarendon Forest. The boundaries were evidently much the same as those of the twentieth-century estate, and many of the place-names of lanes, copses and farms are still in use. In this century the Forest was rigorously exploited, for both Henry III and Edward I were over-generous with their grants of timber. This was the century which saw the building of Salisbury Cathedral, and much of the timber used in the fabric and for scaffolding came from Clarendon. Grants of timber are recorded, too, for building a chapel at Britford, building a house for Franciscan friars at Salisbury, renewing the dormitory-floor in Romsey Abbey, repairing and extending Winchester Castle as well as Clarendon Palace, rebuilding the king's mill under the castle of Old Sarum, building a new church for the Abbess of Wilton, and supplying oaks for the rafters of the queen's house at Lyndhurst. This last grant seems strange, for Lyndhurst is in the heart of the New Forest. Why haul oaks from Clarendon?

The Palace evidently fell into disuse during the Wars of the Roses. The last monarch to reside there was Henry VI, who in 1453 spent the best part of a year there, during an interlude of insanity. When Elizabeth I went hunting there in 1574 the building was evidently in ruins.

Thereafter royalty lost interest in Clarendon. James I granted the entire forest to the Earl of Pembroke in 1606. At the Restoration Charles II gave it to George Monk, the Duke of Albemarle, who parted with it briefly to Lord Chancellor Hyde (who took the title of the Earl of Clarendon) and then re-purchased it. It went by bequest to the Earl of Bath in 1688 and by purchase in 1713 to the Bathurst family, who retained it for over 200 years. Since 1919 it has belonged to the Christie-Miller family.

During the Commonwealth a detailed survey of the Forest was made. Dated 1650, it asserted that the fenced land amounted to 4,293 acres and was worth £1,806 per year. It had five main divisions, namely those of Ranger's, Theobald's, Fussell's, Palmer's and Hunt's, all of which names are known and used today. Palmer and Hunt are known to have been keepers at that time or a little earlier. The Forest then contained 14,919 timber trees, apparently nearly all oaks, but many others had recently been felled for the Navy. The deer in the Forest (all fallow) numbered approximately 500. Within the boundaries of the Forest, too, were several rabbit warrens, and in 1606 they were estimated to yield an income of about £200 a year—a large sum for those days.

Throughout the Middle Ages the underwood crop was evidently a useful source of income. The right to cut the underwood in certain sections of the Forest was sold annually. The system must have been much the same as that which prevailed until within living memory. The underwood was then sold in lots of about an acre when seven or eight years old and was purchased by independent craftsmen living in the neighbouring villages. The wood they valued most was hazel, from which they made hurdles, sheep cribs, faggots, peasticks, bean rods, clothes-props, thatching spars and many other humble but highly essential articles. Ash was also considered a valuable wood, useful for ladders and posts besides having the propensity to 'burn fierce when it is green'.

Parts of the deer-leap which marked the boundaries of the Forest in 1273 are still extant and constitute a quite formidable barrier. The park and woodland are privately owned and not accessible to the public, except by two footpaths.

Presumably red deer as well as fallow and roe roamed the glades of medieval Clarendon. Roe deer are still plentiful, and there are some fallow (though not nearly as many as before the second world war, when large numbers were killed off), but only an occasional red deer wanders into the district. Wild boar were evidently still quite numerous in Clarendon in the fourteenth century, the same century that saw the killing of the last wolf in the Forest. Throughout the Middle Ages the rabbit warrens of Clarendon were regarded as a valuable asset. They contributed £100 a year to the king's household in 1495 and were assessed at more than £200 a year in the reign of Charles I. Medieval Clarendon Forest evidently extended to the Avon below Salisbury, for there are numerous references to swans on the river. A good deal of poaching went on, the value of stolen swans in the year 1345 being put at £100, which is not only a very large sum but also indicates a big swan stock. Records of herons being sent from Clarendon to the royal household in London indicate the

Forest in winter
Photo. Dr Alan Beaumont

presence of a heronry there in the fourteenth century, and local place-names imply that woodcock were quite plentiful.

SAVERNAKE FOREST

The present Forest of Savernake, lying mostly south-east of Marlborough, Wiltshire, although extending over 4,000 acres, is only the shrunken nucleus of the medieval forest, which linked up with the Forest of Chute on the Wiltshire/Hampshire boundary. In the reign of Edward I it reached over the Berkshire border to beyond Hungerford. The name 'Savernake' is Celtic, indicating that it has been applied to the Forest since Romano-British times.

William the Conqueror gave manors in the district to one of his knights, Richard Esturmey, ancestor of the present Marquess of Ailesbury, owner of Savernake and twenty-ninth hereditary warden of the Forest. Although Savernake is not mentioned in the Domesday Book, some of the places in it are, notably Ulfela, which later became known as Wolfhall. Situated about a mile from the village of Great Bedwyn, Wolfhall became in the sixteenth century the seat of the powerful family of Seymour, who had succeeded by marriage to the inheritance of the Sturmeys when the male line failed 100 years earlier. It was on a visit to Wolfhall that Henry VIII met Jane Seymour, daughter of the Forest Warden, John Seymour, who was one of his friends and courtiers. Having executed Anne Boleyn in 1536 he promptly married Jane, who died in childbirth in the following year. Her son, of course, became King Edward VI.

During Edward's short reign his uncle, Edward Seymour, became Lord Protector of the Realm and first Duke of Somerset, but ambition proved his undoing, and Queen Mary, the next monarch, had him beheaded on Tower Hill. The family remained connected by several marriages to the royal family until the time of the Stuarts, when the estates passed by marriage to the earls of Ailesbury. Throughout these turbulent times the Seymours continued to be based on Savernake, at first at Wolfhall and then at a newly built Tottenham House. Both buildings have long ago collapsed in ruins, but a new Tottenham House stands on or near the site of the old.

At the time of the building of this new Tottenham House, in the eighteenth century, the great landscape architect, Capability Brown, was commissioned to re-shape the estate. His work is still in evidence in the superbly planned forest unit that is the present Savernake Forest. Four thousand acres and 16 miles in circumference, it possesses eight magnificent beech avenues leading like spokes of a wheel to the centre of the Forest, and even a casual drive along the A338 (the Salisbury to Marlborough road) will reveal that the woodland is rich in ancient oaks. The Marquesses of Ailesbury, still forest wardens, are said to base their title

Badgers in a typical habitat
Drawing by Kevin J. Dean

to the office and to the estate on the possession of a famous hunting horn, which is believed to date from the Norman period and is sounded whenever a king enters the Forest.

The chief village in the Forest, though now on the edge of it, is Great Bedwyn, which before the Reform Act used to send two Members to Parliament and still has an area of over 10,000 acres. Queen Jane Seymour is buried in the church.

In the late 1930s the Forestry Commission undertook the management of the Forest, on a 999-year lease from the Marquess. The woods are now managed as a commercial unit, though with restrictions on over-extensive planting of conifers. The red deer for which Savernake was long celebrated are still there. Their usual home is a small park near Tottenham House, but some break away and wander from time to time. Fallow and roe deer are quite plentiful.

MELKSHAM AND PEWSHAM (WILTSHIRE)

Until towards the end of the thirteenth century this forest was known as the Forest of Melksham and Chippenham, and the reason for the change in name is not known. The Forest occupied a considerable tract of country between Chippenham and Devizes, the woodlands of Bowood and Spye Park representing what remains of it. The forest courts seem usually to have been held at Devizes.

The Forest seems to have been well stocked with fallow deer though apparently not red deer. Records of 1423, 1424, 1425 speak of a heavy mortality among deer, in 1424 amounting to 140 bucks and 200 does. 'Murrain' is given as the cause of death, but that could mean almost any disease. Most of the area was disafforested early in the seventeenth century, but Bowood was retained by the Crown. It contained some very fine timber, most of which the authorities of the Commonwealth ordered to be felled to pay the Army. The order was partly carried out but some of the trees were saved through the intervention of John Pym, who represented the adjacent borough of Calne in Parliament. A survey of 1653 showed a total of 10,921 trees still standing in 958 acres of forest.

Splendid trees, underlaid by bluebell carpets in May, are still a feature of the estate parks that have replaced the Forest, and fallow deer still browse there.

THE FOREST OF BRADEN

Old beeches in Savernake Forest

Little remains of the great Forest of Braden, or Braydon, which once extended across north Wiltshire from the vicinity of Malmesbury almost to the Berkshire border and covered much of the ground occupied by the town of Swindon. The M4 now traverses it. Its northern edge was just south of Cricklade, the monks of the medieval hospital there having a special dispensation to take carts through the Forest when collecting fuel for the poor.

In a survey of 1222 it was stated to rank second in all England for the number of timber trees, and it abounded in both red and fallow deer. Kings hunted there throughout the Middle Ages, and as late as the reign of James I a swainmote court (held in 1609) could still command the attendance of an impressive muster of forest officials—four foresters, 11 regarders, 41 agisters, 14 woodwards, two herdsmen and many jurymen. However, it seems that enclosure was even then making inroads into the Forest, for it was reported that for many years no-one had cut the stipulated amount of deer-browse for winter fodder for the deer, in consequence of which the deer were leaving the woods and doing much damage in the neighbouring fields. The entire Forest was disafforested in the reign of Charles II, and Cricklade still possesses a charity for the relief of eight poor men and women and for apprenticing children, from funds received from 100 acres of forest land enclosed at that time.

Although the Forest has virtually disappeared, this is still great hunting country, though the quarry now is, of course, the fox not the stag.

THE FOREST OF CHUTE

The Forest of Chute occupied an area of still wild, broken and thinly populated country along the Hampshire/Wiltshire border, the northern extremity being near the point where the two counties and Berkshire meet. Most of it, however, lay in Wiltshire. Near Conholt and the village of Chute the land rises to an altitude of over 800 ft and the hills are so steep that the Roman road from Winchester to Cirencester uncharacteristically takes a broad sweep around one of them to find an easier gradient. The name 'Chute' is derived from a Celtic word meaning 'wood'.

Under the Plantagenet kings Chute and Savernake were sometimes under the same administration, creating an immense contiguous forest area. It was well stocked with red deer, about the disposal of which, as gifts to royal favourites, there are many documentary references. The warden in 1490, Sir Nicholas Lysle, seems to have been a rogue, for at a forest court at Andover he was found guilty of killing 20 deer, of allowing one of his foresters to make off with two hives of bees, and of various other misdemeanours. He was consequently removed from office but was taken before the court again in 1497 for similar offences. Sir Nicholas, whom contemporary records term 'the abbot of Misrule', evidently felt he had a grievance, for he complained to the king that his was an hereditary office held by his ancestors for generations. For it he had paid a rent of 10 shillings a year and had supplied seven foresters at his own cost, and in return he had the use of a forest lodge as a dwelling house. He asked to be reinstated, a request which was finally granted in 1501, on payment of a fine by Sir Nicholas.

Collingbourne Wood and *Conholt Park* are now the largest woodland vestiges of the ancient forest, but there are many smaller woods. Red deer no longer roam the glades, but roe deer are quite plentiful and there are some fallow.

THE NEW FOREST

The New Forest justifiably bears the reputation of being the best and biggest surviving example of a medieval English forest. Despite the pressures of modern urban civilisation, the latest demand being that for a fast motorway through its very heart, the Forest still retains much of its natural charm and character, while its people hold tenaciously to their ancient customs. The glade in which Rufus's Stone stands is still much the same as it must have been on 2 August in the year 1100 when King William II was slain in mysterious circumstances, for modern research has shown that the demarcation line between woodland and open heath must have been the same then as now.

The New Forest occupies, or rather occupied, a quadrangular or a butterfly-shaped territory of Hampshire, bounded on the east by Southampton Water, on the south by the Solent and the English Channel, on the west by the Avon (though the countryside on the other side is very similar), and on the north approximately by the Wiltshire border. Within its limits are about 140 square miles of woodland, heath, bog and enclosed land, of which roughly two-thirds belonged to the Crown until the present century, while the other third was privately owned. A writer of about 1900 put the total acreage at 92,365; at the time of the transfer of the Crown properties to the Forestry Commission those in the New Forest amounted to about 65,000 acres.

In typically English fashion, this ancient forest bears the appellation 'New', given it by William the Conqueror, who established it in 1079. Old-time history books used to describe graphically how the Conqueror ruthlessly destroyed churches, burned villages and generally made a prosperous countryside into a desert in order that he might enjoy the hunting. The allegations, originally set down and repeated by Saxon chroniclers who were no friends of the Normans, are only partially true.

Saxon and Danish kings had enjoyed hunting over this extensive area of poor and thinly populated country. The soil of much of the Forest, especially the heaths, is such that it could never have been of much use for agriculture. Moreover, their Forest laws seem to have fallen little short in severity of those of William the Conqueror. What William perhaps did was to enforce and amplify a code of laws which had fallen into disuse. And when William made laws he saw that they were obeyed.

The Forest in pre-Norman days was called 'Ytena', which is said to mean 'the place of the Jutes', thus identifying the early settlers with the Jutish people who are known to have colonised the Isle of Wight. The official limits of the Forest have in the course of the centuries been pushed back from the natural boundaries sketched in our second paragraph. A belt of land about two or three miles wide is now imposed between the Forest proper and the river Avon on the west, between the Forest proper and Southampton Water on the east and between the Forest proper and Christchurch Bay on the south. This zone represents much of the better and more desirable agricultural land. It seems likely that the process of encroachment on the Forest began in late Saxon times and that it was here that William embarked on his ruthless reafforestation policy.

The records say that he caused about 140 hides to be taken out of cultivation and added to the Forest, which modern research suggests added about 17,000 acres to the Forest area. A 'hide' is generally agreed to be the amount of land ploughable and therefore required to support a family. By that estimate William dispossessed about 140 families, which is bad enough but nothing like the 60 villages alleged by Saxon chroniclers. Details are known of some of the land lost by specific manors to the Forest by the Conqueror's action. Ringwood had to sacrifice 24 'ploughlands' (which probably amounted to about 16 'hides'); Brockenhurst lost the whole of three of its four manors; Burley about three 'hides';

'Folk Cottage' at Furzey Gardens in the New Forest; a typical commoners' cottage, now modernised

Lyndhurst, two manors; the south coast lost land from 19 manors.

On the other hand, Domesday Book records the names of quite a number of Saxon landowners, at Burgate, Brockenhurst, Wellow and elsewhere, who were allowed to retain their property. Some of them, such as Aelfric, a thane of Brockenhurst, was given land in another district to compensate for some of his Forest manor required by the king. And it is worth remembering that making a Forest does not entirely depopulate the area. Foresters, keepers, wardens, woodcutters, falconers, charcoal-burners and numerous other officials, craftsmen and labourers would be needed. Doubtless many of the dispossessed peasants found such employment and probably continued to live in the Forest. The small plots they were permitted to enclose, however, would be inadequate to support them and so the rights of pasturage, pannage, turbary and the rest may well have arisen as a kind of compensation for what they had lost.

By the twelfth century the process of encroachment had begun again. It went on at all levels, from the humble peasant squatter to the powerful baron seeking to extend his estate. The quarrels of King John, a monarch extremely fond of hunting, with his barons were partly due to John's attempts to maintain his rights in various royal forests, including the New Forest, where the lords had been steadily extending their territory.

As the Middle Ages unfolded other interests secured their share of the Forest. One of the most important Tudor ecclesiastical foundations was the Cistercian Abbey of Beaulieu, to which King John, apparently repenting on the rebound some atrocities he had committed on certain monks of that order, made a huge grant of land said to have amounted to about 10,000 acres. Netley, another Cistercian abbey, and the priories of Christchurch and Breamore also acquired substantial holdings in the Forest. The Cistercians, deeply involved in the wool trade, established large sheep flocks at Beaulieu, and some of the farms they held still retain forest grazing rights for sheep.

Medieval Forest records are full of reports on cases of trespass and poaching, though evidently the Forest courts sat at infrequent and irregular intervals. A court held at Southampton in 1330 dealt with cases dating back as far as 1284 and, not surprisingly, it is recorded that on the first day of the session no fewer than 95 persons who had been summoned to attend as plaintiffs, defendants or witnesses had died in the meantime. The severity of the penalties for killing deer seem to have been considerably relaxed, for offences were punished by fines rather than imprisonment or mutilation. The fines ranged from 12 pence to 20 shillings, though to get them into perspective one can compare them with the contemporary value of a good horse, which was five shillings. The status and identity of some of the medieval poachers are surprising. One is 'Sir Wyllium Holmes, a priest of Sarum'; another is the bailiff of Godshill; another, 'Rychard Carter, a yoman'. They were bold offenders, too. Two of them went hunting in the Forest with nine greyhounds and a mastiff and even brought along a white mare to carry the carcases. Some of the cases concerned the unlawful felling of trees.

The 'expedition' of large dogs was a regulation apparently introduced in the reign of Henry II. All dogs above a certain size had to have three claws of each of their forepaws struck off with a chisel, to prevent them chasing and pulling down the king's deer. The criterion of size was a large stirrup, through which the dog was required to creep. If it was small enough to do so it was exempt. A stirrup still kept at Lyndhurst is known as Rufus' Stirrup and is said to be the one used for the purpose, but it probably dates only from Tudor times. The dogs of the Abbot of Beaulieu were exempted from the test, and from the above reference to greyhounds and mastiffs it seems that a lot of local residents ignored it.

From Tudor times onwards royal hunting parties in the Forest became infrequent and increasing interest was taken in the timber, primarily as ship-building material. A succession of monarchs neglected the place, allowing the wages of officials and other employees to fall into arrears and turning a blind eye to encroachments. Charles I even offered the Forest to his creditors as collateral for loans, while Charles II capriciously granted coppices and plots of land to ladies of his court. Charles II did, however, order a survey or perambulation of the Forest, which survives and gives much detailed information. Comparison between it and a similar though less lengthy survey made in the reign of Edward I is full of interest. A further survey, also very detailed, was made in 1801.

During the sixteenth and seventeenth centuries the timber resources of the Forest seem to have been considerably depleted. An Act of William III and Mary, dated 1698, provided for some of the ravages to be made good by planting 6,000 acres of oaks over the next 20 years, to be followed by a further 6,000 acres; in fact, only just over 3,000 acres were planted. The reafforestation required enclosure and met with determined opposition from the forest-dwellers.

After the 1801 perambulation an Enclosure Act was passed for 6,000 acres, while 2,274 acres of existing enclosures were confirmed. In 1851 another enclosure of 10,000 acres was sanctioned. All these enclosures were for the purpose of afforestation, with the idea of keeping out the cattle, ponies and pigs which would otherwise destroy the young trees. Throughout the second half of the eighteenth century and the period of the Napoleonic wars ship-building activity in the ports and shipyards of Hampshire was intense, and particularly in the little yard of Buckler's Hard, on the New Forest coast near Beaulieu, where many of Nelson's ships were built of forest oak.

The 1851 enclosure was accompanied by the Deer Removal Act. Someone worked out that only 120 deer were killed each year and that each one cost £100, making the keeping of them a hopelessly uneconomic proposition. When it was proposed to enclose and reafforest the land thus saved, however, the proposal naturally met with strong opposition from the commoners, especially as it was suggested that much of the planting should be of the alien Scots pine instead of oak. The agreement with regard to the earlier enclosures was that when the trees were tall enough the fences would be taken down and the animals readmitted, but the commoners quickly appreciated that there would be precious little grazing under thickly planted pines. Friction continued until another Act in 1877 limited the area that could be enclosed to 18,000 acres. Even then the commoners continued to deplore the large-scale planting of pines. The long-standing conflict of ideas and interests was at last resolved by the New Forest Act of 1949, since when the Forestry Commission, which had taken over the forest interests from the Crown, and the Verderers, who represent the commoners, have worked amicably together.

The total area of the Forest, by the latest survey, is 67,024 acres. Enclosed woodland and woodland which can be enclosed account for 20,599 acres. Un-enclosed woodland amounts to 11,554 acres. That leaves 32,951 acres of open land, chiefly heath and forest lawns, grazed by the commoners' livestock. In addition, the Forest area contains 27,658 acres of privately owned land. Also there are 6,299 acres of common land adjoining or in close proximity to the Forest commons but just outside the Forest boundaries, including 715 acres in Wiltshire.

In the Forest most of the hardwood trees grow on clay soils, while the thin sandy soils coincide more or less with the heaths, though biggish areas of the latter have been planted with pines and firs. Of the indigenous trees, oaks and beeches are the most numerous. In former times coppicing and pollarding were widely practised, and although they have been discontinued long ago some old pollarded trees may still be found. The most notable example is the Knightwood Oak, which only close examination identifies as a pollarded tree. The ditches and raised banks which marked the confines of coppices may also be traced. Ditch and bank, the latter planted with a gorse hedge, were a barrier intended to keep out grazing animals, particularly deer, for a few years while the young trees inside were becoming established. To the abandonment of this sensible programme the comparative absence of hazel undergrowth, once common here, can probably be attributed, for once protection had been removed the deer would never give the hazel stools a chance. Holly and hawthorn have, however, managed to survive, and are now plentiful. Large numbers of venerable trees, several hundred years old and frequently host to colonies of epiphytes, such as ferns and lichens, add to the picturesqueness of the woodlands. There are also some ancient yews.

The New Forest has all three indigenous species of deer—the red, fallow and roe—including two small herds of the once dominant red. In the middle of the nineteenth century, before the passing of the Deer Removal Act, the estimated number of deer in the Forest was between 7,000 and 8,000. A count in 1947, presumably of all species, recorded 3,196 animals. With the general increase of roe deer it is probably higher now, and there are some Sika and perhaps Muntjac. Of domestic animals, ponies (of the New Forest breed), cattle and pigs are as plentiful as ever, but geese less so. Foxes are common, and badgers on sandy soils.

All the common woodland birds occur, including nightingales, nightjars, woodcock, owls and jays, while whinchats, stonechats, pipits, yellow hammers and linnets are typical birds of the heathland. There is a heronry in the southern part of the Forest. The New Forest is one of the remaining habitats of several rare species of birds, including the Dartford warbler, the hobby and Montagu's harrier. Occasionally a honey-buzzard is reported in summer, and sometimes a wandering black grouse is seen.

Adders abound, especially on the sandy heaths, which warm up quickly in sunshine and retain the heat. They are a constant hazard to ramblers and picnickers.

The heaths are also the home of two rare reptiles—the smooth snake, or Coronella, and the sand lizard—as well as the rare natterjack toad.

The Forest fauna is rich in insects, with a number of species of butterfly and moth rare elsewhere. Here the entomologist may expect to find the Purple Emperor, Silver-studded Blue, White Admiral and Purple Hairstreak butterflies and the Oak Beauty, Oak-Eggar, Crimson Underwing, Lappet, Emperor and Merveille-du-jour among moths. It has a rare insect of its own in the New Forest Cicada, which is related to the grasshoppers.

The Forest floor in the woodland areas is not rich in vegetation. Wood sorrel is fairly plentiful, and almost every sunny lane is margined with foxgloves. There are places where bluebells spread a carpet under the beeches. A very rare flower of certain forest glades, unfortunately easily accessible to picnickers, is the magenta-coloured wild gladiolus. The heaths and bogs carry typical flora, such as heather, cotton grass, bladderwort and gorse. Around the woodland margins large banks of rhododendrons are ablaze with colour in June, those at Cuffnells Park being said to be the largest in England.

Lyndhurst, the 'capital' of the Forest, is, etymologically, 'the wood of lime trees', but lime are not now conspicuous there. Forest business is conducted by the Verderers in the Verderers' Hall, while next door the King's House, rich in relics of Forest life, is the administrative centre.

BERE (HAMPSHIRE)

The Forest of Bere is in no way connected with Bere Regis, in Dorset, but describes what was formerly a very large wooded area in eastern Hampshire, immediately north of Portsdown Hill. The name, strangely, seems to be derived from an Old English word for pasture, perhaps given to it at a time when the trees were already being cleared for farming. In the Middle Ages one gathers that the Forest extended to the vicinity of Winchester, for it was near enough for citizens of that city, and people from Crawley and Sparsholt which lie west of Winchester, to poach deer in it.

A survey of 1688 put the area at not less than 23 square miles, of which two-thirds were open forest land. That leaves one-third of the area enclosed, being the lands of villagers, most of whom had rights to turn horses, cattle and pigs (but not sheep) to graze in the Forest. Bere then had a full quota of forest officials. The Forest held about 250 fallow deer.

The 1688 survey was prompted by an anxiety about supplies of oak for the Navy, and an Act of Parliament in that year was passed for 'The Increase and Preservation of Timber in the New Forest and in the County of Southampton'. Although many trees were planted in consequence, Bere seems to have been somewhat neglected. In 1810 the Forest was disafforested, but the area still bearing trees passed to the control of the Office of Woods. Much timber was felled in the later years of the Napoleonic Wars, and the total area cleared between 1810 and 1855 was 1,169 acres.

It is recorded that the area was re-planted with oak, mixed larch and pine but, be that as it may, by 1923 when the Forest was taken over by the Forestry Commission, there were only 1,450 acres of woodland compared to 16,000 in 1790, and that remnant had been split into three parts. Since then the Forest has been extended through purchase and leasing until it now covers 3,587 acres, though the woodland is not contiguous.

WINDSOR FOREST

Windsor Great Park now covers about 3,000 acres. In medieval times it was immensely larger, extending over much of eastern Berkshire and northern Surrey as well as parts of Buckinghamshire and Middlesex, and having a reputed circumference of about 120 miles. Estimates of its area depend, however, on the definition of 'Forest', and the limits of Windsor Forest varied from time to time according to the policy of the reigning monarch. For instance, although throughout the twelfth and thirteenth centuries there are numerous documentary references to the part of the Forest which lay in Surrey, with records of forest courts held at Guildford; a survey of 1327 stated that the boundaries of the Forest excluded the whole of Surrey and had done for several generations. Six years later it seems to have been realised that this was a mistake, for much of Surrey was then reafforested, which means not that it was planted with trees but that it was recognised as an area to which the royal forest laws applied.

Legal documents relating to 1488, in the reign of Henry VII, establish that courts for forest pleas were held in Guildford (for the Surrey section of the Forest) and New Windsor (for the Berkshire part). On these occasions special liberties within the Forest were claimed by Elizabeth, the queen; by the bishops of Winchester and Salisbury; by the abbots of Reading, Abingdon, Waltham, Westminster, Stratford Longthorn, Cirencester and Chertsey; by the priors of Hurley, Bisham and Merton; by the prioress of Bromehall and Amberwyle; by the dean and canons of Windsor; by the provost and college of Eton; by the dean and chapter of Salisbury; by the mayor and citizens of New Windsor; and by the Duchess of Norfolk and two laymen. This formidable list was the consequence of grants of properties and rights granted by earlier monarchs. The grants largely concerned hunting and timber rights, but as early as the reign of Henry II the king was granting permission to certain privileged persons (in this instance, the abbots of Chertsey) to fence off parks within the Forest limits.

The new park at Windsor was fenced for the king's own use between 1275 and 1278, and there are records of numerous trees being felled for the fencing. Deer seem to have become scarce in the forest by this date, for some had to be transported from Chute Forest in Wiltshire to stock the new park. Possibly the resident herds had been unable to hold their own in competition with the increasing numbers of farm livestock roaming in the Forest. For example, a record of 1257 shows that 10 horses and 100 cattle were agisted to the enclosed Guildford Park (a section of the Forest) from Hocktide to the Nativity of John the Baptist, which means about two months in spring and early summer, and 20 oxen later; also 156 pigs. When Windsor Great Park was being enclosed in 1277 orders were given that the wild bulls and cows in the Park were to be captured and sold. It is unlikely that these were the genuine wild descendants of the ancient aurochs but were more probably feral cattle, escaped from the herds of commoners with grazing rights in the Forest, or possibly they were privately owned cattle turned loose to find their living in the Forest by owners who had no right to do so.

Henry VIII actually extended the afforested area of Windsor by creating a new forest, the Honor of Hampton Court, between Hampton Court and Epsom. The negotiations were protracted, owing to the fact that even dictatorial Henry could not dispossess the existing owners without their consent, which in general had to be purchased. The new forest lasted less than ten years, however (from 1539 to just after Henry's death in 1547), after which it reverted to its original status, the stock of deer being taken back to Windsor.

Under James I a survey of Windsor Great Park gave it an area of 3,650 acres and a circumference of $10\frac{1}{4}$ miles. The area of the unenclosed Forest, outside the parks, was estimated at 24,000 acres. Both James I and Charles I aroused a great deal of opposition by attempting to restore ancient forest customs and to keep the populace strictly within bounds. From medieval times onwards the forest laws had been gradually relaxed and large numbers of local residents had established rights on the un-enclosed land by custom, not excluding the hunting of deer. For Charles in particular the restoration of the old forest laws was a means of obtaining ready cash, for every office-holder within the Forest had to pay an annual fine or fee for the privilege, but the action aroused intense opposition. In 1641 the local populace rioted, killing 100 deer and threatening to demolish the park fencing around New Lodge, but the Civil War prevented the further development of an interesting situation.

Predictably, there were far fewer deer in Windsor Forest at the end of the Civil War than at the beginning. Many of the best trees, too, had disappeared and the Forest area was infested by squatters. After the execution of Charles I the Great Park was sold, but was soon afterwards purchased again for Oliver Cromwell. During the Commonwealth a distinguished lawyer, Sir Bulstrode Whitelocke, who was appointed Constable of the Castle and Keeper of the Forests and Parks at Windsor, prepared a valuable record of the customs and traditions of his office, though under his regime the Great Park was divided up among private owners. At the Restoration the Castle reverted to Charles II, who was later able to re-acquire most of the land. Charles also took an interest in

the re-stocking of the Forest, and by 1731 a census revealed the presence of about 1,300 deer. Thereafter the numbers declined until by 1813, when an Act of Parliament disafforesting Windsor was passed, they were down to probably around 300. As many as possible were then rounded up by a detachment of Guards and slaughtered.

The area thus released and made available for enclosure and farming was about 59,000 acres. Today most of it has long been farmland or has more recently been swallowed by urban or industrial development. A substantial crescent of woodland adjoining the Great Park survives, however.

In 1979 about 900 acres of farmland in Windsor Great Park were taken out of cultivation and re-stocked with deer.

THE FOREST OF ALICE HOLT & WOOLMER

The Forests of Alice Holt and Woolmer may be treated as one, for they have from time immemorial been under the same administration and are separated from each other by only a narrow belt of cultivated and meadow land. Situated near the eastern border of Hampshire, Woolmer, covering some 2,000 acres, has now been taken over by the Army as part of its training grounds.

Throughout the Middle Ages there are incidental documentary references to the deer (both red and fallow) and timber in the joint forest, but the first detailed survey was made in 1635. Their total area was then recorded as 15,493 acres. This was said to have been much the same as in the year 1300, though in even earlier times the Forest had been considerably larger. Little had changed when another comprehensive survey was made in 1790, though by then 6,799 acres were privately owned. Alice Holt supported about 800 fallow deer, but a herd of red deer formerly living in Woolmer had been removed to Windsor in about 1760. This may well have been because Woolmer was steadily losing its trees, grazing animals and the mowing of grass wastes for hay preventing natural regeneration, as described by Rev. Gilbert White in his *Natural History of Selborne*. The Lieutenant of the Forest, Lord Stawell, evidently regarded the fallow herd as his private property, as he held the Forest on a lease which seems to have been more favourable to himself than to the Crown. From the 1770s onwards Alice Holt & Woolmer were required to devote themselves primarily to producing oak for the Navy, although they had been neglected and many of the trees were evidently long past their prime. The Lieutenant of the Forest was relieved of his office in 1811, and four years later the Office of Woods initiated a massive re-planting programme for 1,600 acres of Alice Holt, all oaks. Records have survived of the traffic in oak timber during the Napoleonic wars. The logs were taken not to Portsmouth, the nearest port, but by road to the river Wey at Godalming, whence they were either floated or shipped down to the

Thames dockyards in London.

Most of the oaks planted in 1815 were still there 100 years later, and many were felled during the 1914–18 war. Between the wars replacement of oaks by conifers proceeded on a somewhat muted scale, with some acceleration during the second world war. Alice Holt & Woolmer were among the Crown forests taken over by the Forestry Commission in 1923. Alice Holt then covered 2,142 acres, and Woolmer was slightly smaller. The present policy is to run a mixed forest of conifers and hardwoods, and the Commission has given an undertaking that at least 600 acres will always be oak woods. The Commission now has its research station and library at Alice Holt Lodge, in the middle of the Forest.

Incidentally, there never was a lady named Alice Holt associated with the Forest. The name comes from the Anglo-Saxon personal name 'Aelfsige'. Woolmer means 'the lake of the wolves', suggesting a time when the Forest had a more varied fauna than at present.

THE FOREST OF THE WEALD

The great primeval Forest of the Weald extends from within the eastern border of Hampshire, across Sussex and into Kent. It is the ancient Anglo-Saxon forest region of 'Andreds weald', covering all the country between the North and South Downs, which defied attempts at early settlement and remained a wild, tangled woodland long after it was ringed by well-established villages. These manors in the margins of the Weald tended to be exceptionally extensive, laying claim to great tracts of the Forest not always contiguous to the boundaries of their cultivated land. Thus Tenterden, in the Weald of Kent, derives its name from the fact that it was the 'dene', or forest pasture for pigs, for the people of Thanet, 30 miles away. A location map of the manors mentioned in Domesday Book shows the Weald singularly empty.

Recent research has shown that during the Roman period a number of roads traversed the Weald, mostly linking London with Channel ports but with a few lateral ones in Kent. They were, however, through-roads. Few Roman villas or country estates have been found within the Weald, though 50 or more were situated, like the later Saxon villages, along the fringes. Virtually the only evidence of any settlement within the Forest at that time relates to the iron-working sites.

The Wealden iron, derived from ironstone deposits, was largely responsible for the taming of this inhospitable jungle. It had been known and worked in the century preceding the Roman occupation and continued to be exploited throughout the Roman era. Only one iron-working centre is mentioned in Domesday Book, but thereafter the expansion of the industry was quite rapid, and throughout the Middle Ages the Wealden mines were the main source of iron supplied to London. Production reached a peak in the reign of Queen Elizabeth I, when 80 furnaces and 90 forges, amounting to about half the total for the whole country, were operating in the Weald. The iron deposits continued to be excavated throughout the eighteenth century, and the last furnace closed down in 1824.

Exploitation of the iron ore depended, of course, on the presence of an ample supply of fuel for smelting and this, in the form of wood, the Weald had in abundance. For the purpose the wood was transformed into charcoal, so that charcoal-burning was a major Wealden industry which has even now not died out. At first only wrought iron was produced, but later the development of cast iron required water-power, which was obtained by the damming of little Wealden streams to form 'hammer ponds'. Remains of these ponds are still common features in the Forest. They occur chiefly where a stream runs through deep ravines or gorges, as commonly happens in this broken terrain. It has sometimes been assumed that the decline in iron-smelting in the Weald was due to the exhaustion of the wood supply, but in fact it occurred after the technique of using coal for smelting had been mastered in the eighteenth century. For charcoal-burning only branches and saplings are used, and the forest can in due course produce a new crop.

The Forest has survived longest as a woodland region in the eastern part of the Weald, where *Ashdown Forest* and *St Leonard's Forest* still occupy substantial areas. St Leonard's Forest, once entirely contained in one vast parish, lies to the east of Horsham; Ashdown Forest a little farther to the east. The smaller *Forest of Arundel* survives in a shrunken form in the woods of Arundel Park. There are also considerable woodland areas in West Sussex, between Chichester and the foot of the South Downs, and in East Sussex and Kent, between Hastings and Tunbridge Wells. The large woods between Goudhurst and Hawkhurst in Kent are known as the *Forest of Bedgebury*.

Ashdown Forest was in medieval times a royal forest or chase, extending over about 10,000 acres, and remained so until the reign of Charles II, when it was disafforested. It was divided into seven wards and was well stocked with deer. Hartfield perpetuates the fact that stags once frequented this parish in Ashdown.

St Leonard's Forest, on the other hand, was not a royal chase, having been granted at an early date to the Braose family. A document of 1295 refers to a poaching expedition in the Forest mounted when William Braose was serving the king (Edward I) in Wales. The poachers, it was stated, were after deer, pheasants, hares, rabbits, herons and fish.

The Forest of Arundel was at times held by the Crown and at times by the Earls of Arundel. The Archbishops of Canterbury also claimed hunting rights in the Forest, based on their occupation of the manor of Slinfold. A dispute between the Archbishop and the Earl of Arundel was actually referred to the Pope in the middle of the thirteenth century. It took more than 20 years to settle, on terms none too favourable to the Archbishop, for he was allowed to hunt in the Forest only once a year and with six greyhounds only, and then only after giving due notice in advance. If the hounds killed more than one deer on this occasion the remainder had to be handed over to the Earl who, however, was required to supply the Archbishop with 13 bucks and 13 does during the course of the year.

When the Forestry Commission started to acquire woodlands in 1923–24, a survey of the Weald showed that by far the greater part of the surviving woods were coppiced. That is to say, they were cropped regularly for underwood. In the chalkland regions of England, including the North and South Downs, hazel underwood was normally cut once in eight years, but in the Weald, where sweet chestnut was by that time the predominant underwood, once in 10 to 15 years was the rule. Sufficient large trees were, and still are, left as a canopy; a regulation of 1544, which decreed that at least 12 standard trees should be left in each acre, shows that the coppicing was widely practised even at that early date.

There are still nearly 50,000 acres of chestnut coppices in the Weald, about half of them with a canopy of standard trees, mostly oaks. Coppice wood is now little used for charcoal, the very few charcoal-burners still operating preferring the tops and side branches of mature beeches. The main function of the coppiced chestnut is to supply wood for chestnut or cleft-pole fencing, for which there is a great demand. It also provides poles for the hop gardens of Kent and East Sussex and for gate-hurdles, fence-stakes, props and a variety of other purposes. Standard chestnut trees are much less plentiful than the coppices. The nut crop is very variable in both quantity and quality, and the trees are grown primarily for their timber, which is used in building and for furniture.

Bedgebury Forest, which was transferred to the Forestry Commssion in 1923, then comprised some 2,300 acres, of which 200 acres carried mature timber, 500 acres were chestnut coppice, 150 acres young conifers and 900 acres derelict. The Forest is now managed on good commercial lines but has also a very fine Pinetum, managed by Kew Gardens, as well as a series of Forest Plots run by the Commission's research department: these two features attract large numbers of visitors. The Forestry Commission also has a considerable acreage in the vicinity of Chiddingfold and Plaistow, mostly planted with softwoods.

THE FOREST OF ESSEX

Until the middle or end of the thirteenth century almost the whole county of Essex, except possibly the country around Saffron Walden, was regarded as one great forest and subject to forest law. It was only later, and in the case of *Epping Forest*, much later, that separate sections of this immense forest began to be known by the names of the nearest towns, as *Waltham*, *Hainault*, *Writtle*, *Havering* and *Theydon*. In 1225, following the granting of the Charter of the Forest in 1217, it was held that much of the area was not forest, but three years later Henry III declared that the surveyors had been mistaken. The old boundaries were restored and remained intact till the end of his reign. In the next reign, however, that of Edward I, the question was re-opened, and the king accepted the 1225 ruling in return for a substantial grant of money, of which he was short at the time. That left the south-western corner of the county, nearest London, as the main forest area. The boundaries of this truncated forest, by then known as the Forest of Waltham or *Waltham Chase*, were much the same in 1630 as in 1301, when Edward I's investigation put its extent at 60,000 acres.

It seems that the old forest law was enforced in Waltham Forest far later than in most parts of England, and few encroachments were made until in 1812 a Lord Mornington succeeded to the post of hereditary Lord Warden. He set about destroying the ancient forest system, abolishing rights and customs as far as he was able. His regime was followed by several decades of large-scale enclosures, which effectively transformed the whole of Hainault Forest into farmland. Newly-invented steam ploughs were brought in by a contractor to uproot the massive and ancient forest trees. The same fate threatened Epping Forest but an alert farm labourer, insisting in 1866 on his right to lop hornbeams in the Forest, became the focus of resistance to the innovators. Eventually the Corporation of the City of London stepped in and acquired the remaining woodland, comprising about 5,500 acres, as an open space for its citizens. Management is now by representatives of the City Council and by several verderers elected by the commoners.

The story of the fauna of Epping Forest tends to be a catalogue of last appearances and killings. From the time of Edward the Confessor a rhyme has survived which gives an interesting account of the wild life of the Forest of Essex in those days:

> Ich, Edward Koning,
> Have yeven of my forest the keping
> Of the hundred of Chelmer and Dancing
> to Randolph Peperking and his kindling
> Wyth heorte and hynde, doe and bocke,
> Hare and foxe, Catte and brocke,
> Wild fowel with his flocke
> Partrich, fesant hen and fesant cocke,
> With green and wylde, stob and stocke
> to kepen and to yeinen, by al her might,
> Both by day and eke by night.
> And hounds for to hold
> Good swift and bold
> Four greyhounds and six racches
> For hare and foxe and wilde cattes;

Wild boar, though not mentioned in the poem, were the first of the beasts of the forest to become extinct; the last is reputed to have been killed by the Earl of Essex in the reign of Elizabeth I. Red deer remained in residence until 1827, when the surviving stock was transferred to Windsor.

Hornbeams, formerly pollarded, in Epping Forest.

One or two have since found their way into Epping Forest from time to time but have not become permanently established there.

A thriving herd of fallow deer, however, still lives in Epping Forest, to the occasional regret of some of the residents whose gardens are invaded. After becoming extinct in the sixteenth century roe deer were re-introduced in 1883. Flourishing for a time, they are supposed to have died out in the early years of the present century, but it seems likely that the Forest is now sharing in the general increase of roe deer.

Foxes and badgers still breed in the Forest, and otters may occasionally visit the rivers Lea and Roding. In the realm of epitaphs, the last marten was seen in the Forest in 1883 and the last polecat killed in the 1890s.

THE FORESTS OF BUCKINGHAMSHIRE

The Forest of Bernwood occupies much of western Buckinghamshire, and links up with the forests of Oxfordshire and Northamptonshire. In some medieval documents the Forest of *Brill*, which filled the salient of Buckinghamshire that approaches to within a few miles of the city of Oxford, is treated as a separate entity but in others it is regarded as a part of Bernwood. Brill was a royal manor during much of the Middle Ages, from the time of Edward the Confessor onwards, and several kings held court there. Documents mention the presence of many fallow deer in the Forest, while the village place-names of Grendon Underwood, Wotton Underwood, Blackthorn, Oakley and Kingswood testify to the former extent of the Forest (though Boarstall has nothing to do with wild boars; it means 'The site of an old fort').

There are still some fairly extensive woods on the site of the old Forest, and some fine old oaks survive around Brill. Most of the countryside formerly occupied by the Forest, however, is now pleasant farming country, with cherries as the commonest tree. In the east of the county *Burnham Beeches*, now a property of the Corporation of the City of London, are a popular woodland resort for tired city-dwellers, but they were never a royal forest in the medieval sense. About 800 beeches, of distorted shapes through pollarding up to 150 years ago, comprise the heart of the wood. East Burnham Common, an area of about 200 acres of open country, adjoins the beech wood, and nearby *Egypt Wood* has a number of unusually large silver birches. The Stag Hotel, on Stag Hill, is a reminder of the deer that once roamed the woods but are there no longer.

THE FORESTS OF OXFORDSHIRE

The medieval forests of Oxfordshire were *Shotover* and *Stowood* on the eastern side of the county, linking with the Forest of *Bernwood*, part of which was in Oxfordshire and part in Buckinghamshire; *Woodstock Chase*, which joined up with the Forest of *Wychwood* in Northamptonshire; and *Cumnor* and *Bagley* Woods in the south. In addition, the south-eastern part of the county was covered in woodland and scrub merging with the Chiltern Woods, so all in all the greater part of Oxfordshire was forest. Its proximity to London made it a favourite chase for medieval kings. Henry I had a house at Beaumont, just north of Oxford, and a hunting lodge at Woodstock, where he established what was probably England's first zoo. The animals in his collection there included lions, leopards, lynxes, camels and a porcupine.

In the thirteenth century wild boars as well as both red and fallow deer roamed the woods. The red deer apparently became extinct in the county about the year 1782, but a survey in 1792 of the Forest of Wychwood, which is partly in Oxfordshire and partly in Northamptonshire, estimated a population of about 1,000 fallow deer, of which 61 bucks and 42 does were supposed to be culled annually. Wychwood then had an area of 3,709 acres in the two counties and was enclosed by a stone wall. The chief trees were oak and ash, others mentioned being beech, lime, elm, sycamore, horse chestnut, thorn, maple and holly. Most of the best timber had, however, disappeared by that date, only 173 good oaks of ship-building quality remaining. Eight years later, in 1800, a visitor admired the landscape with its 'vales of finest turf', but saw 'not one very fine tree of navy oak in sixteen or seventeen miles'. The final enclosures of Wychwood took place in 1862.

In the Middle Ages quite heavy demands were made on the Oxfordshire forests for timber for Oxford's colleges. And Oxford students were frequent in the roll-call of prisoners brought before the eyres for forest offences, notably poaching.

THE FOREST OF DEAN

The Forest of Dean, comprising the territory between the Severn and the Wye and thus most of Gloucestershire west of the Severn, has a curious history. Throughout the Middle Ages its story is very similar to those of other royal forests. The Forest and its commoners suffered considerably from the dissolution of the abbeys of Tintern and Flaxley, the nobles who replaced the abbots being more eager to claim any rights attached to the properties they had acquired than to fulfil the complementary obligations. However, calamity really struck when in 1638 Sir John Wintour bought the entire Forest from the Crown for £26,000, payable annually for six years together with a rent of £1,950, doubtless a tremendous boost for Charles I's shaky finances.

Sir John immediately set about getting some of his money back—felling trees, grubbing up their roots and making enclosures wholesale. He was strenuously opposed by the commoners, who destroyed his fences, and by the time of the outbreak of the Civil War the Forest was in a state of near anarchy. Under the Commonwealth the whole transaction whereby Sir John had obtained the Forest was declared null and void, but the Restoration opened the way for everything to be restored to him. He forthwith resumed his campaign of enclosure, again arousing bitter opposition from the commoners, until a commission had to be appointed to report on the dispute.

The commission found that there were in the Forest 25,929 oaks and 4,204 beeches 'as good timber as any in the world', and a new agreement was made with Wintour whereby he agreed to reserve 11,335 tons of timber for ship-building. Two years later it was reported that the tree-felling was proceeding as actively as ever, with 500 woodmen at work, and that very soon there would be no trees left. In fact, of 30,233 trees which he had acquired by the former agreement, only 233 remained standing. This time the controversy resulted in an Act of Parliament in 1668 which decreed that the Crown, or whoever it might permit to act for it, could enclose 11,000 acres but that the remaining 13,000 acres should be retained as woodland and re-planted with trees if necessary. This time the agreement held and the reafforestation of the ruined Forest began. Much of the new planting was done by Scottish woodmen brought in for the purpose, and their descendants still live and work in the Forest. A traveller who saw the Forest in 1705 reported that it was full of young trees, of which two-thirds were beech.

The forest people naturally suffered severely from this upheaval of their environment. With the destruction of so many of their ancient forest rights, mining and sheep were all that remained to them. Totalling about 6,000 souls, they lived in settlements on the margins of the old Forest, on which they increasingly encroached. Throughout the eighteenth century as their numbers multiplied so did their incursions into the woodland. A survey of 1833 found no fewer than 1,462 houses on illegal enclosures.

Although by the Act of 1668 a total of 11,000 acres was supposed to be enclosed and reafforested, enthusiasm for implementing it seems to have evaporated quite quickly, for in 1787 only 700 acres of enclosed woodland could be found. In 1808 another Act, the Dean Forest (Timber) Act, reinforced the former scheme, and for the next few years new plantings, chiefly of oak but with some sweet chestnuts and conifers, proceeded rapidly, in one year alone achieving a total of nearly 1,500 acres. The campaign provoked vigorous opposition from the commoners, who saw their grazing rights smothered by trees, and the unrest reached such proportions that in 1831 a detachment of soldiers had to be sent in to suppress it: some of the captured leaders of the riots were sentenced to transportation. The woodlands, however, now extending to nearly the statutory 11,000 acres, flourished, the oaks doing especially well under their conifer nurse-crop, and in 1850 Dean was stated to be 'not surpassed by any forest property in the Kingdom'.

The Forest of Dean has from time immemorial been associated with mining. It was carried on by the Silures in pre-Roman and Roman times and apparently never ceased in the unrecorded centuries. At some time in the thirteenth or fourteenth century a royal charter was granted to miners, to the effect that

any man born of a free father in the Hundred of St Briavels, who had worked for a year and a day in a mine, might become a free miner, a right that entitled him to mine for iron, coal or stone within the Hundred.

He had to pay the king a toll of a penny a ton for ore extracted. Most of the mines were originally surface mines, their galleries entered by a sloping tunnel or adit, but in time the miners followed the lodes deep underground. Mining operations were strictly controlled by a Court of the

Mine Law which fixed prices, jealously guarded the miners' monopoly and enforced sundry detailed regulations. For instance, no road for public use could be constructed into their territory and no-one other than a local man with forest, mining or common rights was allowed within a stone's throw of a mine. Originally the miners had the right to cut from the Forest whatever timber they needed for use above or below ground, but that was later lost, probably at the time of Sir John Wintour. In the 1830s attempts were made to abolish the free mining system, but the miners successfully upheld their ancient rights and still do so. During the nineteenth century some of the deeper mines were sold to large colliery magnates, but most of the smaller and shallower ones remained independent. They were exempted from nationalisation when the Coal Board was formed and some are still operated by their forest owners, mostly as a part-time occupation.

Another traditional Forest of Dean occupation is that of 'ship badger'. It has nothing to do with ships, 'ship' here being the local pronunciation of 'sheep'. 'Badger' is said to be derived from the practice of 'badgering' or harrying sheep found grazing too near one's own flock. Many of the forest folk combined 'badging' with mining, earning a somewhat precarious living from the two. A black-and-white collie dog, skilled in rounding-up sheep, was the inevitable companion of a Forest of Dean 'ship badger'. Grazing was based on custom rather than rights and was therefore more or less uncontrolled, with the consequence that often there were far too many sheep in the unfenced parts of the Forest. At various times attempts have been made to regulate the sheep grazing. Woodland has been enclosed; areas of woodland have been opened to grazing as soon as the new trees are tall enough, so that new areas may be enclosed and planted —the policy of 'rolling enclosures'; within the past 20 years schemes for creating enclosures *for* the sheep, instead of enclosures for keeping them out, have been prepared. Little has been done, however, to restrict the movements of the sheep, which continue to roam freely, even in the towns and villages, where they act as scavengers and garden robbers. Meantime, under the control of the Forestry Commission softwoods are gradually replacing hardwoods, though oak and beech are still dominant.

In early times, both the red and fallow deer were to be found in the Forest of Dean. King John often came hunting here, and documents from his reign reveal that wild boars were then quite common in the Forest. In the next reign, that of Henry III, they were still sufficiently plentiful for tithes in them to be granted to the Abbey of Gloucester. At this time red deer seem to have outnumbered fallow, but in the latter part of the thirteenth century fallow appear to have become dominant. Roe deer are also mentioned at the same period. Around the year 1300 wolves were numerous enough to cause considerable havoc among the commoners' sheep, but with the lightening of penalties for killing them about that time their doom was sealed. Deer must have been virtually eliminated from the Forest during the period of Sir John Wintour's depredations, but they, or at least the fallow, returned later. A survey of 1788 could obtain no accurate information but witnesses thought that there were about 500 in the Forest. When in 1850 deer were finally removed from the Forest, on the grounds that the measure would save the Forest people from the temptation to poach them (!), about 150 bucks and 300 does were rounded up and killed.

Medieval annals of the Forest are filled with the usual records of poaching affrays, encroachment, illegal felling of timber and chasing the king's deer. In this forest offenders had the advantage of access by water. Time and again instances occur of men coming by boat up the Severn or Wye to remove loads of timber illicitly. On the river Wye the Far Hearkening Rock on the Gloucestershire side opposite the celebrated beauty spot, the Seven Sisters' Rocks, is a kind of whispering gallery, catching and magnifying sounds made in the gorge. Here keepers would listen for the sounds of poachers and robbers crossing the river for deer or timber. The Forest inhabitants also had a bad reputation for not only helping themselves to the cargo of any ship wrecked on their shore but even of engaging in piracy against merchant ships passing up and down the Severn estuary. Through all the turbulent centuries a full quota of forest officials was maintained. As late as 1788 a commission found in existence a warden, six deputy wardens, four verderers, a steward of the long-defunct swainmote court, nine foresters, nine woodwards and six keepers, all of whom were presumably paid in cash or in kind, though they seem to have had only vague ideas about their offices.

An interesting detail concerning the Forest is that a plantation of the then rare sweet chestnut trees was established at an early date. It was large and productive enough by the reign of Henry II for a tithe of its produce to be granted to the Abbey of Flaxley. The former name of Flaxley—the valley of Castiard—was apparently derived from these chestnut trees.

No deer now live in the Forest of Dean, with the possible exception of a few roe deer. Foxes, badgers and grey squirrels are quite common, polecats have occasionally been seen, rats inhabit even the deep mines. It is recorded that in 1814 the Forest was visited by a plague of mice (they may have been voles) which caused a great deal of damage, even stripping the bark from young oaks. All other measures having failed, they were at last eradicated through the ingenuity of a miner named Simmons, who had a series of pits dug into which the mice tumbled wholesale.

A few miles from Lydbrook, just off the Monmouth road, is the Machen Oak, a splendid 350-year-old specimen. Not far away, from a picnic-site provided by the Forestry Commission, a magnificent view can be enjoyed.

TINTERN (GWENT)

Based on old forest land belonging to the Abbey of Tintern and later to the Dukes of Beaufort, modern Tintern Forest is, with the adjacent

Chepstow Forest, one of the important new forest areas of the Forestry Commission. It is situated in Monmouthshire (now Gwent) and separated from the Forest of Dean only by the river Wye. When sold by the Duke of Beaufort to the Crown in 1901 it consisted chiefly of coppices with standard oaks and beeches but with some conifers. Its total acreage is now 7,849 acres, of which 2,629 comprise the Forest of Chepstow. The coppicing of woods has been largely abandoned but, although Douglas firs and other conifers are extensively planted, many of the better oaks and beeches remain, and the yews on the limestone cliffs along the west bank of the Wye are strictly protected. Since the opening of the Severn Bridge, Tintern Forest has become a popular afternoon excursion goal for Bristol, and the Forestry Commission is doing its best to cater for the visitors. The walk based on Symond's Yat is one of the most picturesque in all Britain; there are fallow deer, foxes, badgers, buzzards and ravens in the woods.

THE FORESTS OF HEREFORDSHIRE

Although Herefordshire was and is a well-wooded county, the historic or royal forests seem to have been confined to the south-eastern sector, adjoining the Forest of Dean, and that for only a brief period. There in the twelfth century most of the Hundred of Greytree was proclaimed a royal forest by Henry II and John. Early in the next century, however, the great Charter of the Forests restored the status quo.

The large Forest of Irchenfield, on the far side of the Wye from the Forest of Dean, and the smaller one of Haywood which adjoined it on the north, were privately owned and not royal forests.

THE FORESTS OF WORCESTERSHIRE

The territory which was to become Worcestershire was in early times almost entirely covered with forests. The Weogoran, a Celtic tribe who lived in the woodlands in these parts, gave their name both to the great Forest of *Wyre* and to the city of Worcester. Under the Saxon monarchy the boundaries of the new shires of Worcestershire and Shropshire cut through the Forest, leaving the great part on the Shropshire side (see *Forests of Shropshire*).

The section of the Forest left within Worcestershire was in the Middle Ages more frequently known as the *Forest of Bewdley*. It was much exploited for wood for smelting and for use in the mines which developed in the district from at least the sixteenth century onwards. Mindful of the future, however, the miners and ironmasters tended to coppice woodlands rather than destroy them, and it is likely that most of the woods of the Forest of Wyre on either side of the county boundary were thus managed. The old woodland economy has now, of course, yielded to the overwhelming demand for conifers.

The *Forest of Feckenham* occupied most of the country between the Severn and the Warwickshire Avon, south and east of Worcester. An alternative name for it in medieval times was the Forest of Worcester. In the reign of Edward I it extended as far east as Evesham and as far north as Redditch, so was evidently a very large forest. Records from the end of the thirteenth century refer to foxes, badgers, wildcats and hares as well as the two species of deer being found in the Forest. It was disafforested in 1629.

On the west of the county *The Forest of Malvern* was said in the early sixteenth century to be 'bigger than Wire or Feckingham and occupieth a great part of the Malverne Hills. Great Malverne and Little Malverne also is set in the Chase of Malverne. Malverne Chase (as I hear say) is in length in some places twenty miles.' Chase rather than Forest was the correct description at that period, for it had been granted to the Earl of Gloucester by Edward I. However, it retained the usual forest administration and hierarchy of officials as late as the reign of Charles I, as well as other survivals of its former status as a royal forest.

A sidelight on forest life in the Middle Ages is supplied by the rules on expeditating or lawing commoners' dogs in Malvern, which differ in some respects from those in general use. The dogs had to have their claws cut twice in seven years, and the larger ones had to have further joints of the two middle claws severed. The criterion of size above which lawing was compulsory was that the dog 'could not be drawn through a strap of eighteen inches and a barley-corn in length'.

Two other Worcestershire forests approached the gates of the city of Worcester. On the north the *Forest of Ombersley* extended for several miles along the banks of the Severn and linked up with the Forest of Wyre, of which it was originally a part. To the east the *Forest of Horewell* is said to have extended to the far side of the Avon and must therefore have merged with the Forest of Feckenham. Both were disafforested by the Forest Charter of 1217.

THE FORESTS OF WARWICKSHIRE

In Shakespeare's time the river Avon served as a kind of frontier between the primeval forest land that covered most of the north-western half of the county of Warwickshire, and the tamed and cultivated countryside to the south. The Forest of Arden, the central part of the ancient woodland, was, however, not a royal forest, and a survey made for Edward I in the year 1300 attested that there was no royal forest anywhere in Warwickshire.

The only exception was a narrow strip of territory west of the river Arrow, near Alcester, which technically belonged to the Worcestershire Forest of Feckenham. Several place-names in the old Forest of Arden are reminiscent of its former state. Henley-in-Arden means 'the high clearing in Arden', Wootton is 'wood town', Tanworth is 'a woodland enclosure made of branches', Nuthurst is 'a wooded hill where nuts grew', Haselor and Haseley both refer to hazel woods, perhaps an indication of coppicing in some of the Warwickshire woodlands at an early date. Many snippets of information about life in the Forest of Arden in the sixteenth century may be found in Shakespeare's plays.

CANNOCK CHASE

Though commonly known as a chase, Cannock was technically a true forest in that it was a royal preserve to which the forest laws applied. Confusion evidently arose from the fact that within the limits of the very extensive royal forest the Bishop of Lichfield had his own private hunting-ground, 15 miles round, which was often a source of friction between the rival foresters. Cannock Chase occupied a vast extent of wild country between Lichfield and Stafford, taking its name from the little town of Cannock.

In the Middle Ages it was evidently well stocked with both red and fallow deer, and wolves still roamed the forest in the thirteenth century, for there is a record of a wolf killing a fat buck there in 1281, to the delight no doubt of the lepers of Freford, who were given what the wolf left of the carcase. The Forest was too far from London to be often visited by the king, and so medieval records contain frequent notices of grants of deer, timber and other concessions made chiefly to nobility and clergy but occasionally to humbler people. For example, when in 1278 King Edward I was staying at Brewood near Wolverhampton a fire destroyed part of the little town, and the king generously gave several oaks from Cannock to individual householders who had suffered loss.

An instance of the way in which forest law worked is provided by the account of a case brought before the local eyre in 1286. It concerns a hart which, having been put up by the king's huntsmen in the Chase, was inconsiderate enough to leave the confines of the royal forest and run into Brewood Park. There a man named John de la Wytemore shot an arrow at it. The hart thereupon fled out of the woods into the grounds of a nunnery at Brewood and collapsed in the nun's fishpond. John de la Wytemore followed and fished it out. At this juncture another John, John Gyffard, came along and claimed the carcase, saying that he had been pursuing the deer. So that made three claimants—the two Johns and the nuns, who naturally argued that the hart, being taken on their property, was theirs. Eventually the nuns took half the carcase, John Gyffard had the other half, and John de la Wytemore was left with none. But all were in error, for the deer having been put up by the king's huntsmen in the king's forest, was technically the king's. So, when the eyre next sat (which incidentally was ten years later), all of them, including the nuns, were called upon to give an account of their actions. The nuns were let off 'for the good of the king's soul, as they were poor', but the two Johns were arrested and sent to prison, but were later released on paying heavy fines. One feels sorry for John de la Wytemore who got nothing but a lot of trouble for his pains.

After extensive cutting of wood for charcoal in the sixteenth century, coal-mining and iron-working took a further toll of Cannock Chase, but an area of 26 square miles of open country and woodlands still remain and have now been designated an 'Area of Outstanding Beauty', though 7,000 acres of dark conifers have done little to enhance its appearance. Deer still roam there.

THE FORESTS OF NORTHAMPTONSHIRE

In early medieval times Northamptonshire was extensively afforested, largely because the Norman kings had important castles at Northampton and Rockingham, as well as six other houses in the county, and needed good hunting-grounds in the vicinity. The chief forest areas were *Rockingham*, which extended northwards from Northampton and included all the country between the rivers Welland and Nene (excepting the Soke of Peterborough): *Salcey*, which consisted of the county between the Nene and the Tove; and *Whittlewood*, southwards from the river Tove to the border with Buckinghamshire. A survey of 1286 records that the Forest of Rockingham was 33 miles long by 7–8 miles broad.

Even in the time of the Normans, however, the forests of Northamptonshire do not appear to have been densely wooded. The forest area was already a jigsaw of settlements, private property and clearances as well as open chase country. Significantly, grants in Rockingham Forest made by medieval kings include relatively few concerning timber, an omission which suggests that timber trees were none too plentiful. The numerous population within the forest boundaries ensured that poaching was rife, and the medieval forest records are replete with summonses for killing deer. The usual punishment seems to have been imprisonment in Northampton or Rockingham castles, where numerous offenders remained until they died.

Two interesting forest terms are found in the records of Rockingham. One occurs in numerous references to 'fox-trees', and the context suggests that these were trees the timber of which was granted to foresters and keepers as a reward for keeping down foxes and other vermin. The other is 'houndsilver', which is in some way connected with the 'lawing' or expeditation of dogs. Presumably every man paid a fee when he took his dog to have its toes clipped off, or perhaps the payment was for exemption. Another term used frequently is 'derefal wood', which evidently means the twigs of oaks and other trees lopped off for the deer in winter.

Enclosures and encroachments went on throughout the Middle Ages, but substantial portions of the forests remained intact till the eighteenth century. Between 1704 and 1736 more than 2,000 trees were sold out of Rockingham alone. In 1608 Whittlewood still had 4,500 acres of woodland, while only 32 years earlier Mary Queen of Scots was held up by robbers in Geddington Woods and had her horses and jewels stolen. It was in Tudor times that monarchs began to think more about timber revenue from the forest and less about deer. Both James I and Charles I engaged in tree-felling on a large scale, following up the clearances by granting the land to local gentry to enlarge their parks. However, the rule that 12 oaks per acre should be left on cleared land was evidently observed, and a recent examination of the records reveal that between 1565 and 1608 the number of oaks in the Crown forests increased from 85,000 to 130,000.

A survey of 1792 showed that Rockingham then had 9,482 acres of woodland, though much of it was by then in private hands. This survey was followed by disafforestation by Acts of Parliament in 1795 and 1796. The Forest was then granted a brief respite before large-scale felling began about 1820. Big inroads were made into the wooded area between that year and 1880.

In 1924, 25,087 acres of woodland were found in the whole of Northamptonshire, almost all of it in the ancient forest areas of Rockingham, Salcey and Whittlewood. Considerable devastation occurred during the second world war, but since then more than 1,000 acres have been re-planted. Much of the forest land is on private estates, which manage their woodlands very efficiently, while the Forestry Commission has 2,864 acres in Northamptonshire and Cambridgeshire. As elsewhere, the Commission's early policy was to plant conifers in preference to hardwoods, as being more economic and giving a quicker return, though the popular Norway spruce was often alternated with oak. Now, in the 1970s, the emphasis is on amenity, as an outlet for residents in the urban Midlands, and so mixed plantations are the rule.

HUNTINGDON FOREST

Huntingdonshire, as befits its name (which means 'the huntsman's hill'), was great hunting country, almost the whole shire being subject to forest laws. The woodland areas, of which vestiges still remain, were basically an extension eastwards of the Forest of Rockingham, occupying most of the countryside between the Northamptonshire border and the Fens. Certain place-names, such as Woolley ('the wolf's wood'); Glatton ('a forest glade'); Barham ('bear's home'); and Buckden ('the vale of bucks'), are reminders of the former woodland status of the area. Most of the woods lay to the west and north of the town of Huntingdon and were sometimes known in the Middle Ages as the Forest of Waybridge and Sapley. Incidentally, Sapley is said by etymologists to mean 'spruce wood', which cannot be correct, for spruce trees were not grown in England until the fifteenth or sixteenth centuries, and the name is much older.

The records of medieval forest courts or eyres are full of the usual accounts of poaching and trespass, with some interesting incidental details of the making of snares with 'cartropes'. The fact that a party of eight poachers took 40 roe deer near King's Delph on a single day in 1254 implies that roe deer must have been plentiful in the Forest. By the beginning of the sixteenth century the records of tree-felling indicate that forest clearance was proceeding at a fairly rapid rate.

THETFORD FOREST

Thetford is not an old forest but a creation of the Forestry Commission. It occupies 52,000 acres of what was formerly barren heath and waste land —the Breckland—in south-western Norfolk and the north-western corner of Suffolk, and so is one of Britain's largest forests. This was one of the areas in which the newly formed Commission started work in the 1920s and where it first launched into the planting of conifers—chiefly Scots and Corsican pines—on a grand scale, averaging over 2,000 acres of new plantations a year. The early mistakes of regimented plantings in rectangular blocks were indulged in here, but the effects have subsequently been softened by planting poplars along the edges and more recently mixed woodlands of oak, beech, chestnut and elm have been introduced. Red, fallow and roe deer have all colonised the new forest, which is also one of the remaining strongholds of the red squirrel. Golden pheasants released here many years ago are now thoroughly acclimatised.

The Forest Centre at Santon Downham, where there is a small natural history museum, is the start of a 23-mile long-distance walk waymarked by the Forestry Commission.

THE FOREST OF RUTLAND

Charnwood Forest, as noted under that title, was never a royal forest but a chase belonging to private owners. The other forest land in Leicestershire was over on the eastern side of the county, adjoining Rutland, and as the forest courts were usually held in Oakham, the county town of Rutland, the Forest was generally known as the *Forest of Rutland* even though much of it was in Leicestershire. Towards the end of the Middle Ages when the Forest had diminished in size, it was known more frequently as *Leighfield Forest*, the courts then being held at Uppingham.

Perusal of medieval records reveals that in the thirteenth century red and fallow deer, hares, foxes, rabbits and wild cats were to be found in the Forest, and an entry concerning a forest court held in 1490 mentions the presence of lime trees. At the same court no fewer than 250 forest officials attended, although the Forest had then shrunk in size—evidently a glaring example of overstaffing, for a court order of 1269 had restricted the number of foresters and their attendants to seven. Encroachment went on throughout the Middle Ages, sometimes by officials charged with the duty of preventing it, for in 1269 the chief forester was brought before the forest court charged with, among other offences, turning his own 300 pigs loose 'to the great injury of the pasturage of the King's deer'.

Fire is the most serious enemy of the forester, especially in young conifer forests. This blaze was in Bawtry Forest, Nottinghamshire

CHARNWOOD FOREST (LEICESTERSHIRE)

Ancient Charnwood Forest occupies an area of about 60 square miles of hilly land, north-east of Leicester and between that city and Loughborough. It is now almost exactly bisected by the M1 motorway. Although wild, rough country obviously suited to be a chase, it was apparently never a royal forest but was hunted by local gentry. Nevertheless, it was subject to some of the normal forest administration, such as swainmote courts, which has led some scholars to believe that it probably was a royal chase in Saxon times.

The three medieval manors of Charnwood were Groby, Whitwick and Sheepshed. Groby's swainmote was held at Copt Oak, an ancient crossroads in the middle of Charnwood where a great oak once stood. An old directory states that the trunk attained a height of 20 ft before sending out its first branches and was 24 ft in circumference. It supplies the additional information that the tree, which was blown down in 1855, was fashioned into what was supposed to be 'the symbol of the Druidical Jupiter, made by cutting away all the branches of the tree but two, which, although separated, were suspended like arms so as to form a cross'.

In 1794, on the eve of its enclosure, which was finalised in 1812 in the face of strong opposition by the commoners, the Forest was said to cover 15,000 to 16,000 acres. The terrain has been much disturbed by mining and quarrying.

Hereswood, a forest four miles long by one in breadth adjoining the city of Leicester, was distinct from Charnwood. Throughout the Middle Ages it had important associations for the inhabitants of Leicester, who gradually acquired many valuable forest rights in it, but it was never a royal forest and had no forest courts. It was eventually disafforested and its deer dispersed in 1628.

NEEDWOOD (STAFFORDSHIRE)

The Forest of Needwood occupied much of that eastern salient of Staffordshire situated between the rivers Tame and Dove. Originally it was very extensive, and as late as 1558 a survey records:

The forest or chase of Needwood is incompassed by estimation $23\frac{1}{2}$ miles, and the nearest part thereof is distant from the Castle of Tutbury but one mile. In it are $7,869\frac{1}{2}$ acres, and very forest-like ground, thinly sett with old oakes and timber trees, well replenished with coverts of underwood and thornes, which might be copiced in divers parts thereof for increase of wood and timber, lately sore decayed and spoyled.

The Forest was then divided into four wards, a fifth one (that of Uttoxeter) by that time having been lost to enclosures, and within it were ten enclosed parks, each with a stock of deer.

Enclosures evidently began early in Needwood, for the soil was fertile and therefore highly desirable for farming. Even at the end of the thirteenth century the enclosed demesne lands within the Forest together with manorial rights in the Forest amounted to ten times the value of the Forest itself. An incidental item in some forest accounts of that date mention among the receipts 14 shillings and 3 pence for the sale of the bark of the lime trees, which was used for mats and cordage.

Several local ecclesiastical magnates, notably the Abbot of Burton-on-Trent and the prior of Tutbury, had important rights in the Forest, and the suppression of religious houses by Henry VIII seems to have given the impression locally that their forest rights were anyone's for the taking. Foremost among the opportunists were the forest keepers, who set about helping themselves to the timber, to the extent of 841 loads of it in 1540 alone. In due course they were brought to account, but great damage had been done.

In the reign of Philip and Mary a survey showed that the wastage, much of it illicit, was still going on. This survey revealed that six of the Forest parks still supported a good stock of deer, 777 in all, but that one of the parks was now reserved for the use of the king's stud mares and another for the king's 'race of great horses'.

At the end of the Civil War the entire Forest was offered for sale 'for the satisfaction of the soldiery'—in other words, to pay off arrears of wages. The proposal aroused great indignation locally, and a petition signed by both gentry and commoners was sent to Oliver Cromwell pointing out the hardships that would result if the villagers were to lose their ancient forest rights. It reminded Cromwell that the county had already contributed nearly £8,000 towards the Army's pay and concluded with the words 'the Forest of Needwood is neatly formed by nature for pleasure, no forest in England being comparable thereunto'. The petition had some effect, for after a commission had sat to consider claims a half of the Forest and one-tenth of the timber was reserved for the commoners and all who had rights in the Forest. The State took the rest, and doubtless much wholesale felling and enclosure would have followed if the Commonwealth had not come to an end. Under Charles II the Forest reverted to its former state, at least in theory. In practice the Forest freeholders had new troubles, for Earl Stamford, who had been put in charge of the Forest, proceeded to enforce a new range of heavy penalties for obscure offences, such as turning pigs into the Forest insufficiently ringed and taking thorn-bushes out of the woods.

In spite of the continuing problems, Needwood at the end of the seventeenth century was still a very important forest, the finest in England according to some authorities. 'Many of the treese are of soe large dimensions and length,' asserts a survey of 1684,

> that there may be picked out such great quantityes of excellent plank and other timber, fitt for shipping, as is not to be found in any of your majestie's other forests in England; most part of this where the best timber growes lyeing within 12 or 14 miles of the navigable parte of the river Trent.

This survey showed that in the open forest at that time were 38,218 good timber trees, together with an additional 8,932 in the parks, making a total of 47,150 valued at over £28,637. Hollies and underwood were valued at a further £2,000.

Throughout the eighteenth century the Forest survived and was for most of the time fairly well stocked with deer. Poaching was rife in the open forest, though the deer were more strictly protected within the parks, which were now nearly all private properties. The Forest was finally disafforested, in the teeth of strong opposition, in 1804.

A curious incidental feature of forest life has been the survival since at least the fourteenth century and perhaps earlier of a herd of wild goats in Bagot Park, a vestige of Needwood Forest just south of Uttoxeter. The Park for all those centuries has been and still is the home of the Bagot family, whose crest is a goat's head. Until the Forestry Commission took over the management of the woods in 1957 the herd had the run of about 2,000 acres. Most of them were then transferred to the estate of another member of the family at Levens Park near Kendal, Westmorland, but a few escaped and have formed a small herd still living in the neighbourhood. The Bagot goats have a peculiar colour pattern, consisting of a white body with black head, neck and shoulders. Both sexes are horned; their coats are long and shaggy. They closely resemble the Schwarzhals breed of the Rhone valley, and the generally accepted theory of their origin is that they were brought back by a knight of the Bagot family returning from a Crusade in about 1377. Since about 1380 a goat has featured on the Bagot coat of arms and also as the Bagot crest. Some scholars have suggested, however, that the origins of the goats must be looked for earlier, perhaps to the time of the Norman Conquest.

SHERWOOD FOREST

Sherwood, Robin Hood's forest, occupied the central part of the county of Nottinghamshire, north of Nottingham and extending as far as Worksop. In the Middle Ages its area is given as 25 miles by 10. At about the time of the Conquest most of this territory was included in the huge manor of Mansfield, so it seems likely that what happened was that William or one of his successors declared the entire manor a royal forest and brought in additional territory to round off the area.

Ecclesiastical influence was strong in this region, and the Forest had close associations with the Abbey of Rufford, the priory of Shelford, the priory of Blyth and several friaries, including some at Lincoln. Medieval records contain numerous references to grants of timber and underwood being made to these houses, while the Abbey of Rufford, situated on the edge of the Forest, acquired many forest rights. The castle of Nottingham also made considerable demands on the Forest for timber, both for repairs and improvements to the building and also for making armaments, especially the great catapults known as springalds, the artillery of medieval warfare. There are also mentions of wood for furniture and for charcoal.

Although Robin Hood is a fictitious figure, there must have been many outlaws like him, in Sherwood and other forests. Nor is the Sheriff of Nottingham correctly cast as his chief adversary, for if Robin Hood lived in the reigns of Richard I and John, as tradition has it, the Forest then was administered by hereditary Chief Foresters, Ralph Fitz-Stephen and his wife Matilda, though earlier the Sheriff of Nottingham had been involved. Hereditary foresters ran the Forest from the time of Richard I down to about 1284, when the last one, Robert de Everingham, disgraced himself by hunting the king's deer, or rather, by getting caught. After a period in Nottingham jail he was dismissed from his post, which thereafter was retained by the Crown, to be filled by short-term nominees. About the same time, the forest laws were tightened up, the king, Edward I, being a much tougher character than his late father, Henry III, during whose long reign discipline had become very lax. Among the reforms was the reduction in the number of regarders and other officials, who had apparently multiplied after the manner of bureaucrats without making any appreciable contribution to the welfare of the Forest. The pendulum then swung the other way, for the chief forester, holding the position for life or for a shorter term, gathered every possible office connected with the Forest into his own hands so that he could enjoy the revenues, and appointed low-paid deputies to do the work, a procedure which made for poor administration and many abuses.

One forest official, described as a ranger, is commemorated by a memorial tablet in the church of Blidworth, at the centre of old Sherwood. His name was Thomas Leake. Evidently he spent his whole life in the Forest and ended it there on 4 February 1597–98 when, at the age of sixty, he fought a duel and lost. Whether the quarrel was a personal one or was connected with his duties in the Forest is not recorded. However, the event seems to have attracted a lot of attention at the time, for a stone cross was erected at the spot in the woods where he fell, later to be removed to Blidworth churchyard, where it still stands. The tablet in the church is framed in alabaster on which are carved some of the emblems of Thomas Leake's profession, including long-bows and cross-bows, knives, horns and hounds.

The 'Major Oak' in Sherwood Forest. The lower branches are protected by 15 lb. of lead

From about this date the Forest started to decline. In 1609 a survey showed a total of 49,909 oaks. By 1686 it was down to 37,316 and by 1790 to 10,117. The diminution was partly due to storm damage and natural decay but even more so to the heavy demands for timber, both for local use and for the Navy. After the Restoration enclosures by big estates became substantial. The Forest lost 1,250 acres in that way in 1683 and 8,248 acres between 1789 and 1796. By 1799 only 1,487 acres remained to the Crown, though a further 3,000 acres enclosed earlier in the century now comprised Clumber Park. People were beginning to look back with some nostalgia to the great days of the Forest. Major Rooke, who recorded the 1799 statistics in his book *Sketch of the Ancient and Present State of Sherwood Forest*, recalled:

The Revd. Dr. Wylde, Prebend of Southwell and rector of St. Nicholas in Nottingham, assured me he had often heard his father, William Wylde, Esq., of Nettleworth, who died in the year 1780 in the 83rd year of his age, say that he well remembered one continued wood from Mansfield to Nottingham.

Both red and fallow deer were found in Sherwood from the earliest times, and most of the offences dealt with by medieval forest courts were concerned with poaching. The death of 350 deer, of both species, in 1286 through 'murrain' indicates a fairly dense population; in 1538 the Forest was estimated to be supporting about 1,000 deer. More careful counts gave a total of 1,263 in 1616, and 1,367 in 1635, though of the latter figure no fewer than 987 were listed as 'out of condition'.

By 1708, probably owing to the diminishing area of the Forest, the deer were becoming such a nuisance that a representative meeting at Rufford sent a petition to the Crown asking for their numbers to be reduced. The meeting complained that

so many of the woods had been granted or given away ... that there was but little harbour left for the deer in the forest, and the deer in consequence were distributed all over the country, eating up the corn and grass; that tenants had often to watch all night to keep the deer off; that their servants were terrified by several new keepers made by the present deputy-warder, who threaten them if so much as they do set a little dog at the deer though in the corn; that not only had they to watch their cornfields, where the deer often lay nine or ten brace together, but they so destroy private woods as to injure them to the extent of £10 to £50 a year.

Another petition at the same period estimated a total of about 900 deer in the shrunken forest, which, said the petitioners, was three times as many as there used to be—a statement manifestly incorrect. Neither petition met with any positive response. In a footnote written on the second one an unknown commentator has shrewdly observed,

Tis no doubt but that if there were no more than fifty deer in the whole forest, and if it should happen that they were on any one particular man's two or three acres of corn or turnips, they would be sure to lessen his crop; yet he bought the land with the incumbrance ...

Big estates such as Clumber, Thoresby and Welbeck Parks eventually saved much of the ancient forest from extinction. Among the trees they preserved were a number of hoary veterans, including a celebrated oak, the Greendale Oak, in the grounds of Welbeck Abbey, which survived to this present century. It is recorded that this tree, 35/36 ft in circumference,

having become hollowed through age, the great gap through the centre was enlarged in 1724 by cutting away the decayed wood to such a height and width that a carriage and six, with cocked-hatted coachman on the box, drove through the tree with the bride of the noble owner. Three horsemen riding abreast were able to pass through, a feat often accomplished.

The estates also preserved stocks of red and fallow deer.

Since the advent of the Forestry Commission Sherwood has assumed a new aspect. Of the 6,482 hectares which comprise modern Sherwood Forest, 6,076 are new plantations, mostly softwoods, of course, and with large stands of Corsican pine. Much of the old forest has however disappeared under the urban development of outer Nottingham and of the county's other mining and industrial centres. Arnold, Bulwell, Lenton and Wollaton, now suburbs of Nottingham, were all once forest villages.

DUFFIELD FRITH

Duffield is a small town on the A6 a few miles north of Derby; 'Frith' is another word for forest. In the Middle Ages Duffield Frith was an important royal forest, even though not one of the larger ones. Throughout most of the period it was administered according to forest law, though controlled for much of the time by the Duchy of Lancaster rather than the Crown. When in 1399 the Duke of Lancaster became King as Henry IV the distinction was obliterated.

Unlike the Forest of the High Peak, farther north in Derbyshire, where woodlands were somewhat sparse, Duffield Forest was heavily wooded. The usual process of encroachment, enclosure and development of forest rights went on throughout the Middle Ages, further complicated here by mining operations. From quite early times, however, the entire Forest was fenced, it being the obligation of tenants of adjacent farms to keep the fences in repair, while within the Forest several parks were also surrounded by pale fences. It was well stocked with deer but of fallow deer only, except for an occasional wanderer. In 1314 one hart, 96 bucks and 25 does were legitimately killed in the Forest.

Much poaching and encroachment occurred during the fifteenth century, the period of the Wars of the Roses. Leases of land granted by several kings amounted in practice to enclosures, and the deer greatly diminished in numbers. In 1560 a survey of the Forest was made with a view to its possible disafforestation. This survey itemised the trees then growing there, to a total of 111,968. Of these 59,412 were large oaks, 32,820 were small oaks, and 19,736 were 'dotard' oaks, in which decay was well advanced. The underwood included hazel, holly, maple, crab-apple, hawthorn, blackthorn and alder, but no beeches, elms or other large trees, except birches, are mentioned. Twenty-seven years later another survey revealed the almost incredible devastation that had taken place in the intervening period; only 2,764 large oaks and 3,032 small oaks were left.

A writer in 1600 said that very few deer remained in the Forest and those only in one park, Mansell. This was confirmed in 1605, when at a forest court the number of deer in Mansell Park was given as 76. In spite of local opposition, the leasing of land and rights continued. The question of disafforestation arose, and it seems that this was effected for much of the Forest just before the outbreak of the Civil War, two-thirds of the property going to holders of common rights and one-third to the king. A parliamentary enquiry dated 1650 refers to 'the late disforrested Forest or Chase called Duffield Frith'. However, one ward of the old Forest, the one nearest the town of Duffield, escaped. During the Civil War it was treated as common land on the traditional basis and so remained until 1786, when it was enclosed by Act of Parliament. No vestige of common land now remains.

THE FOREST OF THE PEAK

The metes and bounds of the Forest of the Peak begin on the south at the New Place of Goyt, and hence by the river Goyt as far as the river Etherow; and so by the river Etherow to Langley Croft at Longdenhead; thence by a certain footpath to the head of Derwent; and from the head of Derwent to a place called Mythomstede (Mytham Bridge); and from Mytham Bridge to the river Bradwell; and from the river Bradwell as far as a certain place called Hucklow; and from Hucklow to the great dell of Hazelbacke; and from that dell as far as Little Hucklow; and from Hucklow to the brook of Tideswell, and so the river Wye; and from the Wye ascending up to Buxton, and so on to the New place of Goyt.

Thus the boundaries of the royal Forest of the High Peak are defined in 1286, and anyone can trace them quite easily with the aid of an ordnance map, almost all the places being readily identifiable. They do not exactly coincide with the present boundaries of the Peak National Park, which extends much farther south and east and excludes some western territory, but the heart of the area is the same.

In Anglo-Saxon times the whole region, wild and almost empty of inhabitants, seems to have been part of the hereditary property of the monarchy. As such it was taken over by William the Conqueror, who granted certain of the key manors to one of his loyal supporters, William Peverel. About 90 years later all the properties reverted to the Crown, which retained them for most of the Middle Ages.

Castleton, its castle built by William Peverel soon after the Conquest, was the military centre of the Forest. Here offenders against the forest laws were imprisoned, and it seems that the courtyard or bailey of the castle was sometimes used as a pound for keeping sheep rounded up in the Forest and found to have no legal rights there. The eyres or forest courts were, however, not held there but at a place in the centre of the Forest, about equidistant from Tideswell, Castleton and Bowden. Here a meeting-hall and a foresters' lodge were built and a chapel added later. It became known as 'the Chapel in the Forest' or on modern maps, Chapel-en-le-Frith.

Compared with the strictly controlled royal forests nearer London the Forest of the High Peak was a lawless region. The barons of the north were an independent lot, with scant regard for royal authority when they could get away with defiance. Poaching affrays in which local gentry were involved were frequent. In 1264 an Earl of Derby with 38 companions, eight of whom were knights, were brought before the forest court for participating in a series of poaching incursions, in which they killed 40 or 50 deer at a time. The episodes were primarily political, for they came a few months after the Battle of Lewes, in which a confederation of nobles under Simon de Montfort had defeated the forces of Henry III. The Earl and his associates were in affect cocking a snoot at a monarch who was for the moment powerless.

Discipline was tightened up under the next king, Edward I, who was altogether a stronger character than his father. The records show that in his reign offenders against the forest laws were duly summoned and fined, especially those who were wealthy and influential; commoners were often let off, on the grounds of poverty. But under weak kings or when the monarch was busy elsewhere the Forest quickly relapsed into near anarchy.

Almost incredible numbers of deer, though apparently nearly all red deer, roamed the Peak District in the Middle Ages. Writing about 1194 Geraldus Cambrensis mentions that in his days there were so many of them that 'they trampled both dogs and men to death in the impetuosity of their flight'. As late as 1526 members of a commission appointed by Henry VIII saw no fewer than 360 red deer while walking through the Forest on the first day of their investigation. The deer, however, had to share the Forest with large numbers of farm livestock, and in time overstocking became acute. The commission in question was briefed to enquire into this situation and noted that many of the deer were, in late autumn, already half-starved and looked unlikely to survive the winter. Inviting evidence, they were told that about 4,000 sheep, 903 cattle and 320 horses were at large in the Forest. The cattle comprised five herds, whereas formerly only two has been permitted. The commissioners recommended that sheep should be kept out of the Forest, but attempts to do so aroused a storm of protest from farmers. Over the next few reigns a kind of guerilla war was waged intermittently, the forest officials rounding up sheep and impounding them, while the peasants appealed to the local nobles, who seem to have championed their cause. In Easter week in 1557, for instance, a posse of 19 foresters was alleged to have rounded up 800 sheep, together with a number of lambs, and shut them up in Castleton castle without food or water, as a result of which many of them had died. The foresters replied that they were only acting under orders, that the farmers had been warned previously and had taken no notice, that none of the sheep was hurt, and they were only in the castle courtyard for half-an-hour. It sounds like a classic example of two stationary vehicles colliding.

Whether through competition from sheep or for some other reason the deer population certainly declined. In 1567 it was said to be as low as 30 for the whole forest, though much of the blame was put on two very hard winters just past: hunting was banned for six years. In earlier times wolves were abundant in the Peak District, where an unusual number of place-names containing the element 'wolf' still survive. Wild cats and otters are also mentioned as living in the Forest.

A feature of the Forest of the High Peak from the thirteenth century onwards was the presence of royal stud farms. It is recorded that in 1286 the Queen Consort had 115 mares with their foals there. Unfortunately that was not the complete total of horses in the Forest, for at an eyre in that year 20 foresters were accused of turning horses loose in the Forest illegally. One and all pleaded that the horses were part of the queen's stud, but the justices knew better and ordered the animals to be removed and sundry fines and fees to be paid.

In the 1630s the commoners and other landowners in the Forest petitioned the king to have it disafforested, complaining about the severity of the forest laws and the fact that the deer were damaging their crops. A survey was made and after lengthy negotiations a division of the land between the Crown and the local landowners was agreed. Fencing had already begun when the hostilities which led to the Civil War broke out and the whole scheme was abandoned. The only irrevocable step taken before this interruption was the removal and destruction of the deer, which were completely annihilated and never returned.

The enclosure project was resumed after the Restoration and was finally completed in 1674. In the succeeding centuries a number of the greater landowners, taking a pride in efficient estate management and in landscape-planning, planted extensive woods, to the considerable improvement of the scenic beauty of the region. The Forestry Commission's census of 1947–49 showed 26,000 acres of woodland in the whole of Derbyshire, of which about 15,000 acres carried mature trees, most of them broad-leaved. Sycamore and ash were the predominant species but, of course, the acreage of conifers has now greatly increased. The entire Peak District is now a National Park, with due importance being attached to amenities. The Pennine Way, which leads along the crests of the hills for 250 miles to the Cheviots, starts at Edale.

THE FORESTS OF YORKSHIRE

After the 'Harrying of the North' by William the Conqueror's men in 1069 there must have been plenty of waste land in Yorkshire suitable for royal forests. The most important were the Forest of GALTRES, which extended from Boroughbridge to the city of York, the Forest of FARNDALE, around the river Dove in the heart of the Yorkshire Moors, and the Forests of KNARESBOROUGH, WENSLEYDALE, and HATFIELD CHASE.

Because of its situation, on the very doorstep of York, Galtres was a favourite hunting-ground of English kings, even in Saxon times. A survey made in 1229 designated the entire area between the rivers Ouse and Derwent the royal Forest of Galtres, or Galtrees, and numerous place-names, such as Sutton-in-the-Forest, Marton-in-the-Forest, Huntington ('hill of the huntsmen'), Lund ('a grove or copse') and Raskelf ('the headland of roe deer'), testify to its former extent and character. In 1316 this Forest was said to comprise about 100,000 acres and to contain some 60 villages.

The woods were evidently well stocked with red and fallow deer and to some extent with roe deer. The abbot and convent of St Mary's, York, were entitled by Royal grant to a tithe of all venison taken in Galtres. In 1528 Lord Cromwell, then chief justice of the forests, was entitled in Galtres to the rights to net woodcocks, to collect wind-fallen wood and of fishing and fowling, as well as the usual ones of herbage, pannage and browsing. He was allowed to pasture 240 head of cattle there and to collect tolls of cattle, horses and sheep passing the forest gates. Evidently the tolls on horses had considerable value, for they included 4d. for every packhorse passing through with merchandise for York.

A toll taken only in northern forests and mentioned in connection with those of Yorkshire was termed 'thistletake'. It was levied, at the rate of $\frac{1}{2}$d. per beast, on drovers taking herds of cattle and flocks of sheep through the forest en route to market. The term is derived from the wording of the law, which said that the drovers were obliged to pay the toll if their animals ate anything growing in the Forest during their passage 'even to the snatching of a single thistle'.

Encroachments and illicit enclosures multiplied during the later Middle Ages. Even the treasurer of York Cathedral was not above enclosing 80 acres of forest land, a fact which brought him before the forest court in 1528. Much further damage was done during the Civil War, when there was much fighting around York. After the Restoration the Forest of Galtres was disafforested. Farndale is now mostly open moorland, with extensive grazing rights for sheep.

PICKERING FOREST

The Vale of Pickering is a fertile countryside, watered by many streams and by the rivers Rye and Derwent, between the Yorkshire Moors and the Yorkshire Wolds. The woods were said, in the Domesday Book, to be 16 miles by four miles in extent, presumably lying under the shelter of the moors with the castle of Pickering at their centre. The Forest was reputed to be a great place for wild boars: medieval records contain frequent royal instructions to send boars or, in some instances, boars' heads, from Pickering for the king's table.

The Forest was also well stocked with red deer. Even poachers, when well organised, could account for 40 or 50 head in a day. The tallies of deer killed legitimately by the constables of the Forest also include numbers of fallow deer and, on one occasion in the early fourteenth century, two roe deer with their calves. Following a dispute between two rival constables in the late fifteenth century, an enquiry in 1503 estimated the number of red deer in the Forest at around 200, excluding those in a private park, while fallow deer were said to total more than 500. By 1538, for some unrecorded reasons, the numbers of red deer had dwindled to 50 and of fallow to 140, but whether those in enclosed parks were excluded is not stated. Probably so, for another survey of 1562 found 264 red deer and over 600 fallow deer (these latter in Blandsby Park). An order prohibiting the killing of any deer in the Forest was made in 1591 for three years, on the grounds that the stock was too low. In 1608 about 100 deer (species unspecified) were in Blandsby Park, the enclosing stone wall of which was in bad repair.

Distant from the capital, Pickering Forest tended to become, for practical purposes, very much the property of the constable of the castle—who normally combined that office with keeper of the forest—or with local noblemen, of whom for much of the Middle Ages the Dukes of Lancaster were chief. Eyres were held so infrequently that one in 1335 found itself dealing with all illegal enclosures made during the past 117 years. An early seventeenth-century surveyor complains that 'the tenantes about Pickeringe are so unrulie, as they make their owne pervers wills a law'. Court records show that they frequently made free with the forest timber as well as with the king's deer. Encroachments were plentiful, and forest maintenance generally poor, though from time to time desultory efforts were made to tighten up. Forests rights were, in any case, fairly liberal, for Pickering freeholders were allowed to send any of their animals, except goats, into the Forest to graze and to take any dry wood for fuel without permission. *With* the foresters' permission they were also entitled to green wood for building their houses and making their farm implements. Predictably, there were complaints that they abused their rights, to the detriment of the Forest. In 1619–21 a surveyor complained that few red deer were left in the Forest because they were so often disturbed by 'stealers of wood' and that 'for everye redd deare in the forest there are 5000 sheepe'.

Pickering was part of the property settled on Queen Henrietta Maria on the death of her husband, Charles I, and it was returned to her after the Restoration when it was said that, although there were deer in the Park, in the Forest itself 'the game is almost quite decayed'.

THE FORESTS OF SHROPSHIRE

Shropshire, though not now one of the great wooded counties of England, was once heavily forested. In the Middle Ages it had at least six major forests, namely Wyre, Kinlet, Shirlet, Morfe, Wrekin, Long and Haugmond, as well as a number of minor ones.

The *Forest of Wyre* once covered a vast area on both sides of the Shropshire/Worcestershire border (see also *Forests of Worcestershire*). Though later designated a chase, having become the hunting-ground of nobles rather than royalty, under the Saxon monarchs at least part of it was a royal forest. Etymologically Shirlet was 'the share of the Forest belonging to the shire', while Kinlet—one of the great forest manors—means 'the royal share'. Kinlet once belonging to Edith, the queen of Edward the Confessor.

The Long Forest in western Shropshire comprised the *Forest of Long Mynd*, now an area relatively free from woods, and the *Forest of Steepel-*

wood. It linked up with Shirlet on the east. Haugmond was a smallish isolated forest just north of Shrewsbury. The *Forest of Wrekin* lay north of the Severn, around the towering knoll of the Wrekin. *The Forest of Morfe* occupied the country between the Severn around Bridgnorth and the Staffordshire border and indeed spilled over into Staffordshire. Farther north the boundary between the two countries ran through the Forest of Brewood, which was, however, disafforested as early as 1204.

In 1270, on the eve of his departure on a crusade, Edward I gave orders for a fence many miles long to be erected around the Forest of Wyre to keep the deer out of the adjacent cultivated fields. While he was absent Roger Mortimer, one of the great local magnates, set about diverting to himself as many of the royal prerogatives as possible. He pulled down about six miles of the king's fence and went hunting throughout the Forest and the neighbouring manors.

Some medieval records concerning the Forest of Morfe, or the Forest of Bridgnorth as it is sometimes known, illustrate the severity with which the forest laws were applied in the early thirteenth century, before the preparation of the Forest Charter. When forest officials found venison in the house of one Hugh le Scot he fled to the local church for sanctuary. Having admitted that he and another man had killed the hind, he had no option but to remain where he was, which he did for a month. He then managed to escape disguised as a woman, whereupon he was declared an outlaw, unless and until he returned to stand trial. On another occasion a hart strayed into the courtyard of Bridgnorth Castle, where the garrison dealt with it in the manner that might be expected. Hearing of the episode, the forest verderers insisted that the soldiers should be prosecuted and served a summons on the representatives of the whole town. This although the Sheriff of Shropshire, Thomas Endinton, who was technically responsible for the garrison and the town, was a favourite of the current monarch, John.

MARA OR DELAMERE (CHESHIRE)

With its extension, the Forest of Moudrem which covered most of the country around Nantwich, the Forest of Delamere or Mara as it was known in the Middle Ages, extended right across central Cheshire, from the Forest of Wirral in the north to the Shropshire and Staffordshire boundary. Its name means 'The Forest of Meres or Lakes', which are still a feature of the Cheshire plain but were formerly much more numerous. The soil being good, encroachment and enclosure began early, and in the present century the Cheshire plain has become an intensively managed dairying county with perhaps the highest concentration of dairy cattle in the world.

Examination of medieval records shows that both forests were well stocked with red and fallow deer. In connection with a case before the forest court of Mara and Moudrem in 1271 the chief forester, Richard Done, presented a list of his rights and perquisites which throw an interesting light on forest life of his day. He claimed to have under him eight under-foresters and two grooms, all of whom were boarded out on Forest tenants. He was entitled to

> two strikes [probably bushels] of oats at Lent from every tenant for provender for his own horse; bracken at all times save the hunting season; pannage and agistment of pigs; windfalls and lops of felled trees; crabstakes and stubbs; half the bark of felled trees; all cattle and goats taken at non-agistment times; ½ penny each, and the same of straying beasts between Michaelmas and Martinmas; all sparrow-hawks, merlins and hobbies; all swarms of bees; the right shoulder of every deer taken in the forest; the horns and skins of every 'stroken deer' found dead; waifs [presumably of deer] found in the forest; the hunting of foxes, hares, cats, weasels and other vermin with hounds or greyhounds and the *pelfe*, or best beast of any that committed felony or trespass in the forest and fled for the same, the lord having the residue.

There are still red deer at Tatton Park, near Knutsford, and probably roe deer have moved into the new Forestry Commission forest. Foxes and badgers are still to be found, but of course no wild cats, and the polecat, once common, was last seen in the area about 100 years ago. Sparrow-hawks are fairly frequent, and merlins occasionally come down from the moors on migration or in winter, but no hobbies have occurred for many years. The countryside abounds in small birds and the lakes attract numerous waterfowl.

Delamere was disafforested by Act of Parliament in 1812, the share of the old forest then allocated to the Crown being about 8,000 acres of sandy waste, 'virtually denuded of trees'. The Act stipulated that half the acreage was to be farmed, while the other half, under the Crown's absolute control, should be devoted to growing timber. At that time useful timber meant oak, and so the whole 4,000 acres allotted for the purpose was planted to oak trees. On such unsuitable soil they naturally failed, and in the 1850s the obligation to keep the 4,000 acres under trees was cancelled. About half the 4,000 acres were claimed for agriculture, while poor oaks continued to occupy some of the remainder and plantations of Corsican, Scots and Weymouth pines, which did very much better, were laid out on other sections of the old Forest.

When the Forestry Commission inherited the control of the Forest in 1924 Delamere was almost the only English forest with a heavy preponderance of conifers. It has been managed as a mainly pine forest ever since, with some oaks on the better land. Some of the pines are now magnificent specimens more than 100 years old and responsible for some very attractive forest scenery. With large urban populations all around, Delamere has become a popular picnic spot, and increasing attention is being paid to its amenity value.

THE FOREST OF WIRRAL

The Wirral, that rectangular peninsula between the estuaries of the Dee and the Mersey, is not now well-forested country. Indeed, it is largely industrial and suburban, though islets of woodland and common lands serve as a reminder of what it once was. Leasowe Common, Newton Common near Hoylake, and the National Trust property at Thurstaston were no doubt once rough grazing land within the Forest boundaries.

In the thirteenth and fourteenth centuries the Forest of Wirral was royal property. A document of 1275 records that two stags had to be taken from the Forest, salted down and sent to Westminster in time for the Michaelmas feast. The Abbey of St Werbergh's, Chester, was around the same period granted a tithe on the forest venison for the purpose of building its new church. In 1328 the Forest had a 'riding forester' appointed by the king, for the city of Chester had to find some money to pay the arrears of his salary. The master foresters were the Stanleys of Hooton, who continued to hold the empty title long after the Wirral had been disafforested.

In the fourteenth century the Forest became a refuge for outlaws, who made themselves such a nuisance that the citizens of Chester petitioned the king to have the Wirral disafforested. This request was granted in the 1370s, after which the advance of cultivation and settlement seems to have been rapid.

Certain place-names in the Wirral reveal the former forest character of the countryside. We have Woodchurch, Woodhay, Woodside, Bromborough ('the place where broom grows'), Ashfield, and Westwood, while 'Birkenhead' itself denotes 'a headland overgrown with birch'. A local rhyme,

> From Blacon Point to Hiltree
> A squirrel could leap from tree to tree,

implies that the peninsula was once entirely covered in woodland.

THE FOREST OF MACCLESFIELD

The Forest of Macclesfield occupied a large area of hill and mountain country on the eastern border of Cheshire, now the edge of the Peak National Park. Most of the villages bear purely Anglo-Saxon names and the villagers must have suffered considerable curtailments of their liberties when the Normans made the area a Forest, to which the forest laws in all their stringency were applied. The character of the countryside seems to have been waste-land with scattered trees rather than continuous woodland.

Hare, fox, squirrel, cat and two species of deer are mentioned in connection with the Forest in medieval documents, while the village name Wildboarclough is a reminder of another common denizen of the woods. During the Middle Ages many grants of land and other rights in the Forests were made by successive monarchs, and the Crown finally parted with its property here after the Restoration of Charles II. Several large estates have subsequently preserved or planted extensive woodlands, but on the high ground along the Debryshire border trees are now scarce.

THE FORESTS OF LANCASHIRE

The Forests of Lancashire are best considered together, as they seem often to have been treated in this way, the administration frequently overlapping. In the year 1200 one man, Benedict Gernet, had charge of all the forests in the county, and about 20 years later another Gernet, Roger, occupied the same position. The chief units were as follows:

LONSDALE, situated in the northern part of the county and extending into Westmoreland. The chief sub-divisions were the *Forest of Wyersdale* and the *Forest of Quernmoor*.

AMOUNDERNESS, occupying the territory between the rivers Ribble and Wyre and extending well inland. Sub-divisions were the *Forest of Myerscough*, the *Forest of Bleasdale* and the *Forest of Fulwood*.

BLACKBURNSHIRE, extending mostly eastwards from the town of Blackburn to the Yorkshire border and including the *Forest of Rossendale*, the *Forest of Pendle*, the *Forest of Trawden* and the *Forest of Bowland*.

WEST DERBY, sometimes confusingly known as *Derbyshire*, occupied much of the flat Lancashire plain east of Liverpool. It included the parks of Croxteth and Toxteth.

No overall total for the forests of the whole county is available, but in 1228 the Forest of Wyersdale contained about 20,000 acres, the Forest of Quernmoor about 7,000 acres, and the Forest of Myerscough some 2,200 acres. Much later, at the beginning of the sixteenth century, the Forest of Rossendale, on the high country between Bury and Burnley, had an area of about 30 square miles.

Disafforestation began early in Lancashire. In 1228, during the minority of Henry III a commission recommended that the entire county, with the exception of Quernmoor, Bleasdale, Fulwood, West Derby and certain parks, should be disafforested. Probably the citizens of Lancaster objected to the disafforestation of Wyresdale and Myerscough, and with it the extinction of their forest rights, for in the following year these two forests were specifically excluded. If acted upon at the time, the recommendations do not seem to have been permanently honoured, for most of the forests, or parts of them, were still in existence 200 or 300 years later. The Forest of Rossendale was officially disafforested at the beginning of the sixteenth century, but the Forest of Blackburnshire, of which it was part, was still functioning as a royal forest, with its full complement of officials and a good stock of deer, in 1697.

The value placed on their forest rights by the people of Lancaster is understandable, for in 1201 they paid King John the sum of £283. 17s. for a charter giving them the right to use the neighbouring woods freely, entirely exempt from forest laws. John also treated the leper colony of St Leonard's, Lancaster, generously, granting them the right to take sufficient timber for their houses, to gather dead wood for fuel, and to graze their cattle in the Forest. When in the next reign Roger Gernet, mentioned above, tried to charge them for those rights, they petitioned the king, who immediately confirmed their charter and ordered the sheriff of Lancaster to stop Roger Gernet from interfering with them.

Forest court documents of the Middle Ages indicate that both red deer and fallow deer were plentiful in the Lancashire forests, and there are numerous records of poaching with greyhounds. When the Forest of Rossendale was disafforested in about 1506 the deer were killed off, but in 1697 there were still deer in the Forest of Blackburnshire, though severely harried by poachers.

Most of the woodland in the old forests of Lancashire has long since disappeared, except in a few parks. Much has been lost to industrial development, while the upland areas, such as the ancient forests of Bowland and Rossendale, were until recently decidedly bare. The Forestry Commission now has nearly 2,000 hectares of new plantations in Bowland.

THE FORESTS OF CUMBERLAND

INGLEWOOD, the name of the great forest that once covered much of Cumberland, means 'the wood of the English' and may perpetuate an event of the Dark Ages similar to the establishment of the New Forest by William the Conqueror. When Ethelfrith, the English king of Northumbria, conquered Rheged (Cumbria) early in the seventh century he may well have decreed central Cumberland a royal forest, and the Celtic inhabitants would naturally call it the English wood. The English, however, called it the Forest of Cumberland. It occupied the valleys of the Eden and the Petterill from Penrith to Carlisle and was, according to an early chronicler, 'a goodly great forest, full of woods, red deer and fallow, wild swine, and all manner of wild beasts'.

In early times the Forest of Cumberland, or Inglewood, seems to have included the adjacent forests of ALLERDALE, which occupied the territory between the Petterill and the Solway Firth, and GILDERDALE, on the fells near Alston, but these were later administered separately. In 1300 the forest justice was instructed to parcel up the waste land in Allerdale into

Grizedale Beck

convenient lots and let it to tenants at an annual rent. Through much of the thirteenth century the kings of Scotland possessed several manors with associated forest rights in Inglewood, including Plumpton Park, just north of Penrith. An interesting, incidental reference in forest court accounts of 1315 is to the taking of the young birds from a falcon's eyrie.

A survey of 1539 depicts Inglewood divided into four wards: Ashdale, Wastedalehead, Westwood and Nicholl. Each division had a master of game (a knight) and usually two foresters or keepers, while a chief master of game, assisted by a bow-bearer, had control of the whole. Wastedalehead or Wastdale must have been an outlying dependency, for it is in the Lake District, well away from the central forest. Enclosure and encroachment proceeded piecemeal throughout the centuries. Plumpton Park was disafforested in the reign of Henry VIII, but the main forest remained sufficiently intact to compose part of the royal dowry given to Catherine of Braganza on her marriage to Charles II in 1662. Inglewood passed out of the hands of the royal family in 1696, when it was granted to the first Earl of Portsmouth.

It is recorded that an old oak, reputed to be 'the last tree of Inglewood Forest' died of old age on Wragmire Moss, in the parish of Hesket in 1823. Some 20 years later the ancient forest courts were still being held annually in Hesket, for the payment of certain forest dues. The site was by a venerable thorn, the Court Thorn, under which business was transacted on a stone table.

Cumbria is now the scene of much new afforestation by the Forestry Commission, though many of the new forests lie around the perimeter of the Lake District, especially to the south. Three hundred square miles of the central lakes are excluded from the Commission's activities, it being agreed that much of the charm of the region depends on the present amalgam of mountain, moorland, pasture and mixed woodland. Among the largest of the Commission's forests, in which many of the plantations are now well grown, are Grizedale (3,503 hectares), Ennerdale (3,726 hectares), Kershope (5,734 hectares), Spadeadam (6,707 hectares) and Thornthwaite (2,657 hectares). Kershope, incidentally, is not in the Lake District but in the north-east of the county, along the Scottish border. With the Forests of Kielder, Redesdale and others on the Northumberland side of the Pennines it forms the huge Border Forest Park.

THE FORESTS OF DURHAM

Throughout most of the Middle Ages the county of Durham had no royal forests, though in the late fifteenth and early sixteenth centuries the *Forest of Teesdale* is so designated. A survey of 1538–39 found 140 red deer and 240 fallow deer there. The Forest was situated in the upper part of Teesdale, from the Westmoreland border down the Tees to within about four miles of Middleton-in-Teesdale. It was alternatively known as Forest-en-Frith—a tautology, for 'frith' means 'forest'.

In the next valley to the north the *Forest of Weardale*, around and above the small town of Stanhope, belonged in medieval times to the bishops of Durham. It was reputedly well stocked with red deer.

Chopwell Wood, by the little river Derwent near its confluence with the Tyne on the borders of Durham and Northumberland, became royal property in the reign of Elizabeth I. Under Charles I most of the trees were cut, though the quantity of good timber obtained was evidently low. There was little rehabilitation until the early nineteenth century, when 800 acres were replanted, mostly with oak. The soil was, however, poorly suited to the crop and from 1855 onwards the stunted oaks were replaced by conifers, largely larches but some Scots pines; unfortunately the larches did not do well, either. The Forestry Commission took over the Forest in 1924 and has since re-planted the entire 800 acres of the original woodlands and has expanded them to over 2,000 acres. Situated so near to a heavy industrial area, Chopwell has a high amenity value.

The Forestry Commission has another Forest Park at Hamsterley, in the Pennine foothills.

NORTHUMBERLAND FOREST

Three extensive forests occupied central Northumberland in early medieval times and were collectively known as the Forest of Northumberland. Their centre and pivot was the town of Rothbury, on the river Coquet, from which they reached northwards to beyond Alnwick and southwards to the river Wansbeck. The parish of Rothbury was itself vast, being more than 30 miles in circumference, and all was included in the Forest. Nevertheless this was a clear example of the axiom that in the Middle Ages 'forest' did not necessarily imply wooded country, for it is likely that the woods were confined to the river valleys, with wide expanses of moorland in between.

Central Northumberland is now a pleasant agricultural countryside, with most of its trees along the river valleys and in the parks of private estates. However, since the second world war the Forestry Commission has acquired immense areas of land farther north, along the Scottish border, where they have created vast new forests, including Kielder (16,409 hectares), Falstone (14,966 hectares), Redesdale (5,008 hectares) and Wark (13,745 hectares).

Bibliography

ALLEN, N. V. *The Exmoor Handbook and Gazetteer*, 1974
ARNOLD, JAMES. *The Shell Book of Country Crafts*, 1968.
BIRD, VIVIAN. *Staffordshire*, 1974
BOORER, M. *Forest Life*, 1973
BRIMBLE, L. J. F. *Trees in Britain*, 1946
BRYANT, SIR ARTHUR. *The Mediaeval Foundation*, 1966
CHAFIN, WILLIAM. *Anecdotes and History of Cranbourne Chase*, 1818
COX, J. CHARLES. *The Royal Forests of England*, 1905
CROWE, SYLVIA. *Forestry in the Landscape*, 1966
EDLIN, H. L. *Trees, Woods and Man*, 1956
    Forestry and Woodland Life, 1948
    England's Forests, 1958
EDWARDS, K. C. *The Peak District*, 1962
EKWALL, EILERT. *The Concise Oxford Dictionary of English Place-Names*, 1936
FITTER, R. S. F. & RICHARDSON, R. A. *The Pocket Guide to British Birds*, 1952
FLETCHER, H. L. V. *Portrait of the Wye Valley*, 1968
FORD, E. B. *Butterflies*, 1945
    Moths, 1955
FORESTRY COMMISSION. *See Your Forests*, 1971
    Forestry in the British Scene, 1968
GALTON, DOROTHY. *Survey of a Thousand Years of Beekeeping in Russia*, 1971
GUINNESS BOOK OF RECORDS
HART, C. E. *Royal Forest (Dean)* 1966
    The Verderers and the Forest Laws of Dean, 1971
HARTLEY, DOROTHY. *Made in England*, 1939
HAVINS, PETER J. NEVILLE. *Portrait of Worcestershire*, 1974
HYAMS, E. *The Changing Face of England*, 1974
IMMS, A. D. *Insect Natural History*, 1947
JACKSON, JOHN. *Deer in the New Forest*, 1977
KENCHINGTON, F. E. *The Commoners' New Forest*, 1949
LLOYD, E. R. *The Wild Red Deer of Exmoor*, 1970
MATTHEWS, L. HARRISON. *British Mammals*, 1952
MILES, ROGER. *The Trees and Woods of Exmoor*, 1972
POOLE, A. L. *From Domesday Book to Magna Carta*, 1951
    Mediaeval England, 1958
RACKHAM, OLIVER. *Trees and Woodlands in the British Landscape*, 1976
ROWE, W. H. *Our Forests*, 1947
RYLE, GEORGE. *Forest Service*, 1969
SEEBOHM, M. E. *The Evolution of the English Farm*, 1952
SMART, T. W. W. *A Chronicle of Cranborne and Chase of Cranborne*, 1841
SOOTHILL, ERIC & FAIRHURST, ALAN. *The New Field Guide to Fungi*, 1978
STAMP, L. DUDLEY. *Man & The Land*, 1955
STAMP, L. DUDLEY & HOSKINS, W. G. *The Common Lands of England & Wales*, 1963
STEP, EDWARD. *Wayside and Woodland Trees*, 1940
STRATTON, J. M. *Agricultural Records*, 1969
SUMNER, HEYWOOD. *The New Forest*, 1972

SYMONDS, H. H. *Afforestation in the Lake District*, 1936
TANSLEY, A. G. *Britain's Green Mantle*, 1949
TAYLOR, W. L. *Forests and Forestry in Britain*, 1946
TOWNLEY, H. *English Woodlands & their Story*, 1910
TREVELYAN, G. M. *History of England*, 1947
                         English Social History, 1945
TUBBS, C. R. *The New Forest*, 1968
VARLEY, REV. TELFORD. *Hampshire*, 1909
VESEY-FITZGERALD, BRIAN. *Gypsies of Britain*, 1944
WATERS, BRIAN. *The Forest of Dean*, 1951
WATSON, E. W. *Ashmore*, 1890
WHITLOCK, RALPH. *Wildlife in Wessex*, 1976
                   A Calendar of Country Customs, 1978
                   Folklore of Wiltshire, 1976
                   Somerset, 1975
WILKS, J. H. *Trees of the British Isles in History & Legend*, 1972
WOOLDRIDGE, S. W. & GOLDRING, FREDERICK. *The Weald*, 1953

ACKNOWLEDGEMENTS

The author gratefully acknowledges the help of the staff of Yeovil Library, and of the Forestry Commission.

Illustrations: drawings by Kevin J. Dean pp. 76, 94; drawings by Ursula Sieger pp. 57, 61, 63; Dr J. K. St Joseph & the University of Cambridge Committee for Aerial Photography p. 9; National Maritime Museum p. 32; Cecil Higgins Museum, Bedford p. 34; *Wiltshire Times* p. 37; J. M. Dent & Sons Ltd and Oliver Rackham (from *Trees & Woodlands in the British Landscape*) p. 70; W. Clare Lees p. 122; Men of the Trees p. 138; Peter Wilkes p. 155; Forestry Commission pp. 44, 87, 168; Gerd Franklin pp. 1, 25, 30, 50, 54, 126; the John Topham Picture Library pp. 45, 46, 74, 88, 91, 93, 94, 95. Finally, the publishers wish to thank *The Field* for permission to reproduce the photographs on pp. 12, 43, 52, 66, 77, 80, 82, 84, 85, 108, 151; E. H. Wood.

Index

Abbots, Abbeys 21
Acorn 28, 36, 38, 44, 49, 58
Adder 92, 94, 129
Agister 20, 23, 25, 38, 41, 43, 48, 104, 123
Alder 7, 11, 12, 25, 57, 59, 63, 76, 157
Alice Holt and Woolmer, Forest of 133–4
Allerdale, Forest of 167
Amounderness, Forest of 166
Anemone, Wood 55, 72, 73
Anglo-Saxon Chronicle 24, 112
Arbor Vitae 67
Arden, Forest of 145
Arundel, Earls of 135, 136
Arundel, Forest of 135
Ash 7, 8, 10, 11, 12, 26, 61, 63, 69, 71, 120, 140, 160
Ashdown Forest 135
Ash, Mountain (see Rowan)
Aspen 60, 62
assart 24
Attachment Courts 23, 24, 25
Aubrey, John 12
Aurochs (see Ox, wild)
Avon (Bristol) R. 11, 113
Avon (Salisbury) R. 114, 120, 125

Badger 18, 21, 51, 82, 105, 107, 110, 113, 129, 137, 138, 143, 144, 145, 164
Bampton Fair 107
Bavin 71
Beagle 40
Bean rods 71, 120
Beaters 39, 42
Beaufort, Dukes of 143, 144
Bedgebury, Forest of 135, 136
Beech 7, 8, 12, 31, 44, 47, 49, 58, 61, 63, 71, 73, 75, 76, 86, 106, 117, 121, 123, 129, 130, 136, 139, 140, 141, 142, 144, 149, 157
Bees 45, 46, 95, 124, 164
Beetles 95
Bee-ward 42, 46, 49
Bell-flower 72
Bercelet 41
Bercelletter 41
Bere, Forest of 41, 130–1
Berkshire 92, 121, 123, 124, 131
Berner 41
Bernwood, forest of 139,1
Bewdley, Forest of 144
Bill-hook 42, 69, 81
Birch, silver 7, 8, 12, 57, 58, 63, 65, 76, 139, 157
Blackburnshire, Forest of 166, 167
Blackcap 92
Blackmore Copse 94, 117
Blackmore, Forest of 111–12
Blackmore Vale 111, 114
Blackthorn 7, 55, 71, 72, 139, 157
Bladderwort 130
Bleasdale, Forest of 166
Bloodhound 40
Bluebell 55, 72, 73, 113, 123, 130
Blyth 154
Boarhound 80
Boarstall 139
Boar, Wild 18, 21, 38, 39, 41, 80, 81, 120, 137, 139, 142, 161, 166, 167
Bowland, Forest of 166, 167
Bowyers 42
Box 72

Bracken 23, 38, 49, 53, 55, 73, 75, 164
Braden, Forest of 46, 123
Brambles 10, 49, 53, 55, 71, 73, 97
Brill, the Forest of 139
Bristol 35, 113, 144
Brockenhurst 125, 126
Brocket 77
Brown, 'Capability' 30, 49, 121
Buck 78, 80, 82, 118, 123, 136, 137, 140, 143, 146, 157
Buckden 148
Buckholt 117, 118
Buckhound 41
Buckinghamshire 58, 131, 139, 147
Buckinghamshire, the Forest of 139
Buckstall 38
Bullfinch 90, 92
Burnham Common and Burnham Beeches 58, 139
Butterflies 56, 94, 113, 117, 130
Buzzard 51, 89, 105, 107, 144
Buzzard, Honey 89

Cablish 23
Calf (Deer) 76, 103
Cambridgeshire 12, 99, 148
Campions, Pink 55, 113
Cannock Chase 146–7
Canterbury, Archbishop of 135, 136
Castiard, the Valley of 143
Cattle 8, 10, 15, 22, 26, 28, 29, 36, 42, 43, 44, 59, 60, 62, 71, 73, 81, 103, 104, 105, 116, 118, 128, 129, 130, 132, 159, 161, 163, 164, 167
Cedar—Atlas, 68; Incense, 68; Indian, 68; Japanese, 68; Cedar of Lebanon, 31, 68
Celts, Celtic 11, 13–16, 112, 114, 121, 124, 167
Chaffinch 90, 92
Chalk 8, 12, 15, 58, 60, 65, 73, 75
Chapel-en-le-Frith 158
Charcoal, Charcoal-burners 14, 20, 23, 38, 42, 44, 45, 46, 59, 71, 126, 135, 136, 147, 154
Charles I 27, 28, 86, 120, 128, 132, 140, 145, 148, 162, 170
Charles II 28, 29, 119, 123, 128, 132, 135, 153, 166, 169
Charnwood Forest 149–50
Charter of the Forest 20, 24, 95, 136, 144, 145, 163
Charters 20, 103, 167
Chase 17–25
Cheddar Gorge 39, 110
Cherry, Bird 64
Cherry, Wild 7, 61, 63, 64, 75
Chester, Cheshire 163, 165
Chestnut, Horse 64, 140
Chestnut, Sweet 48, 57, 62, 63, 64, 69, 71, 136, 141, 143, 149
Cheviots, The 98, 160
Chief Men of the Forest 18, 23, 41
Chiffchaff 90
Chilterns 58, 86
Chute, Forest of 121, 124, 131
Cinquefoil 72
Civil War 27, 28, 33, 132, 140, 152, 157, 160, 161
Clarendon, Forest of 28, 39, 41, 46, 51, 78, 81, 86, 116, 117, 118–21

Coal-mining 113, 141, 142, 147
Cobbett, William 44
Columbine, Wild 72
Commons, Commoners 15, 22, 29, 35, 49, 137, 140, 141, 142, 152, 157, 160
Conifers 31, 55, 65–9, 75, 76, 90, 96, 97, 99, 104, 108, 117, 122, 134, 136, 141, 144, 145, 147, 148, 149, 160, 164, 170
Conservation 52, 104, 106
Constables 41, 161, 162
Coppicing 12, 26, 36, 56, 59, 60, 62, 64, 69, 70, 71, 72, 73, 82, 90, 116, 128, 129, 136, 144
Cornwall 8, 103
Court of the Mine Law 141, 142
Cowherd 36, 44
Cows 36, 42, 48, 68
Crab-apple 7, 64, 157, 164
Cranborne Chase 44, 53, 78, 82, 84, 114–16
Creeping Jenny 73
Crow 51
Cuckoo 92
Cumberland, Forests of 167–9
Cypress, Lawson 31, 66, 67

Danes 112
Dartford Warbler 56, 129
Dartmoor, Forest of 17, 21, 103–5
Dean, Forest of 14, 28, 32, 33, 45, 48, 64, 98, 140–3, 144
Deer, general 8, 17, 19, 20, 21, 22, 26, 28, 38, 39, 41, 43, 49, 51, 60, 71, 73, 76, 79, 80, 84, 108, 115, 116, 117, 127, 128, 129, 130, 131, 132, 133, 135, 136, 143, 145, 146, 147, 148, 150, 152, 153, 154, 156, 160, 161, 162, 164, 165, 167
Deer, Chinese Water 80
Deer, Fallow 18, 27, 40, 41, 53, 76, 78, 79, 80, 81, 111, 113, 116, 117, 120, 122, 123, 124, 129, 130, 133, 138, 139, 140, 142, 143, 144, 146, 149, 150, 155, 156, 157, 160, 161, 163, 167, 169, 170
Deerhound 40
Deer, Japanese (see Sika)
Deer-leap 38, 120
Deer, Red 18, 27, 41, 76, 77, 78, 79, 80, 103, 104, 107, 108, 111, 120, 122, 123, 124, 129, 133, 137, 139, 142, 146, 149, 150, 155, 156, 159, 160, 161, 162, 163, 164, 167, 169, 170
Deer Removal Act 128, 129
Deer, Roe 18, 40, 41, 49, 72, 76, 79, 80, 107, 110, 111, 113, 116, 117, 122, 124, 129, 138, 142, 143, 149, 160, 161, 164
Deer, Siberian Roe 80
Derby, Derbyshire 42, 81, 157, 160, 166
Derwent R. 158, 160, 161
Devon 13, 80, 103, 104, 108
Dipper 105, 107
Doe 78, 80, 123, 136, 137, 140, 143, 157
Dogs 20, 21, 38, 39, 40, 42, 47, 48, 80, 127, 142, 145, 147, 156, 159
Dog's Mercury 72, 73
Dog-roses 55
Dogwood 55, 71
Domesday Book 69, 103, 105, 121, 134
Dormouse 86
Dormouse, Edible 86
Dorset 15, 79, 86, 92, 111, 114, 130
Duffield, Forest of 157

Durham, Forest of	169–70	
Dutch Elm disease	59, 108	
Edmund	39, 110	
Edward I	112, 114, 119, 121, 128, 135, 137, 145, 146, 154, 158, 163	
Edward II	40, 48	
Edward III	39, 114, 117, 119	
Edward the Confessor	111, 137, 139, 162	
Elder	72	
Elm	7, 8, 10, 11, 12, 57, 59, 63, 71, 140, 149, 157	
Elm, Wych	59	
Elizabeth I, Queen	19, 29, 31, 48, 119, 135, 137, 170	
Enchanter's Nightshade	72, 73	
Enclosure Acts	29, 49, 106, 128, 157	
Enclosures	24, 27, 29, 31, 38, 42, 43, 44, 49, 123, 128, 133, 137, 140, 141, 142, 148, 150, 152, 153, 157, 160, 161, 162, 169	
Epping Forest	60, 136, 137, 138	
Essex, Forest of	43, 136–8	
Estovers	22	
Evelyn, John	28, 29, 31	
Exmoor, Forest of	17, 77, 90, 104, 105–7	
Eyre	23, 24, 25, 27, 35, 41, 47, 49, 95, 106, 111, 123, 127, 131, 140, 146, 147, 149, 150, 156, 158, 161, 162, 164, 169	
Faggots	26, 44, 71, 75, 120	
Falcon	39, 87, 89, 169	
Falconer	39, 89, 108, 126	
Far Hearkening Rock, the	143	
Farms, Farmers	13, 29, 30, 34, 59, 62, 97, 99, 104, 106, 107, 114, 116, 117, 130, 133, 137, 157, 159	
Farndale, Forest of	160, 161	
Fawn	17, 20, 78, 79, 114	
Feckenham, Forest of	145, 146	
Fence month	20, 82, 103, 114	
Fences	26, 27, 33, 36, 38, 43, 48, 66, 99, 115, 116, 128, 131, 136, 140, 157, 160, 163	
Fens, the	12, 14, 148	
Fermisone	79	
Ferns	75, 105, 129	
Fewterer	41	
Figwort	73	
Fines	104, 105, 115, 127, 147, 159	
Fir, Douglas	31, 66, 144; Grand Silver, 68; Silver, 31, 68	
Fletchers	42	
Flowers, forest	72–6	
Flycatcher, Pied	92, 105, 107	
Flycatcher, Spotted	92	
Forest Court (see eyre)		
Foresters	19, 20, 23, 25, 38, 41, 42, 47, 48, 52, 117, 123, 124, 126, 143, 146, 147, 150, 159, 162, 164, 169	
Forester, Chief	20, 150, 154, 164	
Forest Laws	17–25, 64, 105, 125, 131, 132, 146, 157, 158, 159, 160, 163, 165, 167	
Forestry Commission	52, 56, 65, 66, 67, 83, 86, 96–100, 104, 106, 108, 117, 122, 125, 128, 131, 134, 136, 142, 143, 144, 148, 149, 153, 156, 160, 164, 167, 169, 170	
Fox	18, 21, 30, 51, 55, 78, 82, 83, 84, 85, 86, 107, 113, 123, 129, 137, 138, 143, 144, 145, 147, 150, 164, 165	
Foxgloves	55, 72, 75, 130	
Freeholders, Freemen	24, 36, 95, 162	
Fungi	47, 75, 76	
Galtres, Forest of	160, 161	
Gamekeepers	49, 51, 52	
Garlic, Wild	73	
Geese	22, 36, 43, 129	
Gernet, Roger	42, 166, 167	
Gilderdale, Forest of	167	
Gillingham, Forest of	111	
Gipsies	48, 49, 85
Gladiolus, Wild	130
Gloucester, Gloucestershire	90, 113, 140, 143
Goats	22, 153, 162, 164
Goldcrest	90
Goose-girl	36, 44
Gorse	55, 129, 130
Goshawk	89
Greendale Oak	156
Greyhound	38, 39, 40, 41, 84, 127, 136, 137, 164, 167
Ground Ivy	72
Grouse, Black	90, 105, 107, 129
Grouse, Red	90, 105, 107
Groveley, Forest of	12, 117–18
Guelder Rose	55, 71, 75
Hainault Forest	136, 137
Hampshire	27, 41, 64, 77, 112, 116, 117, 121, 124, 125, 128, 130, 133, 134
Hampton Court	132
Hare	21, 30, 41, 83, 84, 116, 135, 137, 145, 150, 164, 165
Harrier—Hen, 89; Marsh, 89; Montagu's, 89, 105, 129
Hart	24, 41, 77, 80, 108, 111, 137, 146, 157, 163
Hartfield	135
Hatfield Chase, Forest of	160
Haugmond, Forest of	162, 163
Hawfinch	117
Hawk, Hawking	18, 19, 39, 42, 51, 55, 87, 89
Hawthorn	7, 8, 10, 64, 73, 75, 129, 157
Haywood, Forest of	144
Hazel	7, 8, 10, 11, 12, 25, 26, 31, 36, 38, 44, 48, 49, 53, 55, 56, 69, 71, 72, 73, 86, 116, 120, 129, 136, 146, 157
Heath, Heaths	12, 125, 129, 130
Hedgehog	51, 85, 86
Helleborine	73
Hemlock, Canadian	67
Hemlock, Western	67
Hemp Agrimony	73
Henry I	111, 139
Henry II	83, 106, 119, 127, 143, 144
Henry III	24, 103, 111, 112, 119, 137, 142, 154, 158, 166
Henry VII	27, 31, 47, 131
Henry VIII	22, 79, 106, 111, 114, 118, 121, 132, 152, 159, 169
Herb Robert	72
Herefordshire, the Forests of	144
Hermits	47, 48, 49
Heron	19, 89, 120, 129, 135
Hertfordshire	9, 86
High Peak, Forest of	47, 157, 158
Hind	17, 20, 24, 39, 77, 80, 114, 137, 163
Hobby	89, 129, 164
Holly	7, 11, 12, 25, 64, 71, 105, 116, 129, 140, 153, 157
Honey	45, 95
Honeysuckle	55, 73
Hops	64, 71, 136
Hornbeam	7, 12, 57, 60, 63, 71, 137
Horses	18, 20, 22, 24, 29, 39, 42, 43, 44, 49, 68, 103, 109, 110, 127, 130, 132, 152, 159, 161, 164
Hunt, Hunting	16, 17, 20, 21, 26, 38, 39, 40, 41, 78, 81, 82, 83, 86, 89, 106, 107, 110, 115, 125, 127, 131, 132, 135, 163
Huntingdon, the Forest of	148–9
Huntsmen	38, 39, 41
Hurdles	26, 36, 38, 42, 44, 48, 53, 69, 71, 116, 120, 136
Hyrsel	77
Ice Age	7, 60
Inglewood, Forest of	42, 167, 169
Irchenfield, Forest of	144
Iris, Stinking	72
Iron	14, 45, 110, 134, 135, 141
Iron-working	14, 31, 134, 135, 144, 147
Ivy	10, 71, 75
James I	27, 33, 78, 81, 106, 115, 116, 119, 123, 132, 148
Jay	51, 92, 129
John, King	24, 106, 110, 111, 127, 142, 144, 154, 163, 167
Juniper	65
Jutes	125
Keepers	115–16, 117, 120, 126, 143, 147, 152, 156, 162, 169
Kent	14, 48, 56, 64, 134, 135, 136
Kestrel	51, 89
Kielder, Forest of	97, 169, 170
Kingswood, Forest of	113
Kinlet, Forest of	162
Kite	89
Knaresborough, Forest of	160
Knightwood Oak	56, 129
Ladders	71, 120
Lake District, the	77, 97, 98, 169
Lancashire	42, 92
Lancashire, Forests of	166
Lancaster, Duke and Duchy of	157, 162
Larch, European	31, 66, 131, 170
Larch, Japanese	66
Launder	41
Lead	110
Leicester, Leicestershire	149, 150
Leighfield Forest	149
Lepers	42, 146, 167
Lichens	75, 129
Lilies-of-the-valley	72, 73
Lime	7, 8, 11, 12, 25, 46, 49, 60, 61, 63, 71, 130, 140, 150, 152
Lincoln, Lincolnshire	13, 56, 99, 154
Linnet	129
Lizard, Sand	56, 92, 129
London	14, 31, 35, 80, 81, 89, 119, 120, 134, 137, 139, 146, 158
Long Mynd, Forest of	162
Lonsdale, Forest of	42, 166
Lurcher	38
Lymer (or limehound)	40
Lyndhurst	43, 119, 126, 127, 130
Macclesfield, Forest of	165–66
Machen Oak	143
Magna Carta	24
Magpie	51
Major Oak	155
Malvern, Forest of	145
Maple	12, 65, 140, 157
Mara, Forest of	163–4
Marten	18, 38, 51, 82, 83, 138
Martinmas	17, 23, 78, 116, 164
Mastiff	40, 41, 81, 127
May Day	53, 116
Meadowsweet	73
Melchet, Forest of	78, 116–17, 118
Melksham and Pewsham, Forest of	122–3
Mendip, Forest of	110
Merlin	89, 105, 107, 164
Mersey R.	165
Mice	55, 75, 86, 143
Michaelmas	23, 164, 165
Middle Ages	20, 26, 31, 35, 51, 60, 76, 78, 80, 83, 84, 89, 106, 110, 111, 116, 118, 120, 123, 127, 130, 133, 134, 139, 140, 144, 145, 148, 149, 150, 154, 157, 158, 159, 161, 162, 163, 166, 167, 169, 170
Midsummer Day	20, 23, 78
Milton Abbas	79

Mining	103, 110, 134, 141, 142, 144, 150	
Molinia Grass		75
Monks	27, 103, 123, 127	
Morfe, Forest of		162, 163
Mosses		75, 105
Moths		94, 130
Moudrem, Forest of		163, 164
Mountain Ash (see Rowan)		
Mouse, field		86
Muntjac		80, 129
Muntjac, Indian		80
'murrain'		78, 83, 123, 156
Myerscough, Forest of		166
Nadder R.		114, 117
Napoleonic Wars		128, 130, 133
National Parks		48, 52, 98, 104, 106
National Trust		106, 107, 113, 116, 165
Navy	27, 29, 31, 33, 120, 130, 133, 155	
Needwood, Forest of		152–3
Nelson		31, 128
Nene R.		147
Neroche, The Forest of		108–10
New Forest	12, 17, 21, 27, 28, 29, 33, 39, 42, 43, 44, 46, 47, 48, 56, 59, 64, 65, 77, 79, 89, 90, 92, 95, 98, 119, 124–30, 167	
Newt		92
Nightingale		92, 129
Nightjar		56, 92, 129
Norfolk		64, 65, 149
Norman Conquest		90, 108, 153, 154
Normans	18, 76, 86, 108, 113, 114, 122, 125, 147, 165	
Northamptonshire, the Forests of	82, 99, 139, 140, 147–8	
North Petherton, Forest of		18, 107–8
Northumberland, Forest of		81, 83, 169, 170
Nottingham, Sheriff of		154
Nuthatch		90, 91, 92
Nuts		38, 43, 44, 48, 53, 136, 146
Oak	7, 8, 10, 11, 12, 24, 25, 27, 28, 31, 32, 33, 37, 46, 47, 53, 56, 57, 58, 59, 60, 63, 64, 65, 69, 71, 76, 86, 96, 97, 105, 117, 118, 120, 121, 128, 129, 130, 131, 133, 134, 136, 140, 141, 142, 143, 144, 146, 148, 149, 150, 152, 155, 157, 164, 169, 170	
Oak Apple Day		53, 78, 117
Oak—Holm, 58; Oak, Pedunculate, 56; Red, 58; Sessile, 56, 58; Turkey, 58		
Ombersley, Forest of		145
Orchid, Bird's-nest		72
Orchid, Butterfly		73
Orchid, Purple		72
Osier		62
Otter		18, 82, 84, 105, 107, 159
Otterhound		41, 82, 84
Outlaws		38, 47, 49, 112, 113, 154, 163
Owls		51, 55, 88, 89, 92, 129
Ox, wild		8, 81
Oxford, the Forest of		139–40
Oxlip		72
Palesters		41
Palings		42, 48, 64, 71, 157
Pannage		20, 22, 44, 127, 161, 164
Parkers		21, 41, 48
Parks	20, 21, 64, 67, 68, 76, 79, 81, 82, 97, 98, 108, 116, 120, 131, 148, 152, 153, 156, 157, 161, 162, 166, 170	
Parsley, Cow		55
Partridge		30, 89, 116, 137
Pasturage		20, 22, 44, 104, 127
Peak, the Forest of the (see also High Peak, Forest of the)	21, 81, 158–60	
Peak, National Park		158, 160, 165
Pear, wild		64
Peasant	24, 27, 35, 36, 42, 44, 52, 71, 126, 127, 159	
Peasticks		71, 120
Peat		7, 8, 22, 104
Peat-cutters		103
Pembroke, Earl of		117, 118, 119
Penchet, Forest of		118
Pendle, Forest of		166
Pennine Way, the		160
Peregrine Falcon		89, 90
Peterborough		147
Pheasant	30, 39, 49, 51, 72, 82, 89, 90, 92, 116, 135, 137	
Pheasant, golden		149
Pickering, Forest of		41, 48, 80, 84, 95, 161–2
Pigeon, Wood		90
Pigs	10, 22, 29, 36, 38, 43, 44, 118, 128, 129, 130, 132, 134, 150, 153, 164	
Pine—Corsican, 68, 149, 156, 164; Lodgepole, 67; Scots, 7, 8, 12, 31, 65, 67, 75, 76, 80, 95, 96, 128, 129, 131, 149, 164, 170		
Pinguedo		78
Pipit		129
Piscary		23
Plantations	28, 52, 55, 62, 65, 66, 68, 75, 90, 98, 148, 167, 169	
Ploughs		11, 13, 15, 17, 25, 35, 36
Plum, wild		71
Poaching, Poachers	31, 49, 84, 86, 105, 115–16, 127, 130, 135, 140, 143, 149, 153, 156, 157, 158, 161, 167	
Polecat		51, 83, 138, 143, 164
Pollarding	36, 56, 58, 59, 60, 62, 70, 71, 129, 139	
Pollen		8, 10, 58, 60
ponies		38, 49, 103, 104, 105, 107, 128, 129
Poorstock, Forest of		111
Poplar—black, 7, 60, 62; grey, 7, 60, 62; white, 7, 60, 61, 62, 63, 149		
Prickett		78
Primrose		55, 72, 73
Purlieu		21, 22
Purpresture		24
Quantocks		77, 107
Quernmoor, Forest of		166
Rabbits	8, 21, 55, 75, 84, 86, 89, 116, 120, 135, 150	
Rache (or Brache)		40, 41, 137
Ragged Robin		73
Ranger		20, 21, 41, 117, 154
Raspberry, wild		75
Rats		86, 143
Raven		105, 107, 144
Redesdale, Forest of		169, 170
Redstart		92, 105
Redwood, Californian		67
Regarders		23, 41, 117, 123, 154
Rhododendrons		49, 72, 113, 130
Ribble R.		166
Richard I		106, 154
Ring ousel		105, 107
Rining		46, 48
Robin		90, 92
Robin Hood		38, 47, 53, 154
Rockingham, Forest of	28, 41, 49, 82, 99, 147, 148	
Roehound		41
Romans		8, 13–16, 76, 86, 90, 134, 141
Rose, Guelder		75
Rossendale, Forest of		166, 167
Rothamsted		9, 14
Rowan		64, 75
Rufus' Stone		124, 127
Rutland, Forest of		35, 41, 149–50
St Aldhelm		112
St Dunstan		110
St John's-wort		55, 72
St Leonard's Forest		135
Salcey Forest		147, 148
Salisbury	47, 77, 94, 114, 117, 118, 119, 120, 121	
Sallow		62, 73, 105
Sandpiper		105
Sapley Forest		149
Savernake, Forest of		121–2, 123, 124
Sawyers		42
Saxons	7, 8, 13–16, 17, 18, 20, 60, 69, 81, 105, 108, 110, 111, 113, 114, 118, 125, 126, 134, 144, 150, 160	
Scabious		75
Scotland	8, 31, 58, 65, 76, 77, 83, 98, 118, 169, 170	
Selwood, Forest of		111, 112–13
Serfs		24, 36
Severn R.		140, 143, 145, 163
Seymour, Edward		121
Seymour, Jane		121, 122
Shakespeare		53, 146
Sheep	8, 10, 22, 26, 29, 36, 44, 53, 55, 59, 60, 68, 69, 73, 97, 103, 104, 105, 130, 141, 142, 158, 159, 161, 162	
Sheep cribs		53, 120
Shepherd		36, 44
Sherwood, Forest of		24, 28, 78, 154–6
Ship-building		27, 32, 128, 140, 153
Shirlet, Forest of		162, 163
Shooting		51, 52
Shotover Forest		139
Shrew		86
Shropshire, Forests of		144, 162–3
Sika Deer		80, 129
Silures, the		141
Sloes		49
Slow-worm		92
Snake, Smooth		56, 92, 129
Snakes		92
Soar		78
Solomon's Seal		72
Somerset	11, 12, 18, 83, 106, 107, 108, 110, 112, 113	
Sorrel (deer)		78
Sparrow-hawk		89, 164
Sparrow, Hedge		90, 92
Spayard		77
Spindlewood		71
Spruce—Norway, 31, 66, 67, 148, 149; Serbian, 68; Sitka, 31, 66		
Squirrel, grey		86, 143
Squirrel, red		38, 86, 105, 149, 165
Stafford		146, 152, 163
Stag	17, 24, 39, 40, 77, 78, 81, 110, 112, 113, 135, 165	
Staggard		77
Stag-hound		41, 104
Stamford, Earl		153
Stannary courts		103
Steepelwood, Forest of		162, 163
Stoat		51, 55, 86
Stock-Dove		92
Stonechat		129
Stonehenge		8, 11
Strawberry, wild		72, 73
Sub-Atlantic period		7
Sub-Boreal period		7
Suffolk		99, 149
Surrey		27, 31, 92, 131
Sussex		48, 64, 134, 135, 136
Swainmote		23, 44, 123, 143, 150
Swans		87, 120
Sweet Woodruff		72
Swineherd		36, 44
Sycamore		10, 31, 60, 61, 63, 71, 140, 160
Tanning		46
Taxes		103, 112, 114
Teesdale, Forest of		169
Tegg		78

175

Thames R	31, 134	
Thatching spars	71, 116, 120	
Thetford Forest	65, 68, 149	
Thistles, woodland	55, 72, 73, 161	
Thorns	25, 36, 71, 140, 152, 153, 169	
Thuja (see Arbor Vitae)	169	
Timber	27, 28, 29, 31, 32, 33, 36, 44, 59, 60, 62, 64, 66, 95, 96, 98, 109, 119, 120, 123, 128, 130, 131, 133, 136, 140, 142, 143, 146, 148, 152, 153, 154, 155, 164, 167, 170	
Tinemen	18	
Tin-miners	103	
Tintern, Forest of	143–4	
Tits	90, 92, 110	
Toad, Natterjack	129	
Tolls	103, 161	
Trails, Forest	98	
Traps	51, 81	
Traveller's Joy	75	
Trawden, Forest of	166	
Tree-bark	46, 47	
Tree-Creeper	90, 92	
Trent R.	153	
Truffles	46, 48	
Turbary	22, 104, 127	
Turf	15, 22, 43, 104	
Turtle-Dove	92	
Tyne R.	170	
Tyrell, Sir Walter	39	
Underwood	16, 24, 26, 44, 48, 53, 55, 58, 69–72, 99, 116, 120, 136, 152, 153	
Venison	17, 24, 28, 104, 160, 163, 165	
Ventrer	41	
Venville parishes	21, 104	
Verderers	19, 23, 24, 25, 41, 43, 48, 83, 117, 128, 130, 137, 143, 163	
Verderers' Hall	43, 130	
Vert	24	
Vetch, Wood	72	
Villages	30, 35, 36, 44, 49, 104, 125, 142, 160, 165	
Villein	24	
Violets, Wood	55, 72, 73	
Vole	55, 86, 143	
Wagtail, grey	105	
Waltham Forest	136, 137	
Warbler, Dartford (see Dartford Warbler)		
Warbler, Garden	92	
Warbler, Willow	90	
Warbler, Wood	92	
Warden	18, 19, 23, 41, 121, 124, 126, 143	
Wark Forest	170	
Warren	21, 83, 86, 120	
Warrener	41, 48	
Warwickshire, Forest of	145–6	
Wasps, Wood	95	
Water Dropwort	75	
Wayfaring Tree	55, 71, 73	
Weald, The	14, 31, 45, 64, 69, 134–6	
Weardale, Forest of	170	
Weasel	51, 86, 164	
Welland R.	147	
Wellingtonia	67, 68	
Wensleydale, Forest of	160	
Wesley, John	113	
West Derby, Forest of	42, 166	
Westmoreland	153, 166, 169	
Wey, river	133	
Wheat	13, 15, 35, 36, 51	
Whinchat	129	
White, Rev. Gilbert	133	
Whitebeam	7, 64, 65	
Whittlewood Forest	147, 148	
Wildcat	18, 21, 51, 83, 86, 137, 145, 150, 159, 164, 165	
Wild Service Tree	7, 8, 64, 65, 71	
William the Conqueror	18, 24, 26, 52, 105, 106, 108, 118, 119, 121, 125, 154, 158, 160, 167	
William II	17, 24, 39, 114, 124	
Willow	7, 62, 69, 71, 105	
Wiltshire	13, 37, 44, 46, 53, 64, 77, 86, 112, 113, 114, 116, 117, 121, 122, 123, 124, 125, 129, 131	
Winchester	18, 118, 119, 124, 130	
Windsor	27, 28, 80, 83, 131–3, 137	
Wintour, Sir John	28, 140, 142	
Wirral, Forest of	163, 165	
Woburn	80, 104	
Wolf	38, 41, 51, 81, 120, 142, 146, 159	
Woodcock	56, 89, 92, 116, 121, 129, 160	
Woodcutters, Woodmen	36, 42, 45, 126, 140	
Woodpeckers	92, 96	
Wood Sage	72	
Wood Sanicle	72	
Woodside	165	
Wood Sorrel	72, 130	
Wood Spurge	72, 73	
Woodward	16, 20, 21, 23, 27, 36, 41, 42, 48, 117, 123, 143	
Worcestershire, Forests of	144–5, 162	
Wrekin, Forest of	162, 163	
Wren	90, 92	
Writtle Forest	136	
Wyersdale, Forest of	166	
Wye Valley	98, 140, 143, 144	
Wylye Valley	11, 44, 117	
Wyre, Forest of	144, 145, 162, 163	
Yellow Archangel	72	
Yellow Hammer	129	
Yew	8, 65, 67, 68, 69, 75, 129, 144	
Yorkshire	14, 80, 84, 160, 161, 166	
Yorkshire, the Forests of	160–1